WIND OF CHANGE

The Scorpions Story

Martin Popoff

WIND OF CHANGE

The Scorpions Story

Martin Popoff

WP
WYMER
PUBLISHING
Bedford, England

First published in Canada in 2013
This revised edition published 2016 by Wymer Publishing
Bedford, England
www.wymerpublishing.co.uk
Tel: 01234 326691
Wymer Publishing is a trading name of Wymer (UK) Ltd

ISBN 978-1-908724-40-3

Edited by John Kemp.

Every effort has been made to trace the copyright holders of the
photographs in this book but some were unreachable. We would
be grateful if the photographers concerned would contact us.

Front and back cover images © Richard Galbraith.

Printed and bound by
CMP (UK) Ltd, Poole, Dorset, England

A catalogue record for this book is available from the British Library.

Cover design by Andy Francis.

Contents

Preface

Ha ha, get this, as kids we used to come up with these elaborate trades of albums with each other, trades that included tennis racquets, sports cards, two crappy albums for one good one, you know, a 3/7 and a 4/10 for a 6/8 (don't ask). Anyway, my very first was trading *away* my brand new, new release $6.99 copy of Virgin Killer, for my buddy Fiver's copy of the also half-hour old $6.99 Yesterday & Today debut, both of us 13 at the time, spinning records on his parents' console after bringing them back from Kelly's or Rock Island Tape Centre, where we both worked.

I still know why I did it. Virgin Killer was kind of creepy, inaccessible, scraping and scary at the heavy end and depressing at the obscure, weather-beaten Uli end. Yesterday & Today on the other hand (and not Y&T yet), that was just good-time bar room hard rock, by smiling Americans I could relate to.

As the years rolled on, I got to appreciate Virgin Killer much more, and was completely taken with Taken By Force, loved Lovedrive, went animal for Animal Magnetism, and I'm sure Blackout was playing on many occasions when... never mind, it was actually more likely Back In Black that was spinning like our heads during those desperate hours way hell an' gone out at some bush party (er, well, not spinning—it woulda been cassette or 8-track).

After that, well, enthusiasm waned, which made it harder to write this book, I tell ya. But it's no secret, most serious Scorps fans swear by the early stuff and I'm there with that majority. But hey, isn't it cool that it's not isolated to the Uli Jon Roth era or anything like that? That really there are at least as many balls-out classics with Matthias Jabs on lead guitar as there are with Uli.

Seriously, man, we were pissed off at Love At First Sting when it finally arrived after a couple/few weeks of the irresistible *Rock You Like A Hurricane* as breathless advance single. Not only did that turn out to be the best song on the damn thing, it was about the third heaviest. Okay, this wasn't a Starz – Attention Shoppers! debacle, but it was certainly as disconcerting as British Steel following Killing Machine, Pyromania following High 'n' Dry or Metallica shuffling along with pockets full of rocks after the strafing that was Justice. In other words, Scorpions had dumbed down and toned it down and we were angry metalheads who didn't stand for that sort of thing.

But doing these books, there's always a silver lining around the discovery of catalogue gems I had previously glossed over and dismissed. Fact is, writing *Wind of Change*, I reconnected with a bunch of good songs all over *Savage Amusement, Crazy World, Face The Heat*, and much to my surprise, Pure Instinct, a record that is not all that heavy, but is, in my estimation, an overlooked semi-jewel that just might be the band's most wise, mature and intellectually hefty of the Hermanating catalogue.

Then there's a gap where I was barely tuned in, and frankly, didn't find much that held value for me. That is, until the band's ostensibly (or so they said at the time) last record ever, *Sting In The Tail*, which I think is pretty damn solid. And there's the rub—I don't think I could have gathered the faculties an' focus to write this thing if I didn't think it would end on a high note, and Sting In The Tail is high enough, I figure, along with the massive farewell tour of lookin' good and playin' good that had us all dancing in the aisles as these old German friends said kaput. But then of course all that was chucked, and the band cranked out the lengthy *Return to Forever*, along with more exhaustive touring and all is right with the world again.

You know, something that isn't really reflected in the pages you are about to read, but I'll say it here: the spirit and the example of how to live a life that is Uli Jon Roth pervades the story. Oh, it's all very well explained, how Uli's vision was more guitar oriented, Hendrix-like, classical and even Krautrocking, and that—no hard feelings—he'd have to leave the fold. So Herman joins and then Matthias, who together help reinforce a vague notion within Klaus and Rudolf that they would like to explore more of a straightforward, Americanised rock sound. Fair enough, that's what happens and a lot of great music got.

Anyway, still, it's pretty cool that Uli has persevered to the point where he's got a ton of intellectually inspiring records under his belt, but more inspiringly, to the point where he's out putting on fiery concerts, he's looking young, and he seems to re-connect with his old mates on stage whenever he gets a chance. To a lesser extent, so do Michael Schenker, Herman Rarebell and Herman Buchholz, surprisingly sharing the stage again in a drive of love. Pretty cool. Which helps reinforce this idea that many (if not all) of these guys feel like old friends, to each other, as well as to me.

Martin Popoff
martinp@inforamp.net www.martinpopoff.com

Early Days

"I'm a guy from the old days"

Not many bands can claim a dozen years of dues-payin' before breaking, but Rudolf Schenker and Klaus Meine can claim that and possibly more, if one includes those first magic years smitten by original rock 'n' roll and the Beatles and a couple more in the middle of a long ride to the top, if the smash status of Blackout be your definition of the band's true point of ascendance.

Indeed, like many a' classic career arc through the '70s (Rush and Priest most comparatively come to mind)... from the outside it might look like making all those great records from say '75 through '79 represent the band as rock stars, triumphant certainly from a creative point of view, to a discerning metalhead of a certain vintage. But as has become plain over the years, bands like Scorpions and Rush and Priest were still very much toughing it out even as they were making their best records for major labels (by the way, off-topic, I am indeed a big proponent of Scorpions without the "the," but in the writing of the book, I've grudgingly mostly gone with a "the," lower case, for purposes of rhythm—and declining to do so in triumph where I think I can).

I mention this only to set the stage, and to make the point that as pertains to our current saga, the Scorpions guys most definitely paid their dues and should be afforded respect for that fact. Reward was hard won, with the band's craft honed and polished over years of enthusiastic dedication.

So where did it all begin? Well, the root of the band begins with Rudolf Schenker and then very quickly to the fold, Klaus Meine, the two that remain to this day —the Richards and Jagger of the band. Like one hears about kids in the Soviet Union, Rudolf and Klaus became enamoured with each and every early trace of rock 'n' roll as it filtered into their country, West Germany as it was known, with much of the signal coming through American GIs that were based in large numbers in that country butted up against the Iron Curtain.

"I'm a guy from the old days," explains Rudolf. "So it was Elvis Presley,

Little Richard, Buddy Holly, Eddie Cochran, all these people. But of course, when the Beatles came, and the Rolling Stones, the black and the white—the Beatles were white, and Rolling Stones were darkie guys. I liked the Pretty Things very much, and of course The Kinks and Yardbirds I liked. So this is my side, bands who inspired me. When I was a fan of Elvis Presley, I wanted to make music too, but somehow I was also a soccer player, and somehow I noticed how difficult it is to make music on the guitar, and it had to wait in the corner until the Beatles and the Rolling Stones came. I'll tell you one thing, when I had started to really work hard to become a guitar player was when I saw these five guys as friends travelling around the world and making music, to their friends. In my naïve thoughts, which was good to be naïve, this kind of dream came through my way of looking and building the Scorpions and finding the right people, musicians that I could also be in a good friendship with, which was very important for me. That is also the reason that we are still together, because of the philosophy. The basic situation is friendship and enjoying being a gang, travelling around the world looking for adventure. Not looking for how you can make the most money."

"Because we were not looking for the money, but the adventure, this is why later we were travelling and we were going to places where nobody else played before us. So that's the reason we went to Russia and went to the Manaus jungle, rain forest, and the pyramids in front of Cairo. Because we wanted to enjoy it. Because we wanted to really tour and enjoy music and our fans. I think this was the situation, that was the reason, because of these naïve thoughts about four or five friends travelling around the world. This came into the Scorpions truly from the beginning, and that's the reason the Scorpions have stayed together."

"Scorpions in the beginning," continues Rudolf, "starting from '65 already, we were very much focused on guitar playing, especially on lead guitar. Our first guitar player, next to me, was already very good in lead guitar playing and my brother, who joined the band, became very successful. Uli Jon Roth was a very well-known guitar player, or became a well-known guitar player, so we always were saying that maybe we were a continental or European Yardbirds. Because somehow there were guitar players in the Scorpions who made their own careers worldwide by being very good and by influencing many other young bands.

Quite incredibly, Rudolf says that he had started using the name, The Scorpions in 1965. It is an obvious nod to the Beatles, in the same manner Alice Cooper and Dennis Dunaway had first called their band The Earwigs and then The Spiders. However, it should be noted Rudolf came down on the side of the heavier bands against the Beatles: as much as everybody couldn't help but be affected by the Fab Four, Schenker was less so. Other rationales for the name from Rudolf include the fact that in German the only difference is that there would be a "k" in place of the "c," and that the scorpion tail is like the needle on a turntable. There's also a numerology component (with 30s and 39s), the idea that many people are Scorpios, and the fact that there's an "s" in Schenker, and that he was born in an "s" town, Schwetzingen.

"*Hippy Hippy Shake*, you know, from The Swinging Blue Jeans?" riffs Rudolf, when I asked him about his very early experiences of rock in any form. "'Hippy hippy shake' (sings it). Also from Eric Burdon, *House Of The Rising Sun*, or from a little bit later, from the Pretty Things, *Rainin' In My Heart*, or *Don't Bring Me Down* by The Animals, and also from the Stones, *Empty Heart*, maybe? What else was very new? I mean, I was not a big Beatles fan; I didn't play much Beatles. But the Stones was already very much in our repertoire.

"But everything we had in Germany was for us, young guys, terrible. There was more for us from the US, Coca-Cola, Elvis Presley and chewing gum—this was for us the lifestyle. This was for us the way of really enjoying life, because everything else, the German... it was be on time, be good in your job, you know, all this classic characteristics of being German. Don't make any jokes. Here, you have to be and work hard and make sure you have a job which you can maybe do until you are 65 and then you save anyway. So that was exactly the way we didn't want to go. Klaus, too, because Klaus played in a different band called Mushrooms. I'm in the Scorpions, and we said this is not what I want to do. We want to have adventure, we want to make something out of our lives. This was the situation of what I called the third dimension. It was something we picked up and said here is a way where we can live our lives, enjoy life and make other people happy, and this was the forcing drive of our career going forward."

"That was of course, no question about it, two bands: Black Sabbath and Led Zeppelin," answers Rudolf, asked what had inspired him to take the band in more of a hard rock direction. "I can say that also already The Yardbirds had this kind of direction, because of Jimmy Page, because of Jeff Beck, and who else was in there? Eric Clapton. So Yardbirds was a very important band too—*For Your Love*, amazing, great stuff. That was the reason why Scorpions was also the German Yardbirds, because with Uli John Roth, Michael Schenker and Rudolf Schenker we were also very guitar-orientated."

Deep Purple was an inspiration as well, although now we're talking more immediate inspiration, directly informing where Rudolf might take his own band... "They had the right songs. I saw them the first time and—maybe it was '68 or '69, I don't know—first of all how loud they played. Ritchie Blackmore, he was very, very much a great guitar player, and I think the whole combination with the keyboards... I think that this band was an organic rock band. It was really a way of bringing music the most effective way. Power, attitude, everything was involved. Of course *Child In Time*, I think that was the bringer—and *Smoke On The Water*—for Germany. Because on the one hand, that's the reason why Scorpions, from the first album on, we had also two sides: the ballad side and the rock side. That's the same situation with Deep Purple, because Ian Gillan was the perfect guy to sing a song like *Child In Time*. I think the whole mixture, all of this, the right songs, the band, how they're performing, everything was perfect for the German market."

But first it was "beat" groups for the guys, Rudolf starting "The Scorpions," in Hannover, in '65, with both Klaus and Rudolf's very young brother, Michael, joining the band on December 30, 1970, after leaving their starter group Copernicus. In the beginning, Rudolf also managed the band's affairs, as band management as we know it today was illegal in Germany—of note, this is cited as one of the reasons bassist Francis Buchholz was the band's ersatz manager later on, well into the recording years.

What is considered the first real version of the Scorpions dates to 1968, however, featured only Rudolf from the band as we know it, Schenker joined by Karl-Heinz Vollmer, also on guitar, Achin Kirchoff on bass and Wolfgang Dziony on drums. The line-up of the band as it existed in late 1970, was in fact the same one that would record the debut album.

"I think we respect each other," mused Michael, about his relationship with his brother. "The way we grew up, there was no competition and no fights. For instance, I wouldn't go to my parents and ask for money; I would just earn it myself. We had a unique upbringing. At the same time, we are both very visual. In order to get somewhere in life, you need to have a vision. The vision brings you to the table. Without a vision, you just do what everybody else does and you are just there. If you are an individual then you create something unique; it's just the way it goes. My whole family are very emotional people. Everything created is created with a lot of feel."

Rudolf encouraged young Michael right from the start. Every time Rudolf would buy a new guitar, he would pass the last one down to Michael. When Rudolf was too busy and tired from working a regular job, he would pay Michael to figure out guitar licks, for him, for both of them, which came in handy as they worked out the dual parts beginning to emerge through the work of the English invasion bands (other stated influences ranged from Little Richard through British blues boom groups like Fleetwood Mac). Rudolf indeed talks about being too lazy to learn the proper chords, and given that impatience, it perhaps makes sense that he would steadfastly over the years define himself as a rhythm guitarist, a somewhat limiting missive.

Klaus, of course, in the early Scorpions, soon took over lead vocal chores, which had previously been handled by Rudolf. Michael was all of 15 at this point (Rudolf was 22, as was Klaus), but already somewhat of a veteran, having sat in with his older brother's band at the age of 11, and having been bit by the bug when Rudolf brought home a Gibson Flying V one day.

"Is there anything German in our music?" wondered Klaus, reflecting on the nascent days of the band, in conversation with Dmitry Epstein. "I don't know; that's a good question! Obviously, we're from Germany but we grew up with English and American music which was such a strong inspiration for the young band. Very early on, in the '70s, we went to England and France, to Japan and America, we toured and then became an international band. I think our music was never German; it's always had this Anglo-American influence—we never tried to be a German band! We are Germans, yes, but not in our music. When we grew up, there was schlager music, this pop music kind of thing. We went through all those different styles as far as clothing goes, but as for the clothing we were always more close to The Rolling Stones because they also had these kind of fancy clothes."

Of course there was Krautrock... "Yeah! Today it's kind of culty, and people say, 'Ah, Krautrock!' But when the Krautrock thing came up, back then, in the early '70s, it was like all the international stars in big music magazines—they got big articles and nice features. It was like they were putting us down and making us very small. It was like, push, push, push when—especially when we were a young band—we needed support to gain the confidence. We felt there was no support and it encouraged us to go to foreign countries. We went to England in 1975 just to figure out, 'We are German but we sing in English. Are we good enough? Are we strong enough to survive among English who invented rock 'n' roll?' This was always like a challenge, and so very soon we became an international band. When we started, there were Kraftwerk and Tangerine Dream, and both bands also became very, very strong internationally but in a different area, in a different field. They were doing experimental kind of music, and Kraftwerk were amazing, while we played traditional rock. But those were the days!"

Lonesome Crow

"We heard it back through the radio with a special sound"

The line-up that would make Scorpions' first record would consist of Rudolf and brother Michael on guitar, Klaus on vocals, along with Lothar Heimberg on bass and Wolfgang Dziony on drums.

Almost as important to the process was producer Conny Plank, who had figured prominently in the movement of the time known as Krautrock, a daring and almost subversive form or progressive rock that often went pioneeringly electronic, and in the Scorpions' case, among others (Jane, Eloy, Night Sun, Hairy Chapter!), toward the hard rock end of the spectrum.

Conny would work with Guru Guru, Eloy, Cluster, Neu!, Kraftwerk, Ash Ra Temple, and the aforementioned very heavy Night Sun, through '71 and '72, with Lonesome Crow emerging in February of '72 on the storied Brain/Metronome label. Of note, the album was actually issued in the US at the time as well, on a small label out of Chicago called Billingsgate (BG-1004, the fourth release), which also issued early material by Neu! (BG-1001), Lucifer's Friend, Frumpy and Epitaph, modestly educating America on the pleasures of Krautrock.

Plank achieved a solid, chunky sound for the guys, the totality of the stoner rock experience that was Lonesome Crow sounding like Ted Nugent & The Amboy Dukes circa Marriage and Survival crossed with, tantalizingly, the first Black Sabbath album, evidenced by the crashing chords and earthy leads all over opening track *I'm Goin' Mad*. It is pertinent that the band had elected to write all their lyrics in English, the guys all too cognizant that singing in their native tongue would severely limit any shot at international success. It is also surprising that there was a proper production video made for this track, featuring the band playing on top of a big rock pile, Rudolf already with Flying V, Michael with a standard Les Paul, Klaus with a moustache and a huge mountain man beard.

Moving forward through the record, *It All Depends* very much perpetuates the Sabbath vibe, with the band jammy jazzy and capably while Michael peels off leads that sound deadringer-bound toward Iommi, all the while Dziony doing his best Bill Ward.

"Lonesome Crow is my first record," recalls Michael, "and you know, when I was 14, I discovered all the sounds from Deep Purple and Black Sabbath and Jeff Beck and Led Zeppelin and all of that, and that was my world, and that was exactly what I wanted to do. So I started to create stuff that I thought was coming out of me and that I thought I should be doing. Starting to put melodies together, songs together, and doing things and playing them to Klaus. Basically I was writing all the music, most of it anyway, but we ended up giving credit to all of us. But it was just that aspect of the excitement of actually being… It was the beginning of writing my own material, and that material, we actually went into a recording studio, and we actually started to record it, and then we heard it back through the radio with a special sound (laughs). Fascinating."

But if Michael could ably ape his elders, actually doing so would not be part of his modus operandi much longer. "No, I've been very aware for many, many years, for actually 40 years probably, that everything I do, and what I write, and what I develop is actually not influenced outside of myself. It's only as I started when I was nine years old, until I was 17-and-a-half, 18, that I copied other musicians, other guitarists. But when I was 14-years-old and I was imagining playing guitar onstage in my head, it was based on hearing Jeff Beck and Jimmy Page. They're exceptional performers that made me decide that I wanted to do what they were doing. That was the excitement that made me want to practice and practice. I said that I wanted to be one of the best guitarists in the world, but that didn't mean anything other than I wanted to be as good as those people I felt were best. I wanted to be able to create such an effect as they had on me."

"So I copied guitarists, really to focus, until I was 14, 15, and the last person that I tried to play or figure out a lead break that I copied, was *Theme From An Imaginary Western* by Leslie West, and that was the end of it. Since then I've always tried to stay away from music as much as possible. I always knew that the infinite and creativity comes from a deeper source. So I have two choices: one is I focus externally and copy what is out there and try to do it better or whatever, or I just go within myself and try to create new colours and something that maybe hasn't been out there before."

"So I don't really focus on listening to music at all. If I do, I write, I invent. I especially don't listen to rock music, because I want to keep it all fresh and exciting for myself. If I listen to rock music all day long, when it's time to make an album, I'm all worn-out. It's like eating too much chocolate—you want to make sure you keep it special."

Back to the album, *Leave Me* is a bit of an unsatisfying bluesy '60s

7

pop darkened by Moody Blues-styled vocal harmonies. Nonetheless, Klaus sings powerfully, and Conny adds a bit of spice in the form of some spacey Krautrock keyboard effects. At the close, Michael returns with a vengeance screeching out some choice Sabbatherian leads over a double time section which, with this portion's haunting vocal harmonies, has the band sounding like Uriah Heep.

Side one closer *In Search Of The Peace Of Mind* is also steeped in Heep, combining epic rocky bits with *Come Away Melinda*-like dark softness. A lot of creepy and unexpected prog is accomplished within the track's five minutes, and the band's Krautrock credentials are assured. Michael affirmed to me *that In Search Of The Peace Of Mind* was the first song he ever wrote, adding that with respect to his lifelong relationship with spirituality, "I started very early, I think when I was five. Yeah, and in Germany also, as part of school, to be confirmed, you had to study for two years the Bible, so I got confirmed when I was 14. And when I was 15 or 16, my brother and I discovered eastern religion; it just went from there, and I just kept going in all directions."

Over to side two, *Inheritance* demonstrates more of the band's solid jamming skills enhanced by Conny's hot-blooded production and mix, again, the vibrancy of Sabbath's landmark debut coming to mind from both a performance and sonic point of view, this one a cross between, say, *The Warning* and the second album's *Planet Caravan*. Lyrically, it's less English-as-a-second-language-contorted than most of the others, this one being about the evils of money, or at least the lending of it, although there seems to be a few complaints about repairmen as well!

Side two's second track (of only three) was a song about driving fast called *Action*, which, incidentally, was also what Lonesome Crow was renamed for some of its many reissues over the years. The song is a jazzy jam, typical of many bits of the album, again with Michael's full-throated soloing throughout.

The epic title track, *Lonesome Crow*, closes the album, winding its way through 13-and-a-half minutes of... well, exactly what is expected, moody dark bits, power chord passages, jazzy rhythms, and a ton of Michael screeching over the top of it all. Dziony plays very much like Bill Ward and indeed his drums sound sonically like Ward, Conny's work evoking very much a Roger Bain production job. There are also some scary sound effects and haunting shrieks from Klaus, and yeah... Scorpions now had their own version of *The Warning*.

Scorpions would tour Lonesome Crow extensively through '72 and '73, although only all over Germany, combining club dates with billings at festivals. Giving the band a bit of a boost, some of the Lonesome Crow material was used in the Schlesinger-directed German anti-drug movie Das Kalte Paradise (The Cold Paradise), Scorpions connection to the project being their producer Conny Plank. "We went to the recording studio to do three songs for the soundtrack," recalls Schenker. "They were *I'm Going Mad, Lonesome Crow* and one more. Conny Plank was in the studio. He said, 'What?! Do you have a contract?! Do you have a company?! No?! I take care of you.' In October 1971, we did our first album. We put those two songs on it. It was a long time ago."

Support slots on the tour were, variously, for Rory Gallagher, Uriah Heep, Chicken Shack and UFO. In June of 1973, the band's flash blond guitarist, Michael, would be poached by the latter of those, Phil Mogg's precocious UFO, who were nonetheless sounding like Krautrockers at this point, promoting their "space rock" album Flying.

"It's one of those things, really," recalls UFO bassist Pete Way. "Scorpions was supporting us, and Michael was the guitar player for Scorpions. Bernie Marsden lost his passport and we had to play. It was actually Phil who said, 'Well, that bloke's really good, isn't he? The blond fellow.' He filled in. From then on... he didn't speak English and we didn't speak German particularly and that was it. He was in the band."

"That was more circumstances than anything," adds UFO vocalist Phil Mogg, confirming the tale. "Bernie, who was playing with us at the time when we had a tour in Germany to do, forgot his passport, and things weren't great. We'd seen Michael play with Scorpions—an outstanding guitarist!—so we asked if we could borrow him for the gig, and we did two nights with him and then asked him to join."

"I was touring already with the Scorpions before I joined UFO," says Michael upon his fateful decision. "That's how I met UFO, Scorpions being an opener, a special guest, for UFO. They had arrived without a guitarist and without equipment, so they borrowed me and the Scorpions' equipment and that's how they found me. I ended up playing with both Scorpions and UFO for a couple of concerts until the other guy came back; this was like 1973. Then they approached me. I always told the Scorpions that, you know, one of these days, if somebody from England approached me, I would leave and go there, because that's where all the rock music is coming from. In Germany it was very hard to develop. There was no management allowed and it was really, really... it was disco music and it was just kind of dead in Germany. So when UFO wanted me, I said, like, this is it. Then I just kind of made sure I wouldn't disappoint my brother too much, and I found Uli Roth, and so I felt comfortable and ready to go."

"I simply wanted to do my own thing," says Michael, further elaborating on the break with what was to become the biggest band ever out of Germany, and a band that was ultimately much more financially successful than UFO ever became. "I think God wanted it that way. I don't think it would have worked as well for Scorpions or my brother if I had been in the band. I think by moving me out of the Scorpions... my brother is more like a group person and I am more of an individual person. His dream was always to be in one of the biggest bands in the world and my dream was to be one of the best guitarists in the world. The visions show that he is a group person and I am a loner. My brother shares his energy with the others and I just simply go within myself and get it from the essence of my being. I was quite independent. I recorded Lonesome Crow when I was 15. I moved in with my girlfriend when I was 16. I told her, 'See those orange boxes over there? We can make some furniture out of them and we can move into a place.' She told her mother and she was like, 'No way!' She started buying us furniture. I remember being 16 years old and lying there talking to my girlfriend and I told her, 'You can drop me off in the middle of China and I would know what to do.' I always knew. When I was 16, I knew anything was possible. I told my girlfriend then, 'One day I am going to be one of the best guitarists in the world.' She just laughed."

"When Michael joined for Phenomenon, he was the lucky link," adds Phil. "It made our sound, which I think is very British, a little bit European. With Michael in it, you can hear German or Teutonic notes or notations in his playing. So it became a very European rock band, second or third generation."

UFO's then-current guitarist Bernie Marsden (later of Whitesnake fame) did in fact show up after the fated Schenker show for the next night's gig and he indeed did finish the tour. Michael was formally brought into the picture in June, after Schenker had actually been encouraged to do so by Rudolf and Klaus, who were considering throwing in the towel, knocking Scorpions on the head after eight years tooling it around Germany and no further. But instead of folding the band permanently, the key position of lead guitarist within the new Scorpions would be filled by a personality and player every bit Michael's equal, but worlds away in terms of style and temperament.

Fly To The Rainbow

"That's the best guitar sound in Germany"

Ulrich "Uli" Jon Roth, at the age of 19, would arrive within the Scorpions ranks as part of a merger between two competing acts. Indeed all that would remain of the band that fashioned Lonesome Crow would be Klaus and Rudolf, who, as alluded to, had actually briefly broken up the band after Michael had left.

"Uli Roth and I had a four-piece-band called Dawn Road with Jürgen Rosenthal on drums and Achim Kirschning on keyboards," explains Francis Buchholz, at this point the Scorpions' new bassist. "One day Rudolf of the Scorpions called and asked Uli to help out playing lead guitar at some Scorpions shows, because their guitarist Michael Schenker had left the band. Soon the Scorpions broke up and Rudolf visited us at Dawn Road's rehearsal room. He needed new companions for his Scorpions, because everybody else had left Rudolf alone. We discussed how we could start the Scorpions new. Rudolf thought about becoming the singer. But he changed his mind and talked Klaus into joining us. So basically Rudolf and Klaus joined our band Dawn Road, but we named ourselves Scorpions from that moment on, because that name was already better established."

"James Jamerson is one of my early heroes," adds Buchholz, asked about his inspirations as a bassist. "I listened to much of his work. When I create a bass line, I have that '60s groove going through my head. But what comes out as a bass line has nothing to do with that old music; it is something new. I listen a lot to new music letting my inspiration pick up things from here and there. In short words, I have no bass heroes. Most important to me is that a bass line fits into the song perfectly. The bass should support the song, possibly carry it to different shores. But there were no heavy bands. We modelled ourselves on the English rock scene, which was not... the Germans were not happy that they had a heavy band playing in that style, an American/English style in Germany, and singing in English. They thought we should rather sing in German, but we wanted to become an international band. So we went with the English language."

Fleshing out the story of the band's career arc in the early '70s, Francis says that, "After their first album, the Scorpions had split and they lost their recording contract with Metronome Records here in Germany. The 'new' Scorpions were formed: Klaus Meine, Uli Roth, Rudolf Schenker, Jürgen Rosenthal and Francis Buchholz. A concert promoter from Hannover, who managed us at the time, was able to get RCA Records (today it's Sony BMG) interested in the band and we got lucky signing a contract with RCA over five albums. Our first RCA album, Fly To The Rainbow, was recorded in Musicland Studio, Munich with an engineer named (Reinhold) Mack, who later worked with Queen there. I still remember his 1970 Mercedes SL. We got everything recorded with a very good sound in quite a short time. On drums, there was Jürgen Rosenthal and keyboards, Achim Kirschning, both from our former band Dawn Road. Achim was no band member, because he wanted to become a teacher. And soon after the recordings Jürgen had to leave the band and join the German army, through the draft."

"I had been in the band for about less than a year," affirms Uli, on the ramp up to the making of his first album. "I mean, the original Scorpions had broken up, and then there was a big lull, and the band kind of folded, and really only Rudolf was left. I had a band called Dawn Road, which was a four-piece. Which was Francis Buchholz, Jürgen Rosenthal, a keyboard player and myself, and we joined forces with Rudolf, and then Klaus came back in, and then because Scorpions had a record contract and were already a semi-known brand in Germany, we called it Scorpions, and we took it from there. By that time I had very little writing experience. I had written a few things for Dawn Road, but I started writing immediately for the Scorpions, and the first one I wrote was a song called *Drifting Sun*, and then of course, most of the songs, on that album, had already... some of them were already in semi-existence, shall we say. Rudolf already had some chord changes and some melodies, and then we elaborated on them together."

Fly To The Rainbow, issued November 1st, 1974, would retain the band's definite Krautrock vibe, even if hard rock or proto-heavy metal was becoming more prevalent in the sound. But the album's cover art was almost nonsensically surrealistic, an up-ratchet in intensity over the debut's illustration of a hand bitten by a Scorpion—Lonesome Crow's wraparound to the back revealed that the headbanger "at hand" was probably dead, with a black crow having alit on his outstretched arm.

"I'll tell you the story," laughs Uli, asked about the flying scorpion man on the Fly To The Rainbow cover. "Personally I didn't like that cover at all. I tried to convince everybody not to have it. I just didn't like it (laughs). It wasn't done by the band. It was done by a studio in Hamburg. They got the album, it was commissioned, and that's what they came up with. I said, 'Rudolf, look, we can't have this for the album cover; I think it looks ridiculous.' He said, 'Well, the guy did a great job on the very first album,' which was called Lonesome Crow, which I agree, actually, I did like the Lonesome Crow cover. He said, 'Well, obviously that's what he feels like when he hears the album' (laughs). So to me, it just didn't feel like the album. In fact, I remember our then drummer, Jürgen Rosenthal, used to paint quite a bit, in oils, and he did an album cover for Fly To The Rainbow, which I preferred at that time, but in the end the one that you know was chosen."

"The Scorpions were never Krautrock," avows Uli, speaking with Sam Dunn. "The only thing we had in common with Krautrock was we tended to play the same festivals as Krautrock bands, and German progressive bands. I mean I always thought it was a weird kind of title anyway. But most of the German bands at that time anyway, they were rather progressive, you know? Like you had bands like Eloy, Guru Guru, people like that, and those were the people we used to play with on festivals but we were the odd ones out. We sounded a lot more English and I guess the band had a more international flavour, you know? But as I say, we had nothing in common with Krautrock. We really did something else. Also our stuff was highly melodic. Being a rock band that was really melodic, both in terms of vocal and in terms of guitars, dual guitars, was unusual. There were maybe a few bands... you know, in England I remember Wishbone Ash; they had like the dual guitar going and they had melody. But I think Scorpions were a little bit more melodic than other bands, and that was a very important factor in their success."

"I have to say when we did it, we didn't think about doing something new," continues Uli. "With hindsight, I guess I've realised it was new. It was kind of like a variation of what I'd been before, but it was kind of an interesting combination of things. It had an unusual sound. It was kind of a winning kind of mixture of individuals that worked well together as a team, onstage and offstage. We did five albums while I was there, and each one was a part of the journey and we were exploring music and getting better each time around. I guess that was it. We were the lone German band, that's true. But again we didn't really look at things that way. We just did really what we wanted to do—wanted to do new music, you know? Very early on we started playing abroad, started playing France, Belgium, and then England every year. So yes, we were a German band and I guess to some degree also we sounded German, but we were very influenced by British and American bands at that time."

Not much was happening with respect to hard rock in Germany at the time, prompting that comment about Scorpions being the lone German band. "It was certainly very different. I remember when we first started out, like in '73, the bands that were big were like Emerson, Lake and Palmer, bands like that. Yes was starting out. We in Germany were, I think, a bit of an anachronism at that time. I was into Hendrix and I learned a lot from that, but at that time Hendrix was not yet... just died three years before but he was a little bit out of vogue. So we were a very eclectic bunch, doing the style of music that some people in Germany didn't get at all. But once we started playing abroad and the band got better at what we did, we started kind of cleaning up on the festivals, you know? So then it changed. It became kind of more respectable in Germany as well, around '75 or so."

So it's easy to imagine Fly To The Rainbow as a record perched between two worlds, tilting toward a more immediate hard rock, in large part because the band's new guitarist did not have art rock or Krautrock as part of his influence set or repertoire.

"Me personally, not at all," reiterates Uli, asked about the extent of prog in his pudding. "Now, I don't know if that's a good thing or a bad thing, but I was very single-minded and I tended to shadow most things. I guess nowadays I'm more open-minded, but back then, my fascination lay with Hendrix, Cream, and later on a little bit of Led Zeppelin. Those were my main influences, to start with at that time. The German rock scene, whatever there was, I didn't notice it. It completely passed me by, and when we played on festivals with them, there wasn't a single band that really did anything for me, and that was probably also because there weren't any guitar-oriented bands at that time. You had bands that wrote epic stuff. You had bands like Eloy, but I was more interested in bands where the guitar players have a leading role, and in Germany, we were absolutely the only band who did that. At least to my knowledge."

Leslie West and Mountain was making an impact on a young Uli as well. "His contribution has been tremendous, because he is one of the original founding fathers, really. He was around at the time of Hendrix. He was around at the time of Cream, and he was already writing music history at Woodstock, and so he was doing something that other people weren't doing, at the time. He had a very rich guitar tone, the songs have lots of power chords, they were melodic, and he forged a certain sound that others got inspired by, and you can see influences of Leslie West left, right and centre, in today's music. Other people probably wouldn't actually know that, because they don't tend to look for the roots where things are coming from. But I can hear it, and I know it's there."

"I always liked Deep Purple," Uli told me, in a wide-ranging discussion that also revealed his admiration for and friendship with that band's current guitarist Steve Morse. "I saw them live in '72, and thought they were great, particularly Ritchie and Ian Gillan. It was very unique, very musical always. Ritchie was totally a trendsetter. His approach to playing the guitar was very, very unique, when he first came out, and it is still unique. There are very few people in the music business who were able to do like three totally different things and make them all work. You know, like Purple, Rainbow, and then Blackmore's Night. It's a very unique gift that he has, a very musical gift, and a great popular gift also."

"Like, I couldn't write a riff like *Smoke On The Water*. Some people maybe laugh about it because you used to hear it in every music store. But you know, that's an achievement. It's a gift. So Ritchie... I always felt he was a guitar player who sounded exciting, and he was never afraid to go close to the edge—there was always danger in his playing. This is what I like. I like players who don't do the expected thing. They take chances and go for the dangerous moments, and are not just being self-complacent. Very often I prefer those kinds of players to the players who are like all smooth and maybe super-refined, and where every note is in the pocket. I guess I'm more fascinated by the aspect of creativity, in the making—and with Ritchie you always get that."

"I only saw one Deep Purple concert, and it was great, in '72, but of course, I sometimes also saw the odd video appearance, like California Jam or something. With Ritchie, it was always fresh. Even if they played the same songs for the umpteenth time, they weren't afraid to improvise on stage, which most bands are—it basically is played the same. But Purple never played them the same. Also, another thing that I really liked about Ritchie, whenever I saw him live, he always has a great tone. He had very much his own tone, and I respond to that. I respect players that have a unique tone, a very good ear for sound. So he sacrificed the playability of the instrument for a great tone. Because it's not easy to do these sounds with an almost clean guitar, the way he used to play."

"What can I say about Ian Gillan?" continues Uli. "Ian was fantastic from the beginning, when he did Jesus Christ Superstar. You know, that was defining stuff. I would say that if anybody in rock created the quote unquote rock sound that thousands of singers ended up copying, it was Ian. Before that we maybe have Robert Plant in Led Zeppelin, but Robert was a little bit more blues-based, coming from that kind of area. But Ian gave rock this kind of incredible bel canto edge, almost like an opera singer, in rock, without any of the opera kinds of sounds, but equally valid. That is so hard to do for most people, and I think he just singlehandedly created that genre. That's my personal take on it. Or at least he's the first one who really had it down to a fine point, with *Child In Time* and all that."

"In the beginning we were part of a big scene," adds Rudolf, struggling to articulate Scorpions' place in German rock in the beginning. "But a very small point. What we tried in the beginning when we played in Germany, we noticed our way, how we play our music was different to the rest of the German music scene, called Krautrock. We had more the feeling to be connected to American and English music. That was our basic way of Yardbirds, Led Zeppelin and all this kind of... like Sabbath kind of direction. We went for foreign countries, like France and Belgium and stuff, and we noticed that by being German it somehow was a different style than maybe the American and English. It was very much American and English music, but a little bit maybe inspired by classical music—maybe we didn't even know that we were doing that. But later on when I did interviews, they said, 'You know, you guys are more like classical-influenced.' We didn't know because we never were into classical music. So in this case I think coming from Germany, we were different because we had to be noticed by coming out of a country where nobody noticed that from Germany there can be rock music or heavy metal music. So in this case we went different roads than American and English bands, and then we started creating our own personality."

"Krautrock was actually a kind of experimental rock," continues Schenker. "Finding a way of making music without copying the English and American music. Finding your own way of making music, and that was, of course, not commercial. But somehow this trend with Amon Düül, Can, Guru Guru, Kraftwerk, what they did was so different that it became their own brand that was Krautrock. Because the English, they thought anyway that they invented rock music. So in this case, they only could laugh about it. But the moment when they started laughing about it, there were other people in England and around the world who'd think, oh, this is something different. We want to see what it is. So for our way of thinking, to be a rock band, it was not our way of thinking. We wanted to make really straight rock music."

"Uli was very much influenced by Jimi Hendrix," affirms Klaus. "Still is! Absolutely! I didn't know how close Uli was to Jimi until some years later I saw some of Jimi's videos and stuff and I said, 'Ooh! It's like Uli!' (laughs). It was amazing! But Uli is also an amazing, extraordinary guitar player, there's no question about it. In those years, with Uli, we were very strong, but it was a different type of Scorpions that many fans call 'Scorpions Edition One.'"

It wouldn't be out of line to call Fly to The Rainbow's opening salvo, *Speedy's Coming*, Scorpions' first, best form of this new approach Uli is getting at, straight to the gut, like Scorpions' first shot at a *Mississippi Queen*. In effect, this short, shocked rocker represents the band's introduction to the nascent genre which would reward the band so richly in the years to come. No surprise that the song was floated as a single, backed with *They Need A Million*. Sending the song into higher relief, it is the only track deep into heavy rock from the entire album, not to mention comparatively to the sum total of Lonesome Crow. Rudolf emerges as the rhythm guitar master that would launch a dozen smash singles, and as foil, Uli rips aggressive leads that grind and whammy bar-divebomb more forcefully than any we had heard out of Michael.

But then it's into a fairly Germanic, prog rock miasma, starting with *They Need A Million*, the very Spanish melody of which forms a blueprint for a more metallic rendition of the same called *Steamrock Fever* three records hence.

Next up is a fairly heavy track called *Drifting Sun*, of which Uli is the sole author. The descending riff structure derives very much from Hendrix and Cream, and it is Uli's first of a handful of lead vocals he would perform throughout his four studio albums with the band. Pounding the track toward heavy rock almost to the point of distraction is a thumping performance from Rosenthal, with Roth himself helping the caterwauled cause with omnipresent howling leads.

Perhaps it's 20/20 hindsight, but such a visceral capture of drums... one might ascribe that happenstance to the presence of Mack as recording engineer, who shares the engineering credit with Horst Andritschke, Scorpions themselves taking the production credit.

"It was the famous Mack, but back then he wasn't that famous," laughs Roth. "We actually never found out his Christian name. He didn't want us to know (laughs), which was funny. But no, we did have a producer for that album, and it didn't really work out and the record company weren't happy, so in the end, you know, we got the production credit."

Elaborating on how the recording of the album went down, Uli adds that "Musicland was, I guess, a very established music studio by that time. Because the Stones had just been there before we had came; I remember that. But you see, for me that was the first time I was in a studio, for Fly To The Rainbow, so I didn't have any reference points. So I came in there like a complete novice, and to me, it felt claustrophobic. It was tiny—I mean, tiny! It sounded horrible in there. It was just like one of these studios nowadays that are old-fashioned, which are totally dead. They mute everything to the point where there's no more resonance. So it was one of these places, and I was absolutely not happy with the guitar sound. So Mack said, 'Yeah, but that's the best guitar sound in Germany.' Well, it didn't really make me feel any better. But I had no reference points. But deep down inside I knew that this wasn't what I was looking for. I wanted the guitar to sound like on the stage, much more natural, with natural ambience and big. Like, the big Marshall sound is like a wild stallion. Like a big Formula One car or airplane. You can't put it into a little box; it just doesn't work together. That's exactly what they did back then. So yeah, I thought the album was good, but again, these things didn't satisfy me."

As for the record's "self"-production, "Well the thing was, we were supposed to have a producer, and he was the founder, founding member of this band Eloy, Frank Bornemann. But for some reason... He was there when we were recording, but for some reason, it didn't end up that way. We kind of produced it ourselves. It just wasn't the right chemistry, I guess. So that's why we got the production credit. It also had to be remixed because the record company... Back then, you see, we didn't have the experience. We didn't know that we can tell the sound engineer exactly what to do. So the guy mixed the vocals too low; they were too quiet, and I knew that, but he had a different kind of preference. So the record company, RCA, at that time, rejected it. Then Rudolf and myself, we went to another studio, in the north of Germany for a couple of nights, and we tried to correct everything by remixing those vocal passages, and that then became the finished product."

Closing side one of the original vinyl was what one might consider the first of the band's notorious "power ballads," *Fly People Fly* playing to that formula of slow, quiet and dramatic for the verse, anthemic and heavy for the chorus. The songwriting credit for this one is the first of three on the record for the departed Michael Schenker.

"That's because he wrote and co-wrote some of those songs," explains Uli, "because when Michael left for UFO, the band split up, and there was no more Scorpions. Rudolf and Klaus and Dawn Road, we kind of formed a new band, and we made a new Scorpions. But there were already some of those songs, like *Far Away* for instance, and we used them as a basis for that album. Because I had only just started writing songs, and it was good material, and we weren't going to throw it away. So he gets these writing credits, based on his original writing." Uli also confirms that these were not leftovers from Lonesome Crow. "No, no, they were written afterwards."

Onto side two, and *This Is My Song* offers a pert and powerful pop rock, the band accomplishing this by putting their prog predisposition into a succinct and driving structure, adding a memorable twin lead that amusingly sounds more Maiden than Lizzy. Professional video footage exist of the band pounding through this one live, the end effect sounding and looking not unlike Uriah Heep on a tear.

Far Away offers more of the album's acceptably heavy and chunky hard rock, even if the power chords utilised are of an older tradition circa Hendrix, Cream, Humble Pie and even BTO, versus the modern rock to come circa Uli's later records with the band. Lyrically a theme is forming, reaching back to the debut in fact, around flying, fantasy, solitude, loneliness, and the spreading of love.

The album closes, like its predecessor, with a long, involved title track, *Fly To The Rainbow* offering up a pile of prog, a little folk, and again, twin leads of a mournful nature that we would get through Iron Maiden. Interesting that Uli Jon Roth gets a co-credit with Michael, who he never wrote with. It is only Uli's second credit, after his sole ownership of

Drifting Sun.

A few interesting notes on the band's timeline to this point... Uli Jon Roth's first show with the Scorpions would be a mere five months after the February release of Lonesome Crow, a German club show on June 29th '73. Fly To The Rainbow would be worked on in April '74, with drummer Jürgen Rosenthal out of the band shortly after, playing his last show on June 30th '74, five months before the album bearing his credit would be released.

The limited but still substantial tour itinerary for Fly To The Rainbow would find the band, again for the most part, stuck legging it around Germany, playing with the likes of Edgar Broughton and Dr. Hook. All told, response to the record in the western world was minimal. Essentially, Fly To The Rainbow was viewed, very much signalled by the absurdist front cover, as a Krautrock album that somehow escaped and wound up with wide distribution, inexplicably showing up in the record section of your middle American drugstore. As for the contents, the album supported the trending idea that many of these German bands, proggy as they were, quite fancied hard rock, and were intent on using its mechanics, as demonstrated by bands that had visited Germany and done well, mainly Deep Purple and Uriah Heep. Still, it would take another record, and a markedly more focussed one, for the band to break out and demonstrate to the western world proper "why Scorpions gotta sting," in the cheesy parlance of this band trying desperately to communicate.

In Trance

"That is also why he had several heart attacks"

First order of business regarding the discussion of Scorpions' slamming third record is the aforementioned switch of drummers. "He was not replaced," confirms Uli, on the loss of Jürgen Rosenthal, superseded by one Rudy Lenners.

"No, he had to leave for army service. In Germany they have conscription for two years, or one-and-a-half years, and people had to go to the army. I luckily got away with it because I had some Berlin connections, but I was the only exception. Because I didn't want to go into the army. I would've been a disaster, for the army, anyway (laughs). They would've lost any war with me. But no, this was the reason why Jürgen left, and after Jürgen there was another drummer. His name was Doobie Fechter (ed. also known as J.F. Doobie, when he was with Viva, who also at one time included in their ranks the Schenkers' sister Barbara!) and he was there for almost a year, but he didn't make it onto any records, because just before In Trance, he decided to leave because he was with a girl, and it was all a big... I don't know. It was all overwhelming for him. Anyway, he left the band, and that was when we found Rudy Lenners. Nobody got thrown out of the Scorpions. They always just left (laughs)."

Lenners had seen the band play in Belgium, and already, word was out that they would have to replace Rosenthal. Lenners auditioned for the band and actually somewhat failed the test, but then asked for another go 'round, got it, and satisfied the requirements, immediately hiring on for a French tour. Interestingly, Lenners, Belgian, could only communicate with the band in English, until he managed to pick up a little German.

New drummer firmly on board, Scorpions also raised their game by finding one Dieter Dierks to produce the band, Dierks quick to become as synonymous with the band as Martin Birch would be with Deep Purple, or maybe even perhaps George Martin with the Beatles.

"Dieter was... foremost he came as a producer/businessman to us," begins Roth. "We didn't know him beforehand. But we started to work, and I liked working with him in the studio. He was a tremendous workhorse. I was very impressed, I remember, he would be staying there night after night, with full concentration. That is also why he had several heart attacks, which I didn't know at that time (laughs). But yeah, that was amazing, his sheer stamina in the studio. I learned something from that, apart from other things. But there were also a few differences. I wasn't happy with the way our time was structured in the studio, because the lead guitars were all of a sudden in a hurry, just at the end of it, and we spent like ten days on backing tracks, which should've been easy, and then I remember being upset about that. I thought it should have been the other way around."

"But it was a longer recording session than Fly To The Rainbow. First of all we did a demo for it at Dieter Dierks' studio, and then I don't know how long the album took, maybe two or three weeks to record. I do remember quite clearly that I had to do all the lead guitars at the end in two days, and I was pretty annoyed about that. Because everything else had taken so long, and I was annoyed about that. But there wasn't much I could do, because we were working according to an old school kind of time schedule."

"We didn't cross paths with any of the major bands at that time," answers Roth, asked if anybody else was in and out of the studio around the time that they were there. "That was always separate, in terms of studios. You know, we bumped into people on the road, but not in the studio. It was very much a private kind of thing. Also, being in Germany, it was a different scene. When we went, for instance, to Dieter Dierks' place, it was pretty much in the countryside, outside of Cologne, and you had to drive quite a long distance to get there. If other bands recorded there, they did it while we weren't there. But when you are in London, you had Olympic Studio, and if you have a session at Olympic Studio, yeah, sure, you would have your session play 'til seven, and then maybe in the night time Eric Clapton comes in or something like that. But that doesn't happen in Germany. Well, it didn't happen in Germany in these kinds of studios, because you were not in London, you are not in New York, you are not in Paris. You know (laughs), we were stuck in the countryside. That suited us just fine. We were just fully concentrating on the albums and we worked very, very hard, morning 'til exhaustion, frenzied. Very intense."

Adds Francis, "Dieter had invited us to his studio in Stommeln, which is a village near Cologne, after Dierks had attended one of our concerts here in Germany. We engaged Dierks as our producer for In Trance. Our first musical differences had to be worked out, especially with the song *Robot Man*, which led to long-lasting discussions in the studio. Also, Achim Kirschning visited us at the studio and did a couple of keyboards."

"Dieter is a workaholic," continues Buchholz. "Sometimes I thought he was crazy, then again I felt he was very smart. He used to start early in the morning in his office and when the band appeared in the studio after having breakfast, Dieter was at his mixing console already trying things out. Every day he was almost the last to leave the studio late after midnight. He was very concentrated during the recording eliminating mistakes at the spot. Dieter is a very good vocal coach; he used to work with Klaus for hours and hours on expressions in the singing. But sometimes we felt working together with a dictator. He always wanted to be No.1. If there was something he did not want, he would not let it work." Amusingly, Lenners, who holds Dierks in high regard as the fount of the Scorpions sound, figures he was spared much of Dieter's attention in the beginning simply because Lenners couldn't speak German.

"I was already successful before I met them," remarked Dieter, to Pete Makowski. "I had worked with a band called Atlantis, which was the first group that I took to the US. At that time they were the No.1 band in Germany and the only band that was internationally respected. It took quite a while for German music to be respected abroad. I could help them break the batter. First of all, I'm a musician. I played with several bands and for two years I played with black musicians, and that is where I learned to feel a grove. The truth is that the American groove is not in German blood so this was all very good training for me. I also went to the states and listened to American radio and checked out the whole scene to get a better understanding of what other markets were about. I started working with non-rock bands like Atlantis, a funk band. I've always been into rock, but I also like other stuff like Supertramp, The Eagles, hippie Californian style music. What I need is good melodies and harmonies. I am not so much into brutal hard rock."

Dark Lady, opening track to In Trance, certain reflects Dierks' aforementioned working over of Klaus. Even if the main verse parts are sung by Uli, it is Klaus that leaps from the speakers, howling, growling, on the edge of nervous breakdown. Of course it helps that the song is the band's heaviest track up to this feverish point, with all sorts of guitar madness from Uli and a penultimate sped-up close before a grumble of guitar makes it known that Scorpions would be enthusiastic participants in the forging of a new heavy rock.

"There wasn't any technology used," laughs Uli, asked about all the crazy sounds on the record, particularly within *Dark Lady* and side two opener *Robot Man*. "I just cranked the amps, and had the odd pedal, my wah-wah pedal. There wasn't really a lot of technology. It was all very, very bare-bones. You know, we did the best we could with what we had. The band was very real. It wasn't really a studio band, as such. We played this stuff live pretty much the same way as we did in the studio, although in the studio it might've been a little bit more perfect, in the way you would overdub things."

"*Dark Lady* was more like a jam band kind of thing, which wasn't even really like a song," continues Uli. "It was more thrown together like a jam, I guess. Originally I wanted Klaus to sing it, but in the studio, I don't think it was really that suitable for Klaus to sing. But Dieter pointed that out. He said, 'No, Uli sings that one' because it's more kind of free-flow, that kind of style. And I guess he was right. My early songs weren't really suitable for Klaus to sing, because the vocals were more Hendrix/Dylan kind of vibe, and that's not a classic, melodic rock singer's vibe. Klaus always needed some very definite melody to get his teeth into. Which I love, but my first attempts at songwriting were more... the vocals were more along the bluesy lines, so they weren't really for Klaus. That's also why I sung *Polar Nights*. *Evening Wind*, I remember, that is the one that I did want to sing, because I did think it was suitable for me. But Klaus said, 'No, no, no, that one's for me' and you know, of course he's right. He was the singer; I was not (laughs). It's that simple."

Next was the title track, another power ballad of sorts, although the emphasis in this one is on the metallic chorus. As for calling the whole album In Trance, "I think that was Klaus's idea," says Uli, "because of the song *In Trance*, which was definitely one of the highlights of the album, that song. And he wrote the lyrics to that, and I think that's why we picked that. It seemed the right title."

The cover art to the record featured the first of many sexy girls to grace a Scorpions sleeve, along with the first of a few controversies, given that she is flashing a bit of breast (this was blacked-out during some subsequent reissues). And the guitar? That's Uli's white Stratocaster, which can be seen illustrated on the cover of his Fire Wind solo album.

But as significantly, on this cover we get the first use of the band's iconic logo. Says Uli, "That logo was actually... believe it or not, it came from a movie called Rollerball. I think it was the record company; somebody just swiped it, and that's where that came from. I've never seen the movie. I don't know whose idea it was to do it that way, but I don't think we had an issue with it."

Back to the record, third track in was another one of the band's dirge-like power ballads, *Life's Like The River* featuring a liquid Uli construct for the verse that kerrangs into a big chorus pounded by power chords and lead licks. Despite the song's drag, there's no questioning the extent to which the explosive production enhances it. Lyrically, *Life's Like A River* perpetuates the band's mystical themes around mortality, the changing of the seasons, night into day, solitude, transcendence.

Further on the impact Dieter Dierks had with the band, Uli says that he was, "shall we say, co-director. I don't want to take anything away from Dieter, because particularly after I left, he had a particularly big impact on the band, and he was also important to their success. But when I was still there, everything was a little bit more experimental, and it was very much like a team effort. For instance, Dieter, he didn't impose anything, other than this timeframe. It was very much, you know, we did what we did live, and what we felt we had to do, and particularly those first albums, they would've sounded rather similar, I guess, with any producer in any studio, because all the studios back then were relatively small-sounding, except if you went to London, Olympic Studios or whatever, where you got these big classic Led Zeppelin-type sounds. But at that time that wasn't fashionable in the German music industry."

"We always used to record our albums in the summer," continues Uli, "except for Fly To The Rainbow—that was the only one that was recorded in April. But from In Trance onwards, it was always the summer. So In Trance was also definitely recorded over the summer. Maybe it was a period of three weeks or something. I remember we did a demo first, at Dieter's place, we spent a few days and we recorded the songs. Then we took them home, and we refined a few things, and then we recorded. What I definitely recollect was like we took about ten days or so for the backing tracks, and I was annoyed that we didn't have enough time. Rudy and Francis took a little longer to get their act together, I think, for that. Then we did the vocals. Rhythm guitars, and the lead guitars, all of them actually done in two days. I remember that upset me, because I thought they should also have a decent amount of time. Because in the studio, I saw myself as very much of a perfectionist."

"I remember doing *Life's Like A River*. I had written this intro guitar solo, a dual harmony lead, and we recorded it in the morning, I think on the second morning of those two guitar days. I wasn't happy with it, because there were a few glitches in the execution. Dieter overruled me and he said, 'Uli, every album has to have an end!' (laughs). I still remember that. I literally went outside and I think I was actually crying, because that was the only time somebody made me cry in the studio (laughs). I didn't... you know, I wasn't in a position to put my foot down, but I was very upset about it, and I never forgot that. That very much made me want to be my own producer afterwards, because I just didn't want to deliver anything on vinyl that I knew I could do a lot better. Because somebody afterwards would hear it like that and say, 'Oh, that's not so cool, that solo.' Maybe not; it's just a question of principle. So that's what I remember."

"Other than that, I think back later, we were largely happy with the album," concedes Roth. "But I have to think. People comment that they sound good, and I think they certainly sound very fresh. You can feel the energy, but it was felt that live we tended to sound better, sometimes. Whereas in the studio, we would've needed more time to do it full justice.

But I guess, in hindsight it doesn't matter. It is what it is, and it's probably a fair representation of what we were able to do at the time. Although, when I listen back to it today—not that I've done that in a long time (laughs)—but I remember that I can still hear the same mistakes, exactly in the same spots, that I wanted to change back then; mixing mistakes or whatever. I think that's still the same. I guess to outsiders that doesn't matter."

Next up is *Top Of The Bill,* which is the fourth Scorpions track from the early days—others being *Speedy's Coming, Dark Lady* and *In Trance*—to have made a lasting impression through the decades. "*Top Of The Bill* was very much Rudolf's riff," notes Uli. "A very typical Rudolf; like, it's almost like a German oak, totally clear-cut, power chords—nobody can do that like Rudolf (laughs). And it's incredibly Germanic, but it's also international, in a strange way. There's something compelling about it. Nobody can write these riffs like Rudolf."

Indeed *Top Of The Bill* is classic Scorpions, Klaus singing powerfully, urgently, adding harmony vocals to a structure that is tribal and primitive and yet Queen-like in its flourishes and sense of punctuation. The track culminates in an insane rave, Klaus screaming the title before Uli and Rudolf battle it out over a military snare beat from Rudy Lenners, before some of the pressure is let out for a return to the song's melodic premise. As with *Dark Lady* and *Speedy's Coming, Top Of The Bill* demonstrated that this band could write energetic and cerebral heavy rock, at least from a musical point of view. Lyrically, it's a throwaway, but for a much needed spell, away from the band's usually heavy spiritual themes to this point: like *Speedy's Coming,* it's about rockin'.

Side one of In Trance closes out with the band's most extreme epic dirge yet, *Living And Dying* creaking and sobbing and moaning as it rises to a crunching chorus, Klaus singing with passion about loneliness, a recurring theme, power chords a' plenty filling his empty room. Still, the band checked their tendency to drag it out, which would be In Trance's major distinction from the first two records, the album offering five tracks a side and only one over five minutes.

Over to side two and the band hit hard with the punky and compact *Robot Man,* and for all the writing credits Uli Jon Roth gets on the album, you can tell this was a Rudolf Schenker backslapper. Roth returns for another dark and bluesy epic in *Evening Wind* on which he exercises his deftness of tone as well as yet another lyric about loneliness and the change of seasons. *Evening Wind* gives way to *Sun In My Hand,* a pounding stripper blues on which Roth sings about the magic of music. The vocal in unison with guitar is a celebrated Hendrix conceit, and the trashiness of the drum sound gives the track grit and drive, over which Roth turns in a grinding, metallic solo in amongst the blues, as well as a cool, composed, almost Celtic twin lead.

Longing For Fire, a Schenker/Roth composition, is a strange kind of bluesy pop number, somewhat a predecessor to *Backstage Queen*, but not entirely as successful, lending the album a modicum of Krautrock integrity, buoyed by a nice bass line.

In Trance closes with a bit of a lullaby in *Night Lights*. "You know, each of them has their own little story," muses Roth, sole author of this instrumental. "I mean, I've had just as much input into the other songs as well, but the credit is basically there because I wrote those songs by myself, you know? But no, they all have their own little story. Some of them, I remember, more vividly than others. That one I wrote pretty much at home. I wanted to branch out into something more, shall we say, more elaborate melodically. Because this was the second album. On the first album I was still kind of finding my feet, because up 'til then, I had played a lot of classical guitar, but I kind of abandoned the electric guitar a bit, at the time. So when we started doing the Scorpions stuff I picked it up again. So on In Trance, I was probing the elements, the instrument a bit more. I started to compose guitar leads rather than just improvise them. One of the first of these was *Night Lights*. I guess it was very Jeff Beck-influenced. But also, it was basically an exercise for me to delve into something that was a little bit unknown territory. Luckily, in the Scorpions at that time, one could do that. We weren't bound by anything. We were probing the unknown, you know? Whatever came to us, we just did. It was very unrestrained."

Perhaps still a bit too unrestrained for mass consumption, not that that should be any artist's concern. Still, as well-regarded as In Trance is, the record is perceived as possessing more accessible tracks, to be sure, than its predecessors, but not enough to really cohere. In fact, if there's any cohering at all to the record, it would be in the direction of deep thought set to ponderous, almost claustrophobic dirge rock.

"Fly To The Rainbow was promoted in '74, and in '74 we played mainly in Germany," recalls Uli, explaining the extent of the band's tour history during this era. "We played some big festivals, but also a lot of club gigs. Then in '75, we started branching out abroad. We went to Holland, France, Belgium, and after In Trance, also to England, for the first time. That made a big difference, because we gathered more and more inspiration on these tours. In '75, now that you are asking, we did several tours, as a support band. We went out with the English band Sweet, which was a glam rock band who had several hits. They basically played to 14 to 16-year-olds. It wasn't quite suitable for us, but we held our own when we did our tour supporting them."

Speaking of Sweet, also in '75, The Scorpions went under cover as The Hunters and recorded a single comprised of German versions of that band's *Fox On The Run* and *Action*. The front of the picture sleeve was a cute and cuddly fox.

Asked about the band's first major touring experience outside of Germany, Francis figures that would have been the UK. "We played about 20 or 30 shows in small clubs. The highlights were the Cavern Club in Liverpool, where the Beatles used to play in their beginner days—The Marquee club in London, which was the most important show, because everybody from the record company and from music magazines showed up. The booking agency booked the London show always as the last concert. I think they did it this way because they were afraid that the band would go home after having played London and would not worry about all the other less important places. Especially because our payment was so little that we had to sleep in the cheapest guesthouses available. I remember the terrible bed sheets made of some easy-to-wash no-iron sheer fabric. Some of the guesthouse owners did not care about washing the bed sheets. I remember Rudolf sleeping with gloves on his hands and a scarf over his mouth because he was afraid to get into contact with that fabric."

Specifically speaking, in '75, Scorpions played their native Germany from late April through to the end of the year, with one French date thrown in. Touring duties resumed in February of '76 again in Germany, with an extensive run through France, and into the UK in early March.

"My mother runs a hotel in the North of England, right?" begins Rob Godwin, book publisher and issuer of the early Uli Jon Roth solo catalogue on CD, offering a slice of life from these times. "I'm kind of like the general dogsbody DJ, you know, cellarman, bartender, you name it. Quite often we would have musicians and a lot of American tourists. So one day I walk into the lobby and there's these guys standing at the checkout desk, and instantly you know they're rock 'n' roll guys. They've got hair down to their ass, practically. Five guys in the band, and three road crew. I got all excited, 'Oh, hey, are you guys in a band?' They said, 'Yeah, we the Scorpions,' you know? (laughs). I knew there was only one place in town that they could play, it was a place called Nelson's Column, and it was a big music hall in the town of Nelson. The Beatles had played there and Hendrix had played there. So I said to them, 'Where you guys going?' They said, 'We're playing Nelson's Column.' I kind of looked at them and said, 'No you're not.' 'Yes we are.' They looked at me like I was stupid. I said, 'No, trust me, you're not playing there.' 'What you talk about?' They barely spoke any English at all. Couple of the road crew did, but the band didn't speak much English. I had been in town the day before, March 18th, in Nelson, walking around town with my camera around my neck because I was taking a course in photography, when a fire broke out at Nelson's Column—burnt it to the ground. I was the only guy in town that was like there with a camera when it happened, so I got these photos of the place burning down, famous music hall. My photos were in the paper that day."

"So I said to the guys, 'You know, it burned down yesterday.' They looked at me like I was daft. I said, 'No, I'm not kidding. It burned down yesterday.' Showed them a newspaper. They're like at loose ends. They didn't know what to do with themselves, because they were going straight from the hotel to do soundcheck. They just kind of sat around looking lost for a while, and we got them checked into their rooms. I basically offered food and stuff, because the hotel was really quiet. There was hardly anybody there."

"We hung around for a little while, and Uli just seemed so cool," continues Godwin. "Uli Roth had like white blonde hair right down his back. Anyway, instead of them playing a gig, which is what they thought they were going to be doing, they came into my... well, for want of a better word, disco. It wasn't a disco in a sense as we know disco today; it was kind of early for discotheques. But it was like a room in the hotel where I played music at night, and people sat around drinking and had a good time. So the band came and sat in my disco, sat down next to me, and just started requesting records. So like for the next three hours or something, I was just sitting there playing DJ for them, playing stuff they wanted to hear."

"Cut to the end of the evening, the hotel closes at one, and they had a few drinks, they didn't want to pack it in. So I said, 'Why don't you come over to my cottage?' which is kind of attached to the hotel, and said, you know, 'We could carry on drinking, and I'll play you some Hendrix bootlegs.' Well, Uli Roth got really excited about that. So three or four of them came to my cottage and I pulled out Hendrix Live At The LA Forum, and Uli just got really excited and we sat and listened to that. Then I pulled out the brand-new Pretty Things album, which they were just gaga over. They thought it was the best bloody album they'd heard all year. I hit it off really well with the road crew, the three roadies, a Belgian guy called Bernard, a German guy called Axel, and another German guy, Langer.

"The drummer, Rudy, I think spoke English the best, and we got on well. Klaus, the singer, didn't, or gave the impression that he didn't speak English at all, at the time. The road crew... I said to them, 'How the hell does he sing all the songs in English?' They were telling me he basically does it phonetically. There was no indication at all to me otherwise, because he never spoke English to me. Rudy was really nice. Uli Roth spoke English really well, and I got on really well with Uli. So the next morning, he wanted his breakfast in his room. I got there, and he's sitting on his bed with his white Strat hooked to a portable amp. He was practicing at 11 in the morning, sitting on the mattress in his hotel room.

So I took him his breakfast and I sat there listening to him, and I was just absolutely blown away about how good this guy was. It was awesome. Then he told me, he said, you know, he practiced every day. That was one of the things that he pointed out to me. Like, this doesn't just come easy; I work at this every day."

"I'm chatting with him, and he said, you know, we're playing a gig tonight, and I want to say it was a place called Accrington. So they started packing up everything, and I rode down there in the truck with Axel and Langer and Bernard. On the way driving down there, Axel started telling me that he'd just come off roadying for the Yes Relayer tour, which really impressed me, because I was a huge Yes fan at the time. So anyway, we get to this gig in Accrington, and I helped them load all their gear into this tiny club with a really low ceiling, and help them set up. I remember that Uli was using an Orange amp, which I'd never seen before. Because everything was Marshalls and shit like that. He pulls out this bright orange amplifier, like something out of a candy store."

"Then I basically sat up at the soundboard and watched the set. One of the things that really struck me was, they seemed like two bands at the time. Because they came out and did a set, four or five songs, with the five of them, and then Rudy and Klaus left the stage, in this little club. I don't know where they went, whether they went to the dressing room or just went to the bar or something and left Uli with the bass player and drummer to basically do a power trio set. It was pretty evident that Uli was fashioning himself to some degree after Hendrix's thing. You know, he was a huge Hendrix fan; he had already told me that. But they were like Uli Roth tracks from In Trance and stuff. I just thought it was the weirdest thing that a band of five would play a show and the singer and a guitar player would leave the stage and let a threesome do their thing."

"So anyway, he did like his own little set in the middle of their set, and then Klaus and Rudy came back on, and they did the rest of their set and that was it. Then I helped them pack up and they went back and decided they were going to use my mother's hotel as the base of operation for a short time. She kept the place spotless, very nice place, perfectly clean rooms, which probably made the difference."

Rob figures there were three or four songs to the Uli bit, and that those to witness it were numbered somewhere south of a hundred. The next night, Doncaster, Godwin skipped out on, but he duly finished his roadying days for the Scorpions with the following night's show in Huddersfield.

"I went out twice with them, and I think they stayed there for a couple more nights and did some more shows in Blackpool or something like that, and then they checked out and had gone. The weird thing about it was years and years later, when we had Griffin Music, we got offered Uli's three solo albums to put out on Griffin and I just thought that was the coolest frickin' thing. Because I remember how impressed I was with Uli. So we signed up these three Uli Roth solo albums onto Griffin, from EMI Special Projects. When I got to put them out, shortly after that we were doing a Hendrix book, and the author told me he had been offered this really cool painting of Hendrix that was done by Monika Dannemann, and we could use it on the cover of the book. So he put me in touch with Uli and we had a chat, I thanked him for letting me use this painting for the cover of the Hendrix book. I reminded him of my short stint as a roadie for Scorpions (laughs). He remembered it, just really cool, because this was like 30 years later."

Last contribution from Godwin to the story is a description of Musicland Studios, where Scorpions recorded Fly To The Rainbow, plus a bit about that record's erstwhile producer, Reinhold Mack, granted, as he was years later.

"I was there with some friends of mine who were a blues rock band I'd rather not name," recalls Rob. "I was pretty happy to be there at first because I knew Led Zeppelin had recorded Presence there. The studio had been built by Giorgio Moroder. There were gold records hanging all over the place, like ELO, Queen, Deep Purple and most recently Billy Squier. It was in the most unlikely place, right under a hotel. No windows. About the only cool thing about the place was that the drum booth had doors that opened out directly into the underground parking lot. John Bonham had apparently recorded Presence with the doors open behind his kit to get that epic sound. Mack was a fixture at the place. He had a solid reputation as a producer at that point. I had spent time at quite a few other studios in Los Angeles with some big name engineers and producers so Mack's methods were immediately noticeably different to me. Very soon after we arrived he brought a drum machine into the mix. I was appalled. The drummer we had brought with us was a fantastic drummer and I simply couldn't understand what Mack was thinking. At first he encouraged the drummer to play to a click track, which seemed odd when you were trying to play blues. Then when the drummer just couldn't get the feel he wanted, Mack asked him to program his parts into the drum machine. Eventually the drummer left in frustration and flew home. The bass player was next. I followed shortly after, partly out of disgust and partly because there was nothing for me to do. The resulting album was critically acclaimed but bore little resemblance to what the band was about. Technically Mack was as good they get, but the room and that venue stripped all the emotion out of the music. The end result was technically flawless but completely devoid of emotion. The technical sterility pioneered by that place during the late '70s; you know, drum machines, click tracks, MIDI synths and over-production, represented to me everything that was wrong with rock music in the '80s and '90s. With a guy like Mack in the driving seat, he was meticulous to the point of obsession, but the technology took over and the music was sanitized and homogenized and became like McMusic."

"In Trance to Fly To The Rainbow... that was a progression," muses Uli Roth, in summation. "You know, I thought all the Scorpions albums, and all my later albums, they were all almost like snapshots in time. As an artist or musician, you move forward, and we certainly did this. Every year we started to learn new things and we spread our wings. We were growing musically. So each album, we tried to do something different. The songs started getting a little bit more, I don't know, I wouldn't say sophisticated, but we were growing in terms of songwriting. We were experimenting, and each album that we did—we did one each year—just took it a step further along that path. Speaking for myself, the first one was done very, very quickly, in the studio, with very little studio time. I think it was done pretty much in a week. We didn't have much studio experience. We really had to learn the ropes by doing it. On the second one we were already a little bit more experienced, and the album maybe reflects that, although some people prefer the first one. It had the title track, *Fly To The Rainbow*, which was kind of a precursor to certain things that happened later."

After the major '76 push through the UK, which saw the Scorpions play nearly every night in March, it was back to continental Europe for dates from April through to October, the lion's share of them in Germany. Finally, the band closed the year out with about a dozen additional UK dates in November.

"America was on the cards a few times, but it never really happened," notes Uli, lamenting missed opportunity. "We were with the record company RCA at that time, and I think the boss of the record company in New York wasn't really a great Scorpions fan. It almost happened, but it didn't. I guess we became kind of like a cult band in the states. But at that time we didn't know it. We found out about that really around the time when I was leaving. The band tried to convince me to go to America with them, but by then I was done, and I really just wanted to leave."

"Kiss came to Europe, to Germany, for the first time," recalls Uli, asked about early live milestones that *did* happen. "Paul Stanley had heard In Trance, and he spoke to the powers that be and said, 'I want that band to be our support band' in Germany. But we didn't know who Kiss was; at least I didn't. I had no idea. I remember on the first gig, riding the elevator, in my moccasins ready to go on stage, and I look and see this monster right next to me. It's Gene Simmons in his full attire, with the full platform heels etc., just smiling down at me. I thought, what the heck is going on here? Then I saw them on stage and he was spitting blood all over the stage, and I said yuck! But at the same time, I saw that it was kind of funny (laughs). So that was way before they became this massive band. It was funny because, I think, at the last NAMM or the year before, I don't remember, I bumped into Gene Simmons again, and we got to talk about the old days, and he said, 'Is Rudolf still doing the headstand?' I said no. He remembered everything about that first tour! But the thing he remembered the most was the ticket prices! He said, 'Oh yeah, it was only ten bucks a ticket or something!' That was unbelievable, after all these years, that he was still annoyed about the ticket prices being too low or whatever."

Virgin Killer

"Everybody knew where the train was heading"

As a bit of framing to the story so far, the heavy rock world was still sparsely populated in 1976, a few eclectic behemoths wandering the earth and on their last legs. But that was about to change with an onslaught of viable baby bands that would ramp up the world over, toward the New Wave Of British Heavy Metal and the golden age for metal that was all of the '80s. One of those bands by this point was the subject of our tale, the Scorpions, who would deliver, on October 9th '76, their most metallic record yet, Virgin Killer, housed, at least in their German homeland, in a scandalous album cover featuring a pubescent and very naked girl with a sparkle-burst oblique-ing the naughty bits.

Asked about the album, vocalist Klaus Meine cringes. "Well, I always think, first of all, about the embarrassing album sleeve. Where, it was like, it was nothing like you wanted to walk home and show it to your folks back home. It was just embarrassing. Most of all, it was the record company, leading guy back then at RCA, who pulled the plugs and wanted us to do this to get the kind of attention, scandal, outrageous, sexy cover. I mean, looking today, you would never do something like that. You wouldn't even think about it, with all the child porno that is on the Internet—you would never come close to doing anything like that. So it is something that at the time, it grabbed worldwide attention, and that's what the record company wanted to do. It's not an album sleeve we are proud of. Right after that we started working with companies like Hipgnosis who did so many great covers for bands like Pink Floyd, Led Zeppelin, and we did Lovedrive and Animal Magnetism, and we did great stuff with them. That was also sexual and about sexual attraction, so from our point of view, let's go for that, yeah, that's rock 'n' roll and that's cool. But with Virgin Killer, it was just too much. It's nothing I am proud of today. It was a good album though."

"Our record company was RCA then," recalls Francis, on the delicate situation of the sleeve. "Their A&R manager and their album cover design department came up with an idea: they suggested a photo of a—I believe she was 13 years young—beautiful but naked girl of the family of the guy of the art department. She was his niece or so. At that time I did not know anybody who had heard about 'child pornography.' I did not even know that word. Innocent and without any bad thoughts, we believed the idea was great. There was just some broken glass needed to cover the nudity of that girl. Even though the whole thing was absolutely questionable, the album got released and nobody in Germany had a problem with it. But our Japanese record company RVC called and said it was impossible to release an album like that in Japan. They designed a different cover with a rose, which I thought was very average. But for Virgin Killer we received our first gold record award in Japan. But yes, we liked the idea of the title and RCA came up with a—today—questionable album sleeve."

"It was the brainchild of a German journalist who was prepared to go to jail to defend it," noted Rudolf. "We couldn't get accepted in our own country in those days, so we had to go right to the edge to get noticed. A record company wanted us to do copies of what Deep Purple were doing, so we thought we would shake things up a little!"

"Maybe we went too far," reiterates Klaus. "I'm sure we wouldn't put it out now. But for us in those days, it was a very big thing. We always thought that using sex in artwork was better than using blood. We had to push the whole thing as far as we could. Thankfully no one ended up in jail!"

The naked girl on the cover was in fact a ten-year-old named Jaqueline. Rudolf has talked about the situation, explaining that it was only a ploy to get attention, and that the lyric to the title song itself really doesn't relate to the image. Furthermore, he says, they've talked to the girl years later as an adult, and she seemed to take the situation in stride. As well, the photographer for the shoot, Michael von Gimbut has explained that the girl's mother and aunt were present at the shoot, along with his own wife and three female assistants.

As Klaus alludes to, the record enclosed was quite good, a serious, artistic affair despite its cover (and don't forget, the cover was changed to a straight band shot in North America, and a third image for Japan). Virgin Killer possessed a sense of everlasting dimension through tried and true happenstances, namely the fact that its writers were a diverse but still functional set of evolving individuals, and the fact that its heavy rock operating platform was still, in 1976, not yet compartmentalized to death. As well, notes Francis, "Virgin Killer was recorded on a 32 track analogue recorder, which was state of the art then." Creativity, personality and technology... it was the perfect storm, one that blew across the straight and then the larger pond, establishing the goodly reputation of this German band amongst a growing gaggle of hard rock fans whose earliest musical memories date from the mid-70s and not much earlier.

Providing a bit of lead-up to the record, Rudolf figures that, "The Fly To The Rainbow stuff, we went through it, after my brother left the band, working with Uli, Uli and me, and we really started controlling the progress of the music. We tried to make it… that was the first influence, of Jimi Hendrix, the song that sounds like *All Along The Watchtower* (sings it), this kind of part; I forget the title. Anyway, so that was the first time that much material came from my brother still and from me, and Uli started writing. So, in this case, it was a very good beginning for us, especially working in the Musicland studio, under the situation of Mack as the producer, who works these days with Queen. He was the engineer for Rolling Stones when they did the album in Musicland studios, so in this case, it was a good experience for us to work with this kind of guy. The only problem with this guy was, in those days, he had a big problem with mixing. He put the vocals very much into the music, so that we had to take the tapes and go to a different engineer to remix the whole thing, to change the vocals. That is the Fly To The Rainbow story. I think In Trance and Virgin Killer was a really good start with Dieter Dierks, who found a way to give a signature sound for the band. I think there are no things we could have done better with Virgin Killer. It was a moment in time, the right moment, the right way, to make this kind of music."

Adds Francis, "During the recording of the album Virgin Killer, our drummer Rudy Lenners had to be taken to a hospital due to a nervous breakdown, because our Dieter Dierks had forced Rudy to record the same take over and over again." Clearly, it wasn't all fun and games working with Dieter.

In any event, Virgin Killer was studded with captivating peaks and quixotic valleys, the winding trails linking the two being equally eventful. Some of the best alchemical rock from the band to date was on this record. *Catch Your Train*, basically about keeping your nose to the grindstone, sounds much like its title, coal-driven, smoky, fixed on the horizon. *Virgin Killer* is clear-cutting and fangs-dripping like nothing previously conceived within the Scorpions catalogue or rarely by any other band— those are indeed some of the most caustic guitar sounds cut to vinyl as of 1976.

"*Catch Your Train*, it's like very, very close," remarks Rudolf. "Because I noticed already that this is a very special song, when I started to write it. I remember, I had a conversation with Uli, because when I put the solo background together, this (sings it), Uli said, 'No, no, do something else. I can't do anything on top of it!' And I said, 'Uli, try, please.' He said, 'No, look, it, why are we not going this way through it?' 'It's boring. Let's try, let's make one try.' Now, he's happy that I really forced him to do it. He comes up so often to me and says, 'Rudolf, the best song you guys ever did, *Catch Your Train*.' The solo, this solo inspired many guitar players, because it's really outstanding. Uli rose to the challenge and put some fantastic great stuff on it."

Elsewhere, *Hell-Cat* was a hard nut of a Krautrock freak show, as was *Polar Nights*, the latter possessing the same degree of oddity as the former, but with more gravity—it is perhaps the first bleak winter black metal song. Bleaker still was the yearning *In Your Park* (night quietly becomes day yet again) the monstrous and sad *Crying Days* (the world is bad) and dour, introspective psych-progger *Yellow Raven* (take me away from this bad world, fantastic dreambird).

"*Crying Days* was a song that is, let's say, different," says Rudolf. "It's not a commercial song but it has a special vibe. I remember, because Dieter Dierks always tried to commercialise the songs, you know, and when something was too far away, he said, 'okay, let's do another one.' I said to Klaus, 'You know, I think Dieter will have a problem with that.' He said, why? I said, 'Because it's not so straightforward. It's more vibe than song-like.' He said, 'Oh, let's see.' To our surprise, Dieter liked it, because there is a special vibe. It's so different, that it really gives a different kind of reaction to the people."

"There is some good stuff on there," adds Klaus. "There are songs that Uli did, songs that Uli was singing, that are beautiful songs, like *Evening Wind* or *Yellow Raven*—they are still beautiful. When I listen back to those songs. They still have something very, very special. I still like those songs. A lot of the stuff with Uli, I don't make the connection anymore, really; there are some songs where he was already on his trip, what he wanted to do, there are songs he couldn't sing but I did, where, looking back, it doesn't really make the connection anymore. But like I said, *Yellow Raven*, listen to that, it's like wow! Beautiful. We just played recently with Uli, and played a couple of old tunes like *Pictured Life*, *We'll Burn The Sky*, very beautiful song, but I think was written by Rudolf. But Uli's girlfriend, Monika Dannemann wrote the lyrics. And *Pictured Life*, and then some old songs like *Fly To The Rainbow*. It's amazing, and fans loved it."

But the album's less eccentric regular rock was proud, defiant and defining, tracks like the Queen-like *Pictured Life* and the near southern rocking *Backstage Queen* pointing to a possible new future with bigger wallets. Indeed the album broke the band in Japan, where it rose to No.32 in the charts and went gold, as would its follow-up Taken By Force, those two records' only accreditations anywhere. *Pictured Life* features one of the band's most vivid lyrics yet. Hard to tell what Roth is on about but the imagery and sense of the mystical is palpable.

Recalls Rudolf, "*Pictured Life*, I presented this song, we were working at one festival. I don't know if it was the festival where Bob Marley, Wishbone Ash and Offenbach were working in Germany, '74, '75, I don't know. So, I came into the dressing room and I played this riff, and Uli said it, 'Hey, what's that?' I said, 'It's a new song.' 'Hey, let's go; next time we go into a rehearsal studio, let's work on it.' This was the situation."

The first premise to making great rock records in the '70s was for bands to go glassy-eyed at those who would dare call or consider them heavy metal. Schenker is one of those—like Page, Plant, the Thin Lizzy guys, the Deep Purple guys, Queen—who held that healthy disdain for the limiting label.

"You know, I think we were never a metal band. We've always told people that but after awhile you shut your mouth because you can't tell people that. They aren't going to listen to you anyway. As far as we were concerned, we were always a rock band. And we are always open to put different spices in. And in this case, we're living here in Europe, and here the music changes faster than in America. It was like this. We always had in mind that we had to do something very different from what the others were doing. We respected other bands like Deep Purple, Led Zeppelin, but we said no, no we want to do it different. We were a different generation. I would go into the studio and write something and then Uli would write something with his influences. We wanted to make something interesting, but very guitar-oriented, that people would go and say, 'Wow, what's that?!'"

But surely *Virgin Killer*, the song, would be considered an early milestone of this as-of-yet not full-defined thing known as heavy metal. "Yes, no question! Let's say it this way. It was a mixture, because Uli was very much Hendrix-oriented, and Klaus and me already had a type of Scorpions thinking, and to mix that Uli Roth sound with our feel, it was very interesting. It was like having Jimi Hendrix playing modern rock."

Uli concurs that the early years of the band were marked, then later marred, by this meeting of influences. For the writer of the band's most celebrated early rock track, *Virgin Killer* (as well as crushing predecessor *Dark Lady*) it seems odd that Roth professed to be wholly lacking in metal influences.

"I don't think I had any whatsoever, aside from Jimi Hendrix. Because I never did listen to metal and I never really liked it. It was never my world and I always felt like an outsider stepping into it. At one point I really wanted to step out of it, and that's what I did. I was always trying to bring different aspects into rock, aspects that I didn't see there before. I guess that's what made the connection of Scorpions with metal; I guess that's what made Klaus, Rudolf and myself an interesting band at that time. Because there was quite a variety of influences in there. But I mean, yeah, some of these pieces do sound a bit generic, *Dark Lady* or *Virgin Killer*. I guess, if I said I wasn't influenced, of course that is a black and white answer. I was influenced in the sense that I did see bands like Deep Purple, and of course being in the Scorpions and having two guitars, I did a few experiments in various directions. But they were usually short-lived."

"Like for instance I never wrote another song like *Dark Lady* again, I never wrote another one like *Virgin Killer* again. Most of my songs are complete one-offs. If you look at my entire catalogue, I'm usually trying to create something that I find interesting, and once I've done it once, it's enough for me (laughs). Which is totally confusing for my audience which is why a lot of people don't get it. I'm basically just an explorer, and I'm not interested in exploring anything once I feel I've explored it enough. I guess that's what sets me apart from most other people in the business. Because a lot of people make their success by doing precisely the opposite, finding a good thing and then basically constantly repeating it. I can't blame them for that. I guess it's a normal human way. But I'm not normal. I'm totally abnormal in that sense, and I don't want to be normal. And I don't care about being successful for success's sake. Otherwise I would have stayed in the Scorpions because they were getting really successful at the time of Virgin Killer and Tokyo Tapes. Everybody knew where the train was heading."

On his classic signature track *Virgin Killer*, Uli figures that "was basically me trying to be funny in the rehearsal room. Because we had just supported Kiss on their first tour in Germany and we didn't know anything about Kiss (laughs). It was funny to watch them every other night because they were so, well, out there and outrageous. Their lyrics were also outrageous. So in the rehearsal room I just jammed the riff and I started singing to it in front of the band just basically making fun of Kiss in a way and started singing, 'because he's a virgin killer.' Klaus went, 'Hey, that's a great line; you should do something with that, you know.' So then I had the added trouble of trying to make a meaningful lyric out of that line, and it was quite a big challenge actually. It gave me no end of trouble and headaches. But in the end, I was quite satisfied with the solution I came up with. Mind you, most people don't understand that lyric because I think it wasn't printed in there. So Tipper Gore, when she did her campaign against the evils of metal, she included that one. Sure, the title was obscene, but the lyric is just the opposite of that. Virgin killer basically means the demon of our time, all the negative influences that come toward people when they grow up in society nowadays, and how people get corrupted by it. We're born in a pristine condition with a clear conscience, and then something happens and we get corrupted by the pressures of everyday life and society. Nobody escapes that. Nobody dies in a pristine condition."

So it's about becoming worldly and losing one's innocence? "Yes. The virgin killer is the demon of the zeitgeist that kills people's innocence. That's what it is. It wasn't helped by the album cover. I'm still blushing with that one. Luckily that wasn't my idea, although I have to admit I didn't do anything to stop it either. That was a big mistake. It was just unnecessarily obscene and I don't like obscene things."

Adds Schenker on this barnstormer of a track, the band's heaviest song to that point, "*Virgin Killer* was interesting because we did it in a rehearsal room in the basement of a school, and we started playing this song, and Uli was singing the song, and I heard something like 'virgin killer.' I said, 'Hey Uli, what's that? What's what? What are you singing there? You are singing something, virgin killer, that's a fantastic title, that's great, we have to do that!' So that became the title track and the title of the album."

"I have no idea," shrugs Klaus, asked where the band found influence to be so ragingly heavy as this track and *Dark Lady*, when such extremity simply didn't exist on much of a scale. "We started before the term heavy metal was even invented. I don't know. For us it was not so much about doing a heavy metal album. We did some music where we wanted to do our own music. With Dieter Dierks, he made me scream like all those big screamers from those days, and I trashed my voice as good as I could. That's just what we wanted to do and it just came out in the studio sessions, and the songs, and also as a live band. That's what we did live. It was always a pretty wild live act, Scorpions, and it still is. But in those days, there was nobody we went like, 'Let's sound like Judas Priest or Iron Maiden.' We always wanted to sound like Scorpions."

"I really enjoyed recording that album," continues Uli. "It was a really good time. Scorpions were at a peak. How shall I say this? I was never happy in that studio, because I wasn't happy with my guitar sound. As ridiculous as that may sound to some people's ears, the sound that I had onstage was always better to my ears. I just can't get it in most studios with dead walls. I was always frustrated there. I mean, the reason that it still sounds good is that they were close mics and that's pretty much what came out of the amp but you cannot actually hear the room and the ambiance. So that's one thing I always found grating. Then the thing that annoyed me was that we were spending ten days on just bass and drums and then rhythm guitars and then I would only have a couple of days for the lead guitars. I thought the priorities were wrong. But having said all these negative things, on the positive side there was a lot of inspiration and I remember each track as we did it. Of course, we did record separately. We did a drum and a bass track, and then rhythm guitars were usually overdubbed and then I overdubbed my leads. On Fly To The Rainbow, it was different. On things like *Speedy's Coming*, the whole band played in one go. But for separation later on, we didn't do that anymore. Production-wise, Virgin Killer was the album I had the strongest hand in the production. Tracks like *Polar Nights* or *Yellow Raven*, I was virtually in control of the production, whereas with Rudolf's songs, I would add my guitars and my ideas, and then everybody would be chipping in."

Uli's English has always been pretty good because his father started teaching him the language when Roth was five years old. But Klaus had a hard time with the language, the resulting texts, well into the '80s and arguably the '90s, sounding stilted and awkward under too powerful a microscope. Did Uli dust off Klaus's lyrics and fix them up? "Yes, sometimes, of course. I did have a hand in it, but it was only the occasional word or line. A few of them we did together. But I mean, Klaus and Rudolf are great songwriters so they'll always have something going for them."

Rudolf offers this remark on Klaus's early attempts. "His English is getting better, but at first he wrote with a lexicon? A translation book? He was working with a book next to him and he was always looking up to see what the word means. He was writing like a German trying to write English."

But Uli's songs were usually sole credits, while many others were Schenker/Meine collaborations. "I did all my song on my own, even the lyrics," states Uli. "I would say that 90%, I played all the guitars on them, and often the bass. That's also why they sound different. Rudolf and Klaus, their story is different. They tend to write either together, or Rudolf would come with the main idea and Klaus would add something, or a lot of the songs were Rudolf's music and Klaus's lyrics. The only stuff that went on is that I played bass on songs like *This Is My Song*, *Yellow Raven*, quite a few. But Francis was a really good bass player. It wasn't necessary. But it was usually when we didn't have time in the studio or maybe Francis didn't know the song so well. It was more just a convenience thing."

Other bit comments from Uli on some of Virgin Killer's tracks: "I think *Pictured Life* was a good song. It was based on a band who had a similar riff, but I forget who it was. It was certainly sparked off by some idea. I mean, for a lot of the songs there was some kind of direct precursor (laughs). And *Hell-Cat*, that's basically a Jimi Hendrix rip-off, although I was trying to do it in an innovative way. It has something going for it but it's certainly not one of my better efforts."

Uli is well aware that people found his attempts at lead vocals a bit rough. "Unfortunately, I'm not blessed with a good voice, but you know, I get by, particularly with stuff like *Polar Nights*. I guess it's authentic, you know (laughs), let's put it that way. I mean, I've just got the kind of voice that a lot of people hate and some people like. I guess that's the best that can be said about it (laughs)."

Finally with respect to Virgin Killer, one wonders if the record's more commercial, straight-ahead songs like *Catch Your Train* and *Backstage Queen* represented the beginning of the end for Uli's tenure within the band... "No, they weren't. It wasn't my style as such, but they were humorous, and I saw them as humorous. At that time I was still so much part of the band that it was still natural for me to play that stuff. *Catch Your Train* was a great platform for a guitar solo (laughs)."

The tour for Virgin Killer indeed represented a bit of a milestone, with the band mounting a second, more intensive assault on the UK that saw them perform nearly every night beginning on April 22nd of '77 in Manchester, through to May 5th in London, before heading back to Germany for a second exhaustive leg.

Taken By Force

"In my mind, I had already left the band"

C ajoled into talking about his last studio album with the Scorpions, "Why Taken By Force? That's my least favourite album. You want to torment me," laughs Uli Jon Roth, which, despite his thumbs down, is a fast fan favourite of the catalogue.

So what seems to be the problem? Was there perhaps more tension in the studio this time around?

"No, not more tension. I would have to say that I was not in the right frame of mind for that album. Because in my mind, I had already left the band, and I had already told Francis about it. At the same time, the drummer, Rudy, left, and so I said, okay, I'll stay on. So I wasn't as committed. I regret that, because on that album, I didn't necessarily give it my best. I just didn't fight as much. When I say fight, I don't mean fight in an aggressive way, because we never fight in the Scorpions. But I didn't fight for the quality on the album as much. I just did my thing, so to speak. If I had involved myself to the degree that I did on Virgin Killer, In Trance, and Fly To The Rainbow, I think it would have been a much better album. Because there are certain things I don't like about this album, and I could have, and I put my effort into it, it would have come out different. So I regret that. It's the only album where I had not given it 100%, and that's not good. Anyway, I wasn't so happy with some of the songs on the album, whereas of course, *We'll Burn The Sky* is a great song, no question about it."

As might be predicted, it's the bright and headbanged rockers on the album Uli takes most umbrage with, including the wall-of-sound "Spanish" metal stylings of *Steamrock Fever*, which is actually considered a proto-metal classic by watchers of this stuff.

"Yes, absolutely awful. I mean *Steamrock Fever* was just like a big joke," scoffs Roth. "I mean, it's okay for some bands who play that kind of stuff, but it shouldn't have been a Scorpions song. It's just like some kind of misguided pop attempt. I didn't even play on it. I said no, I can't really play on this. I think I played some slide guitar, because there was nobody else around, a couple of notes... don't you even remind me of that. *He's A Woman - She's A Man*, just the most awful lyrics. That was exactly the kind of lyrics I did not want to get involved in; it was inane, immature, pseudo-sexual kind of rubbish, and that's exactly... I mean, it was totally anathema to everything I stood for in my mind. I didn't want to have anything to do with it. But it still ended up there, despite my protestations. Okay, I'll play a lead, so I played a lead on it. It's not something I really want to be associated with, but I am associated with it (laughs)."

Rudolf figures that "*Steamrock Fever* was maybe influenced a little bit by the punk generation in England, because we had seen a lot of that on tour that year. I think punk was similar to the Seattle thing, you know? It was a similar situation, but the timing was different because in England at the time, the country is much smaller, and word travels faster. But anyway, we were in a position where we said we wanted to do everything different. But Uli Jon Roth made a decision at that time, because he had met Monika Dannemann, the old girlfriend of Jimi Hendrix, in the Speakeasy Club in London, and he started to fall in love with her. From this point on, he had in mind that he wanted to do a solo album. He was half-hearted on this album. I think the material of this album is so good, but the situation, how we play it wasn't really the way it could have been done. It had the potential to be as strong as Lovedrive. But because Uli already had in mind to leave, we never really finished the album properly."

Steamrock Fever, lyrically, pretty much lays down the band's new goals, albeit with the inarticulateness characteristic of writers who couldn't be bothered with getting their words checked out by a native English speaker. Substitute the "word" "steamrock" with heavy rock, and a pathway to fame and fortune is paved. Presciently, Klaus even locates the fever in Los Angeles. Its one nod to eccentricity is the sound effects intro, which the band intended to sound like heavy machinery.

As far as Uli is concerned, the aforementioned *We'll Burn The Sky*, side one, track two... this one's fully within the realm of the band's intriguing dual nature, as represented by Schenker to one side, Uli to the other. It's the type of composition that, if there might have been more of them, Roth might have stayed with the band.

"Oh well, it is a great song, and with great lyrics by Monika," comments Uli. Monika Dannemann, last girlfriend of Jimi Hendrix and at this point, girlfriend and later wife to Uli, strangely, a major Hendrix devotee sadly committed suicide in 1996 at the age of 50. "A beautiful intro sung beautifully by Klaus. To me, it was probably my favourite song of Rudolf's. From the beginning, I just thought it was unusual and it had a certain ethereal quality about it, although it was a rock song. It seems endless at the end. It seems to go somewhere. It's one of these songs that could go on for a long time. I did like the guitar lead, you know, the harmony leads, which I wrote for it, in triple harmony."

As for the rare Dannemann lyric, in fact the only one for Scorpions, Roth says, "This one, I think came about because I think Klaus didn't have the lyric. I don't quite remember how this came about. I mean, Monika was always travelling with us at that time because we were inseparable. So she did spend a lot of time with the Scorpions in 1977. She was on a lot of tours because she came with me. I don't quite remember how this lyric ended up with her doing it."

Before we get any further, it must be mentioned that Taken By Force found the band embroiled in yet another album cover controversy. Explains Buchholz, "Because we did not have an album cover idea, RCA put photos of the band members on the cover. The record company in Japan, RVC, did not like that idea and took a photo they already had in one of their drawers: children fighting with their toy guns on a cemetery. We liked the double meaning of that photo and that is how the album got released in other countries."

We fans over in North America indeed missed out on the striking cemetery sleeve (its actors don't quite look like children), instead settling for small individual shots of the members of the band, arranged along the top, oddly, each named, with the album title in a sea of black for the bottom two-thirds. The layout was essentially repeated on the back, making for a cover that seems ill-executed but kind of striking, mildly iconic with the passing years.

Additionally, as Uli has alluded to, the band had experienced yet another change of drummers, Herman Rarebell joining the fray for this, the band's fifth album, issued December 4, 1977 in Europe, and into the new year in North America, with Japan putting it out in April '78, with the aforementioned superior cemetery sleeve. Rudy Lenners indicates that he was in fact part of the decision process, himself having left not because of heart problems, as reported in the press, but simply because he needed a change of pace. After about six months, he was back in various bands, while teaching, and then had moved on to production work. Even after seeing the band's success in the '80s, he wished them well, having long resigned himself to the fact that he was not as ambitious to be a star as the rest of the band was.

"Taken By Force was recorded with our new drummer Herman Rarebell, whom we had auditioned in London before a show," says Francis. "Herman had moved there hoping to get an engagement in a English band! The recordings were a tour de force because before hitting the studio we had not yet integrated Herman's drumming into the style of the band."

"We listened a lot to Led Zeppelin," continues Francis, on the subject of shared influence. "They were especially Rudolf's and Herman's heroes. They liked the heaviness of Led Zeppelin; they were not so much into Deep Purple. I liked Deep Purple also, because I felt that the band had a lot of power. We never thought about being a heavy band. We just recorded the songs the way we played them."

"I was 12 or 13," recalls Herman Rarebell, asked by Jeb Wright when he first got the drumming bug. "I remember I was at a wedding and there was a drum kit there. I got behind the kit and I got my passion then and there. If you get passion for it at that age and you stick to it for the next three years then you will end up a great drummer. When I was 16 or 17, I was in high school and there were other boys who wanted to make a band. I was not a great player then, but I had a lot of passion; they were not great players either. We all grew up with our instruments. We had one drum kit and three guys all plugged into one amplifier (laughs)."

"The Scorpions were not big in those days at all," notes Rarebell. "They were up north in Hannover. Klaus played in a band called Mushrooms and Rudolf had just formed a band called the Scorpions. They were a school band; this is back in 1967-68. I played in a few semi-professional bands. One band was called The Mastermen. I went to England when I turned 21 and that is where I actually met the Scorpions. They were touring in England."

"So yes, I had moved away," continues Herman, filling in the interim bits. "I studied music here in Germany, and then after four semesters I had enough of classical music and I thought England is waiting for me, so I went to England and I was hoping maybe to join there, Uriah Heep or any of the bands that were popular in those days. This was 1971, '72. Then of course after four weeks, my money was gone so I survived as a taxi driver, as a gardener, as a barman, until about 1974, when I joined a band called Vineyard, and we played like Friday, Saturday, Sunday, and Wednesday, universities, schools and pubs. Then I became a studio musician. I played studio sessions for pretty good money. I made a good name being a fast drummer in the studio, which is, every is producer like that, you come in, you play the song and you go out."

"I played on different songs; I cannot name them anymore," continues Herman, on these early studio gigs. "Not major hits, just productions. Somebody calls me up, come in, you play. I had once, a conversation with Michael Monarch from Steppenwolf, and the guys who later played that song, *My Sharona*, The Knack. So those two boys, we had a band together, and then with different musicians in England. Alexis Korner was one of the guys I worked for, then the sax player from Gary Glitter Band, I worked for. People like this who make their own productions, who just called me up. Then in '77, in May, I met the Scorpions at the Marquee club. I met Rudolf, and we had the same interests. Next there was an audition at the Sound Center, I played there, they liked what I played, and then they asked me two days after, 'Would you like to come to Hannover?' Then I said yes, and then from then on is the story you know. I joined because we had the same philosophy. We had the same approach to making music. I got on really good with Klaus and Rudolf. You could say we were on the same wavelength."

But before Scorpions there really wasn't much auditioning for bands in Herman's fairly uneventful English experience. "No, there was only Melody Maker, and I thought there were big bands, you know, but the biggest thing I auditioned for was Sharks—do you remember the Sharks? I didn't get the gig. I was too loud for them. The guy with the moustache, (ed-Andy Fraser), he told me you're much too loud, you must play quieter. All the dance bands I auditioned for, I never got the gig. Always play too loud, too heavy, so in the end I ended up with a band called Vineyard, and there at least they had work; like I say, they played every Friday, Saturday, Sunday, and every Wednesday, and then I could quit my job as a taxi driver. I was a gardener, and I played two years with Vineyard, and then I got the line-up with the Steppenwolf guy, Michael Monarch, and then the last one was the guys from The Knack, and then after three months came the Scorpions. But for me, the six years in England was hard surviving. It was not easy living."

Of note, Herman had a long history of playing even before his move to England, including stints with The Mastermen, Fuggs Blues and R.S. Rindfleisch. In fact, having gotten the Scorpions gig and finding out they weren't nearly as far along on home soil as they had played themselves up to be, he wondered if he'd find himself playing gigs in support of some of his old bands.

"My biggest hero is John Bonham," offers Rarebell, on the subject of influence. "I think when it comes to rock drumming, that's an absolute master there. There are other masters like Ian Paice, Carl Palmer, and since Pete York worked with Ian together, I was very happy when he said yes to working with me recently. I also like the drummer from The Police, Stewart Copeland? I think he was a great drummer. One of my early influences was Ginger Baker, those great songs he did with Cream, like *Toad*. From the American side, I like drummers like Carmine Appice and Alex Van Halen. Tommy Aldridge as well—Tommy's an old friend of mine. I've played many tours with him. I remember when he was with Pat Travers, amazing band, amazing guitar player, 'Boom boom, out go the lights.' It was a pleasure to see this every night on stage. Believe me, the same thing with AC/DC, Ted Nugent, Aerosmith. I really had a good time, I must say. I really met the best in those days it. It was a really good environment to learn in."

As for the man Herman replaced in the Scorpions... "Rudy Lenners, the drummer before, he was a teacher in a school for handicapped people, and he wanted to go back to his job. He had enough in those days of going into cold England and sleeping in two star hotels on the damp floor. So he was quite glad that I took the job. He went back to his pupils, and I arrived in Hannover, they rented me a room there under the roof of the house (laughs), and that's how we started. It was May 18th, '77, the day of Klaus's wedding."

Back to Herman's first record with the band, Taken By Force, next up is another well-regarded hard rocker, *I've Got To Be Free* moving briskly, arranged smartly with some unexpected guitar textures from Uli, who is somewhat dismissive. "It's okay, it's okay. It's not one of my better efforts, I would say. I don't know, the lyrics are maybe a bit tongue in cheek. Definitely not one of my better efforts."

How was Uli getting along with the new drummer at this point? "Very well. No problem there, but then again we were on such different wavelengths. I mean, he was very much into the rock star thing, and all that was kind of anathema to me. I just wanted to be free in the music. That's what *I've Got To Be Free* is all about. I needed the freedom to explore and he was more concerned with actually, physically, making it. That was irrelevant for me at that time. I mean, we were very successful anyway, at least by our standards back then, and I just wanted to carry on my path. My path and his path were pretty much diametrically opposed in terms of music, although we did play together, and I did enjoy his playing. But I don't think that he understood me in any way. I even got Herman into the band. It was me at the rehearsal room who decided on him."

Says Herman, "Uli's song *I've Got To Be Free...* when you listen to those lyrics, you could tell he had already made up his mind, then and there, that he was going to leave the band. He was not very happy with the direction that I wanted the band to go in. I wanted us to have songs that had hooks but he wanted to do his Jimi Hendrix-type stuff, which I thought had already been done by Hendrix. I thought Jimi had already done a great job of it. So, he left and did his solo thing, like he always wanted to do. As my mother always said, 'If a train is rolling then let it roll. Don't jump on it because you could get hurt.'"

Even when Herman first joined the band, he could see the rift beginning. "I talked to Rudolf the night before and I told him I would come and check the band out at the Marquee. Rudolf asked me what I thought. I said, 'You have two bands here. One band backs up Uli Roth and sounds like Jimi Hendrix and then you have another band that is Klaus and you who sound a little bit like early Uriah Heep.' Rudolf said, 'Yeah, but we will never find another guitar player like Uli.' I told him that if that is the case then let's play like that. We have to decide one direction. Either we go the way of Uli Roth or we go the direction of Klaus, you and me."

The first side of Taken By Force closes out with an eerie, almost apocalyptic song called *The Riot Of Your Time*, which caps a side of music that is pretty much entirely exotic and even Latin of melody. If anything, any fairly studied Scorpions fan would imagine the record so far, and in fact much of it going forward into side two, to be very much the kind of music the apparently quite dissatisfied Uli Jon Roth, would appreciate. Blackout and Love At First Sting this most definitely isn't.

Says Rudolf of this song, "Always, in the early days, when we started to write our own material, we were always into trying different sounds, like the reggae number we did on Love At First Sting. And *Riot Of Your Time* is somehow... I had a chance about half a year ago, to listen to this song and I said, 'Oh, interesting.' I think having these different songs has made Scorpions different from all the other bands. Other bands find their sound and then composed within that sound, and we always tried to see songs from different sides. I think *Riot Of Your Time* is a number like that too."

Over to side two, the Latin or Mediterranean or Moroccan or Zeppelin vibe continues to pick up steam, the Scorpions crafting for our exotic pleasure *The Sails Of Charon*, widely considered the greatest song of the entire Scorpions catalogue, at minimum, a classic of an epic ilk that includes the esteemed *Kashmir* from Zeppelin, as well as *Stargazer* and *Gates Of Babylon* from Rainbow.

"Well, that was really my only venture into, I would say, the metal field," figures Uli, not that accurately. "You know, a little bit of a Zeppelin touch there, bands like that. That's probably why it's such a favourite in the states, apart from the guitar solo. I mean, it's an interesting song. It's also been covered quite a bit. But it's not a piece that is close to my heart. It is, perhaps, more experimental. I was experimenting with those modes, and with the sheer heaviness of it. But it wasn't really... as I say, I don't think it really came out of my heart, you know? I don't want to disown it; don't get me wrong, but it's never been a song that's been all that close to me. The message of the lyric is simply an anti-black magic lyric; that's what it is."

"Don't forget, we never performed *Sails Of Charon* live," notes Herman. "Unfortunately, one of my favourite drum songs ever. Because simply, I only did with Uli Roth a few shows in Japan at the beginning, and that's all I did in terms of live performance with him. We had already involved our program with all the other stuff in there. Okay, we did a mixture. We did *We'll Burn The Sky*, but we never did typical Uli songs like *Hell-Cat, Polar Nights*, all that stuff, never. Never did *Virgin Killer*, we did *In Trance*, yes. We did *Top Of The Bill, Robot Man*, but we did not do typical Uli Roth songs. For him, it was a bit too much at the time to sing and perform at the same time. Because what he used to do in the studio, he did all his guitar work on one track, and then afterwards sung the song."

"We only recorded it in the studio; we never played it live," confirmed Uli on this tantamount Scorpions track, in conversation with Sam Dunn. "I play it live nowadays but back then we didn't. So that was something I wrote at home and then I just brought it to the guys and we just recorded it. Like with all the stuff that I'm writing I'm always trying to do something new, and then once I've done it, I'm done with it. So it's part of the journey. So I've never written another song like *Sails Of Charon*. I don't even know if it's a song. It's kind of like a theme and it's a little story. It was never really quite finished, I thought. Later on I wrote an orchestra arrangement, which actually is finished, but the original wasn't. Maybe for good reason. But the thing that was new, if there was anything new, I think the guitar solo was maybe pointing to that fast Phrygian thing that was new in rock. To me, it was like taking a flamenco kind of approach to electric guitar playing. That's what it was: a flamenco rhythm. In fact a really good flamenco player in the states, Ben Wood, he just sent me an album where he played *Sails Of Charon* just on the flamenco guitar on his own and he did a great job, and he did exactly what it should be, you know? Yeah, it's basically metal flamenco. People don't know that, but I knew it."

As for the track's material influence on generations of heavy rock guitar players over the ensuing years, Roth says, "That one puzzled me for years because people kept referring to that song and it wasn't even anywhere near my list of favourites of things that I have done. Until I did this orchestra arrangement and suddenly I started to like it a lot. I don't know what they saw in it. Certainly the guitar was new. The fast triplet runs being smooth and all over the fret board, and at the same time being melodic. Maybe that's what it was. The riff was maybe unlike any other in rock at that time, although I don't know because I certainly didn't take it from anywhere. It just came, and it came very fast. It just kind of wrote itself, you know? So I don't even remember. Certainly there was no blueprint or template other than it felt like a flamenco in a way, a heavy flamenco. Every generation has a different perspective. So what the kids who came after me see in it, I can't see. Just like they can't see what I'm seeing and heard in Hendrix. But I know when I played it that it felt new and it felt like something I hadn't heard before. Maybe that's what it was. Maybe it captured something. It was a little strange because I had never done a song like that before and I haven't done one since."

Ask Rudolf why the song holds so much sway over Scorpions fans, Rudolf answers, "Because it's an outstanding riff, it's outstanding guitar playing and it has a magical kind of feel inside. It's a very strong and powerful combination of different things fitting together, the composition and all the melody. Everything came perfectly together and it builds a very strong impulse when people listen to it. It's a song that influenced many young bands—I know."

Back to the album, *Your Light* is one of those quiet, under-rated songs on Taken By Force that bolsters the record's integrity, enriches it. Not pop, not blues, not funk, not metal, it's an intriguing and Hendrix-like combination of all three, Herman driving the track with gorgeous groove. The production is plush, superlative, cymbal-smashingly bright. Uli plays a liquid, funky riff, and the end effect... one mourns for the loss of this side of the band with the departure of Uli, but then the changed band made a stack of pretty amazing records as well.

"I like *Your Light*," comments Roth, sole author of the track. "Lyrically, that is a song addressed to Jesus. So it's basically a spiritual song. But for me it was a foregone conclusion I would leave. Because you see, at the time of Taken By Force, I had already written quite a few Electric Sun songs, but they would absolutely not fit into the Scorpions format. I had already written *Earthquake* the following month, and pieces like that. There was no way I could perform these in the Scorpions format. So my mind was on that. It was high time for me to leave, simply. I was not a happy camper anymore toward the end. Although I did enjoy the Japan tour."

Quite understandable why Uli would treat with disdain, *He's A Woman - She's A Man*. Sure, mainly it's the clumsy transvestite lyric, but it's also the rote heavy metal rhythm 'n' riffing, which—one has to give the band credit—was not all that tired and travelled territory in 1977, '78. In fact, Scorpions were busy forging some of the first good examples of the heavy rock form, along with the likes of Rainbow, at this point into their third album, similarly Judas Priest with Sin After Sin. Indeed, it is perhaps that band that is the crowning example of thinkers and doers a fair leap beyond the proto-metal skills of the Scorpions. Fact is, Priest was crafting a gleaming cache of these now time-honoured heavy rock anthems of a type Uli found boring.

But we have the new guy, Herman, to blame for the *He's A Woman - She's A Man* lyric, which constitutes Rarebell's only credit on the album.

"Don't forget, I joined the band on the 18th May, and already most of the songs were then written," says Rarebell, who would go on to wordsmith many of the band's biggest smash hits, a rare role for a drummer. "On Taken By Force, all that was left was *He's A Woman - She's A Man*. This was the first song I wrote. In those days, the whole band... you had to do a promotion for the French record company. When we went to France, everybody said, let's go to the red light district in Paris, where the hookers are; let's go look, you know? So we went there, and there's this beautiful girl who came up to the car, with a great deep voice. She appeared and said, 'Hey guys, don't think I'm a chick. I'm a dude, you know. I recognised you. I'm a big fan, yeah. Keep on rocking.' She was a German transvestite, you know? So we were all shocked. *He's A Woman - She's A Man*. So nobody had an idea about the song. I just loved the riff Rudolf wrote, and I thought, hey, isn't that perfect? *He's A Woman - She's A Man*. Everybody went, 'Yeah, great. Write the rest of the lyrics.' This is how I came in to become the lyric-writer for the band. Because after that, everybody liked what I wrote, and then the next album came—Lovedrive of course—and I was asked to write some more, and then there was a good reaction, and then I wrote nearly everything on Animal Magnetism, and on Blackout and the others. Because more of them came. Klaus and myself shared the ideas, but in the end he said, 'I don't have enough ideas to fill the whole album; you're going to have to help me.' So that's how it all came together. My English was the best because of all the years I lived in England. Our producer, Dieter Dierks, liked my words. I wrote about what happened to us while we were out on the road. I think people could associate with that."

"My philosophy is to have fun because then people can have fun," says Herman, on his penchant for not so literary penmanship. "It is that simple. Remember that I didn't have as many words to play around with because my vocabulary is not as big as yours because English is your mother language. I had to learn English in England from 1971 to 1977; that is really when I learned all of my English. If you were to come to Germany tomorrow then you would speak fluent German in six years without a problem. Now, most people could answer you in English but if you were to have come 30 years ago, nobody would be able to answer you in English because nobody spoke it. If you would have come to East Germany they would have spoken Russian."

So this transvestite vignette served as Herman's only lyric for the record. "Yes, just that one. At the time we had Uli in the band and Uli presented us with a finished song. He would say, 'This is called *I've Got To Be Free* and you can put the drums on there.' He had the structure and the lyrics of the song ready. The direction he wanted to go when I joined the band was more of Jimi Hendrix style music with an orchestra. But when I joined I told Rudolf that we should become a melodic hard rock band who writes songs that people can sing along with. Uli wanted to do his own thing and so he formed Electric Sun."

"Monika was writing a lot of his lyrics," says Rarebell, as regards Roth's mysterious partner. "She was also the original girlfriend of Jimi Hendrix. She was the one who was with him in the night when he died. She claimed that she told him to take a quarter of a sleeping tablet but he took four tablets. That is the story that has been told all of these years but I don't believe it. I don't buy that at all. I think the US government killed him because he was too popular for a black guy at the time. He was opening up his mouth for freedom. The CIA or the Secret Service took care of him just like they did Kennedy. For me, I think that is what happened to him. Don't forget that he was perceived as more dangerous than even Martin Luther King at the time. He was the hero to the white kids. For a country that has so much racism, like you have in America, it was unthinkable that a black man could have that kind of power in the United States."

Taken By Force closes with *Born To Touch Your Feelings*, a throwback to all those morose ballads about the pains of life and love dotted throughout the past four records. Comments Uli, "That's one I remember as being potentially a very good song, *Born To Touch Your Feelings*, but we didn't really get to grips with it. It shouldn't have a guitar solo at the end, but you know, I don't think I could be bothered."

"Actually, I know that Uli, in his mind, had left already when he did this album," muses Rudolf, in agreement with Uli's recollection. "I think if Uli had been more connected to this album, this album could have been even better than it was. Because the material on this album is excellent. But first of all, it was the first album for Herman, who, in the past, with Rudy Lenners and with all the other drummers, we had more up-tempo kinds of players. With Herman, we had for the first time a really laid-back drummer. We didn't have enough time to really groove together, to get closer. I mean, the album is good but I know that a little bit more time for getting together more, and knowing each other better, it would've been a better album."

"Also Uli was already gone. But, I like very much the material. *Steamrock Fever* is outstanding, because it's somehow different. It's commercial, but it's different. And Uli isn't playing very much on *Steamrock Fever*, because he never liked this song. There was already this split between the Schenker sound and the Uli Roth sound, because Uli Roth was more Jimi Hendrix-oriented and he didn't like things like *Steamrock Fever* and *He's A Woman - She's A Man*, and he only played the solos on this. Everything else I played by myself. Because he said, 'I don't play on this stuff.' But because I'm not a solo player, we convinced him to at least play the solos there."

"He's good! I mean, Uli always did good solos. Actually, stuff like *Catch Your Train*, which is not on Taken By Force. But when he had to be on... I mean, look at *Sails Of Charon*—amazing solos, amazing playing! I think it's one of the best songs he ever did. So when he played guitar solos on songs that Klaus and I composed, he did great stuff."

"But somehow, it came to a head with Taken By Force, where he already had his solo project in mind. *We'll Burn The Sky*, he was more involved in it because Monika brought the lyrics to it, and all these lyrics were about Jimi Hendrix. So in this case, he was strongly connected to *We'll Burn The Sky* and he put excellent parts on this song, because he wanted to support this song about Jimi Hendrix, and the love of Monika Dannemann to him. Uli played excellent on it. But the songs are coming from different corners, even though both are great on their own."

Tokyo Tapes

"They told us they massage the cows"

Quickly after Taken By Force, Scorpions found their way to crafting Tokyo Tapes, a flash double live album every bit as cool as the celebrated gatefold spreads at the time. Golden era of the live album this was, with Blue Oyster Cult's single live album Some Enchanted Evening being one of the band's best selling records, and with UFO's Strangers In the Night, Thin Lizzy's Live And Dangerous and Judas Priests Unleashed In the East being some of the most beloved albums by those bands. Then again, let's not talk about Live! Bootleg, On Stage and The Song Remains The Same.

A manic, rocking front cover adequately got across the violence of the music enclosed, with the biggest treats for fans being the two non-LP tracks, *All Night Long*, a brisk, technical riffster, and *Suspender Love*, a sex-and-glamour party rocker with a sophisticated twist of a chorus. Could have done without the Uriah Heep Live-like '50s throwaways *Hound Dog* and *Long Tall Sally*, or for that matter *Kojo No Tsuki*, but the propulsive *Speedy's Coming* and *Top Of The Bill...* pure German rock invasion of Japan.

"That was to be our farewell kind of statement," explains Uli. "It was the idea of Klaus Meine; he said to me... because originally, I didn't want to do the Japan tour. But he said come on, let's do it, it would be our farewell thing and we would do an album, and it would be the end of that era. I'm glad he did, because it was a very good experience. So I'm glad he talked me into it."

In terms of those apocryphal patch jobs you hear about for these live records, Uli says, "No, there wasn't much additional. Well, maybe a couple of vocal overdubs. There were no guitar overdubs. We tried a couple of things with the guitars, because I wasn't happy with one of the things, but I couldn't get the sound, because the sound at Sun Plaza Hall was fantastic on stage, and in the studio it was horrible in comparison. I couldn't get anywhere near it. So I forgot about that right away. Then we didn't choose these tracks. No, most of the time... for instance, I wasn't there for the mix on that album, because I had lost interest. I had already left the band and I was already working towards the Electric Sun songs, and in hindsight, I regret that I wasn't there for the mix. But unfortunately, when it was recorded, with the mobile, there was a horrible mistake that was made in that the Japanese engineer who recorded it, he recorded the tracks with EQ, so some of it sounds too brittle, and it was over-EQed. A mistake like that can't be rectified. They should have recorded it flat, and I guess this was not done, because nobody in their right mind normally would do such a thing. It's standard procedure to record everything flat, but for some reason they didn't. They EQed it. So once again, I wasn't happy with the sound (laughs), and you know, I don't want to sound like the eternal moaner, but it's just the truth. I was always somewhat dissatisfied. But whether people say it's great or not…"

As for his own playing, in particular, the guitar solos… "With most of the songs, we tried to stay faithful to the original idea, and particularly if it was a written or structured solo, like say these harmony leads in *We'll Burn The Sky* or *In Trance* or *Catch Your Train* or whatever. These things I tended to play very much note for note, because that's not the kind of stuff you jam on. Other things were very much spur of the moment. Like *Kojo No Tsuki* was pretty much made up during the soundcheck, because Klaus came to me with the vocal melody, which he had been given by the Japanese, I think, by the fan club or something like that. So he sang me this vocal melody a capella, on stage, and I put the chords to it, and made an arrangement on the spot and we played it and that was pretty much it. That's what you hear on the album. We played it that night."

"*Suspender Love*, I remember, we did record it as a b-side of a single once, so there is a studio version somewhere, if I'm not mistaken. *All Night Long* is very much a jam thing that I threw together during a rehearsal. I didn't consider it a real song, actually." The studio version of *Suspender Love* was in fact the b-side of the studio *He's A Woman - She's A Man*, failed single from one record back.

As for the totality of the sessions, the band's performances on April 24th and 27th 1978 had been recorded. "We did three nights in Tokyo," says Uli, "one in Osaka, and one in Nagoya, and a couple of appearances, one on TV, which was a playback appearance. We recorded two nights at Sun Plaza Hall, where we played three nights, and that was a shame, because the very first night, to me, still to this present day, sounds like the best show that we had ever done with the band up to that point. It sounds like everything came together perfectly that night. Unfortunately, that was one that wasn't recorded. The other two were good as well, but they didn't have quite the same magic that this night had."

"When we came over the first time in the spring of '78, first it was amazing to have a reception like the Beatles in Tokyo airport," recalls

Herman, who spent the trip with "Montezuma's revenge" due to some ice cream he had eaten in New Delhi when the DC-10 they were on had to divert there after experiencing engine trouble. "All those fans, girls, it was amazing. And Mr. Udo is a very powerful promoter in Japan. He really knows all the radio stations and the TV stations, and without him, I don't think any band would have been very successful in Japan. He has like a monopoly down there. In those days, everything went to Mr. Udo, you know? He was, in my opinion, a very good promoter."

"Also, I have a memory of him taking us to those Japanese beef houses, where they make this very, very soft beef, where they told us they massage the cows to make them eat very, very soft and very good to eat. I remember those days. I remember the first visit to the bathhouse (laughs). I'll never forget those girls sitting on you, doing the whole massage with their body, with the oil, and not with their hands, they do with their pussy. It was unreal, so with Mr. Udo, I think of the first visit in the bathhouse, these massages, it's nothing like we have here in Germany with the normal whorehouses and brothels. This is pouli-massage, which was another name in their country for no fucking. Unreal. When you ask me about Mr. Udo, this comes to mind. I remember the cherry trees in Kyoto in springtime. I remember the fast train; it was a wonderful visit. We played places like Sun Plaza Hall, which was like 2200 people. I remember it was funny, when we had to do a TV show, Uli did not want to play the parts on *He's A Woman - She's A Man*. He said this is not my style; I'm not playing this. What will my fans think of me? (laughs). He said it was cheap. You know, in the quality. I think it's a great solo. Later, as you know, he got replaced by Michael Schenker and anyway this is my first memories. I was running around in a kimono for weeks even after, when we came back. We were a young band; this is nothing like Germany, and suddenly super stages in Japan."

"It took us years to be big in Germany," noted Rarebell back in 1980, "because German people don't accept bands coming out of Germany. You know, the prophet doesn't mean anything in his country. We had to go to Japan to prove ourselves." But the Germans at least understood the band's English lyrics. "You know why they know the words so well? I tell you. After the war, the American soldiers who stayed here screwed the German chicks and the kids picked up the language. In rock 'n' roll, there is only one language and that's English. We don't want to be a band who are just big in Germany. We want to be big worldwide. If we sang German in England, they wouldn't understand us. They'd be too lazy to learn the language."

"In the early days, there was very much a difference between countries, of course also continents, because people were acting differently," adds Rudolf, on the subject of cross-cultural differences. "In

Japan we heard from the promoter that it's sold out. We were backstage in the dressing room, and there was no noise (laughs). Mr. Udo was the promoter and we said to him, 'Mr. Udo, you told us it's sold out!' He said, 'Yes, it is!' We opened the curtain and looked that the place was packed but there was no noise, nothing. Everybody was sitting there and the moment we came out on stage it changed."

As discussed, it was well-known that Uli would be leaving after the tour. "Oh yes, he had already said so," explains Rarebell. "I joined the band and I tried to make the band more commercial, more the American way, to write more for American hit radio, where he was always more heavily Hendrix-influenced. He says he thinks he is the rebirth, like Frank Marino from Canada, and he could not equate with going such a way. He always said to me, I want to go out and I want to do the Hendrix direction, so it was obvious that sooner or later, it was either him, making his own band, or we always play this music. That was the step at the time, and I'm glad we decided to work as a band, as a team, because it became very successful in the '80s. But he was always spiritual. Always before the concert, he would put out the candles, together with Monika Dannemann; she was still alive then. It was very simply getting into contact with the spiritual way, and he told me, that Hendrix's spirit is entering him, during the time of his performing. Now, you can believe a thing like this or not, but for sure, Uli is an excellent Hendrix player, that's for sure. As good as Frank Marino. I saw Frank a few times, and he's a very good Hendrix copy too, you know."

"Not only are we really good friends, but we believe in the same things, also, and I think he's absolutely brilliant," says Uli of Frank Marino. "I think most people don't even know how brilliant he is. He should have a bigger heyday now than he had then, because he plays better than ever. But nowadays the business has become so difficult for virtually everyone. It's difficult to find the right kind of outlets for someone as different and as special as Frank. The entire industry is so formalised and narrow-minded. Unless you dance to their tune, you've got very little chance of actually doing anything. Frank is not the kind of guy to dance to anybody's tune. He's always gone his own way, and that's what makes him Frank Marino. The people outside, the people in the music business or whatever, they're the ones that are losing out, by not checking into him more."

There's most definitely a commonality between Frank's career and the one Uli was now about to embark on. "Yes," laughs Uli. "I never compromised in that respect either. I stayed truthful to the path I chose, against the odds. I'd have to say that I was usually swimming against the stream in the Scorpions; I always did my own thing. In the long run, I think that's something that makes for results that are something different from the mainstream. It is definitely harder to survive, when you're swimming against the stream. But it's not impossible, and I'd have to say I've always been very, very lucky. So I can't complain. Things are always coming my way."

"Uli left the Scorpions because of artistic differences," is how Francis frames the departure of this major force in the band. "He could not get along with our producer Dieter Dierks anymore, I believe, because of Uli's different approach to music. Also, Uli wanted to do his own thing and felt not comfortable playing some of the songs written by other band members. With some of the compositions we had lots of discussions going on in the studio during the recording sessions. He wanted to leave the band directly after recording the album Taken By Force and I was very happy having been able to convince Uli to doing the Japan tour as his last tour with the Scorpions, which resulted in the great album Tokyo Tapes. It was a very good album showing the live qualities of the band. I was proud having played very well and emotional without any mistakes."

Roth reflects back on his time with the band. "My time in the Scorpions was a little bit like an apprenticeship, in terms of regarding the whole music scene, the whole business, touring, making records. I did enjoy it very much, but only for the first four years. Then in the last year I became very, very dissatisfied. It was like a growing dissatisfaction because of the direction that the band was taking, which was more and more alien to the direction that I wanted to go in. The band had its own framework which we basically established ourselves. Some of the things I wanted to do would have completely split this framework. For instance, at the time that we did Taken By Force, by that time I was already writing things like *Earthquake* and *Sundown*. I could never have played *Earthquake* in the Scorpions. So for me there was no alternative. Leaving was a necessary step and we parted on very good terms, and that's the way it had to be."

But Uli disagrees with Francis that the decision had much to do with Dieter. "No, I mean, he was just producing the albums in the sense that he was there in the studio trying to make sure things were recorded in such a way. The choice of material was always our own, at least in the time that I was there, and we never had a problem actually choosing the songs, because we tended to agree on the choice of material quite easily. There were only a couple of songs that I really didn't like and did not want to play on. But in the end I just did it anyway. But on the whole, we didn't have a problem choosing the material. It just developed kind of naturally. We just did what we felt like doing at that time. Toward the end, I would have to say yes, the others were casting an eye more deliberately on commercial success, thinking about what we have to do to sell more records. That kind of thinking was an anathema to me because I was only interested in exploring really, expressing what I saw or what I felt during these explorations. Of course, very often that wouldn't always be the commercial thing, particularly not in the short run. Because the short run is always trend-driven. I see myself rather as a trendsetter, and then when I set the trend... pretentious as that may sound, but very often I do stumble on things that later on become quite fashionable. But by then I've moved on."

"Back then it was his decision, first of all," said Klaus, to Jeb Wright, on Uli's tenure with the band. "He wanted to play his own music. He had his own formula of writing songs. It was very exciting but we could see we were drifting apart musically. We remained friends and we could respect that he wanted to do his own thing. When Matthias Jabs joined the band then Rudolf and I could follow our own way and do what we wanted to do. It was the next step up for us. We had Lovedrive, Animal Magnetism, Blackout and Love at First Sting. With Uli we would have still been a very powerful band but I don't think we would have survived the next ten years. We were just too different. We are all more relaxed now. Uli is more relaxed too. He can also enjoy this part of his life and his career. He loves to come back and play with us."

As for Uli's vast body of solo work in the ensuing years... "Well, it's hard to choose," says Meine. "I mean, as much as I admire Uli for his genius guitar work, I never really followed his albums, because that's maybe because I'm a singer and he's a guitar player. It's special, but his songs are not so interesting for me, as far as singing goes."

As it happens, there was no tour for the Taken By Force album. Before heading to Japan, the band had played but a handful of dates in France and Germany, in December '77 and January '78. Without Tokyo Tapes, we'd have nothing.

If you read the tealeaves in the Tokyo Tapes track list, it becomes apparent pretty quickly that Scorpions were moving toward a riffier and more rhythm-guitar oriented heavy rock sound. Fly To The Rainbow's only clearly heavy rock song, *Speedy's Coming*, was here. In Trance's three heaviest rock songs, *Dark Lady*, *Top Of The Bill* and *Robot Man*, were here (additionally, the title track was slammed with a few extra power chords). Virgin Killer... not so much, with the absence of *Catch Your Train* and the vicious delicious title track; still, we got the forceful, four-on-the-floor of *Pictured Life* and the party rockin' *Backstage Queen*. From Taken By Force we get both tracks that helped send Uli to the exits, namely *Steamrock Fever* and *He's A Woman – She's A Man*. Then finally, both new non-LP tracks are fairly simple hard rock (even if *All Night Long* turned out to be a Roth/Meine composition), and both sport lyrics about some hot chick driving you mad.

What's more, the band's new drummer, Herman Rarebell, seemed bent on driving the band's compositions forward with insistent whacks of his mighty bass drum—the subtleties and textures of the band with Uli and various past rhythm sections was making and quaking way for a sound that could compete with all your Ted Nugents, Aerosmiths and Kisses of the world, not to mention the bands out of England that had been building upon the deaths and wanes of Sabbath, Zeppelin, Deep Purple and Heep.

"I think it was my influence, actually, and I said, at that time," affirms Herman. "At the time there was Uli Roth in the band, there were basically two directions in the band. You had the Uli Roth direction that was very Jimi Hendrix-oriented, and then you had Rudolf's songs and Klaus Meine's songs, which were very melodic rock. I tended more to that side, because I was a big melodic rock fan. Remember, in those days you had Foreigner with *Cold As Ice*, a big rock song. I said, it if we want to get to America and get big there, we have to go to the American side and write commercial songs for American hit radio. Which we did, with songs like *No One Like You*, especially for America. In those days, when we saw all those bands perform live, we knew this is what Americans want to hear, so let's produce for this market. That was the aim in those days."

"Tokyo Tapes has its high points," reflects Herman. "I still like my drum solo there, in the middle of *Top Of The Bill*. Tokyo Tapes has a lot of fresh excitement. Don't forget this was the beginning days of the band. So of course you can feel that vibe. You can feel that everything is new, first time in Japan, first time with Japanese groupies; we never had this before. Don't forget, before that, we played in Germany and clubs, and nobody screamed. I remember one of the first gigs we played, in Le Havre which is in the north of France. Because in those days, the record company said, if you get a gig outside of Germany, we will release the record in that country. So we went to France, we got a gig there, but we played in front of 30 people. First song is over, nobody claps. The second song's over, nobody claps. Imagine, very quiet, okay? Then the third song—this is punk time, '77—some guy screams, 'Hitler, go home!' Can you imagine? Great atmosphere. Then you go to Japan and you get hundreds of Japanese girls screaming at the airport. Of course, you feel completely different. It took me a month to come down again after Japan, in Hannover. People always said, 'Why are you wearing a kimono here?'"

Lovedrive

"Storm, come on, make us a really crazy cover"

The immediate post-Uli Jon Roth era of the Scorpions would be marked by an album somewhat seen as transitional. Lovedrive, issued February 25, 1979, was in fact clouded and shrouded by a bit of messiness. Was Michael Schenker, escaped from UFO, in the band or not? The new guy, Matthias Jabs... was his job assured if Michael was in fact staying?

"It was a bit strange, that whole situation," explains Matthias Jabs, newly arrived lead foil to Rudolf's increasingly mastered rhythm, and still lead guitarist in the band to this day. "I just joined the band in June '78 and we went into the studio in October; played a few shows before that. We had recorded most of the songs and then Michael split with UFO and came to Germany, on a honeymoon with his new wife. Michael at this time was more popular than the Scorpions altogether, because they had never really gone to the States. They went to Japan once, for Tokyo Tapes, but that was about it. So obviously, they're brothers and I thought well, maybe he can join the band. He tried, went on tour, and he played on three tracks on the album—it was almost finished anyway. Then they went on tour in Europe and after three weeks he left for the first time, and I helped out. He called me before he called them so we were still getting along great. We never had a problem, Michael and myself. So I said, 'okay, I'll just finish the German tour and after that, do what you like.' They went on tour again, and they called me from Lyon in France a week later and said, 'okay, he's gone again; he's left and that is it. There's only one way; this is it.' It actually helped in the long run because we got that problem out of the way forever."

To clarify, Mathias played a handful of dates at the end of 1978, but then Michael was good for a dozen or so shows, essentially in February and into early March '79. Then it was back to Mathias for ten or so shows in mid-March, after which Michael returned for a similar number of dates through late March into early April. By April 4th, 1978, in Lyon, as Matthias accurately states above, the musical chairs were over and Jabs was permanently the lead guitarist for Scorpions.

In typical Michael fashion, he was, in a sense, just passing through... "The way it goes is that when I started making my first record, every next record was an amazing development. All the way up to Lovedrive. Basically, the period where I did develop, in those few years, I developed so fast, and what happened to me was always from one album to the next, an incredible step. Every step was an incredible improvement, and then by the time I came to 1979, it was Lovedrive with the Scorpions, which worked out pretty good. Then it was time to focus on other aspects. So that's what I did. I learned so much, and all the things that I didn't see before I started to see, and then I experienced things that I didn't even know were there (laughs). It's amazing, but I guess that's my custom-made journey. Every person has their own custom-made journey going. Mine just worked out with those kind of extremes."

Explains Herman, "I think with Michael, when he was in the period when we did the Lovedrive album, he was in and out on the situation. I remember we played in Lyon, France, where there were 6,000 people sitting out there waiting for the band to perform, and he wouldn't even show up to the concert. The promoter told us, 'You guys better leave now because I think they're going to demolish everything here in a minute.' Nobody did, thank God. We said to the audience, 'We cannot play. Our guitar player's missing.' He was on a little motorcycle on the way to Spain, God knows why. Then he shows up a few days later again, comes to a few rehearsals, disappears again, and this went off and on, and in the end we said, 'Look Michael, we cannot work like this. We're going to take Matthias Jabs now as our guitar player.'"

To clarify further, the band never played with three guitarists, i.e. Rudolf and both Matthias and Michael, which might have sounded reasonable, given the band credit to all three on the back of the record.

"No, never," continues Rarebell. "What happened was, after this in-and-out-going story with Michael, we finally took Matthias, and then he came back after two weeks, and he wanted to be back in the band again. We said, 'Look Michael, we cannot do this, kick Matthias out and bring you back in again. We did this once before.' So he said, 'Aw, it'll never happen again,' and then it happened again. Matthias said, 'Look, you took me one time, and now you want me to leave again because you're taking Michael back? I tell you one thing now, this is the last time. The next time Michael leaves, don't you phone me.' So we said to Michael, 'you've done it before, you fucked us up again, let's forget it, let's stay friends and you do your thing, we'll do our thing.'"

"Michael has a very big ego," noted his brother Rudolf, not long after, in 1982. "He needs to be in the spotlight, writing and playing his songs. In Scorpions, we are very much a team and we try very hard to have everyone pull in the same direction. Michael has always wanted to do things his way, which is why he has MSG. He needs to have his own band. There has always been a very special feeling between my brother, Klaus and me while we play, so that's why he came to us later and will still play with us occasionally live."

Assessing Michael's style, Rudolf explains that, "One reason why I like my brother's playing is that he takes feeling and technique, two very different things, and combines them in his playing. He is very, very good technically, yet he is quite aware of melody and feeling when he is playing. Even when he is playing very, very fast. But if you get too much technique, the music becomes too hard to listen to and nobody wants to hear it. I play music so that other people can hear, not just for myself. If you get too much into feeling, it's easy to get into drugs searching for more feeling. I think that is what happened to Eric Clapton and Paul Kossoff."

"So with Michael, and Uli Jon Roth, we had fantastic guitar players, but not team players," reiterates Rudolf, expressing his role as well. "So with Matthias, one guy came in the band, he was ready to be part of the team. Which is very important if you want to make a career. Then you only can do it when five guys really connect like a puzzle fitting together. So in this case, of course, Dieter Dierks, longtime producer, he was a very important guy as well, because he found out my energy, my karate kind of guitar, rhythm, because I was also into being a little bit of a solo guitar player. But somehow, that was interesting. Uli Roth said to me, once he saw how I was doing my finger techniques and stuff like this, he said, 'Rudolf, you know, its much better to be a great rhythm guitar player instead of being an average solo guitar player.' I understood that very well, especially by seeing Keith Richards and also Malcolm Young—that the rhythm guitar player can along with the drummer and bass player, make a solid basic rhythm section."

"You know, I see a group of rock musicians more like a soccer team," continues Rudolf. "Matthias and Klaus are the guys who are kicking the goals. I'm the guy in the middle, sort of like a Beckenbauer, the bass player is more the guy, the defender, and the goalkeeper is the drummer. So in this case we have a very interesting thing. When we work with Matthias and me, and Dieter Dierks, we try to really make the rhythm. Not that we played the same thing always—no, we try to make it like a cluster. That everybody has his role and make a strong rhythm, and also a strong energetic rhythm foundation for Klaus's beautiful voice. That's why Dieter Dierks always tried to force Klaus to sing very high, because he found out that when Klaus is singing very high, the energy—which is the fuel of rock music—is even stronger. That makes the Scorpions sound: great melodies, very, very strong and high vocals, and of course, the great rhythm machine with great solo licks."

Years later, in conversation with Tim Henderson, Michael mused about the divergent paths taken by him and his brother. "We were together for two years when we were doing the Lonesome Crow album and touring it. That's the only time I knew him. He is seven years older than me. So, I know very little about him. I know we are both very spiritual people who meditate. He told me he had a dream once where he was a monk and the main person there who was deciding which way to go—to Buddha or not—and he chose to be in the physical world. I believe that is what he is doing now with his life. So, it's basically, he is in the world of physical and I'm more in the artistic realm. I love music and I love to be creating it."

"Rudolf had a dream to be in one of the biggest bands in the world and have an extremely successful career. But, he needed a tool to achieve that, and I think I was the tool. I didn't need what he needed so therefore he has freedom to enjoy it because he doesn't get stopped in any way because I don't need it. In a way, we are helping each other indirectly and not consciously. That said, it appears to be more than meets the eye, if you look at it from another dimension. There was something he really needed for his life to be fulfilled. But, he needed to be in a particular spot on this planet at a particular time. Maybe this is a little farfetched for some, but I don't want what he has. So, I am happy for what I have. My involvement as his brother and member of the Scorpions enabled him in many ways to step up, and that I was able to withdraw after Lovedrive to do my own little experiments and stuff like that. It makes it look like a puzzle, two elements that are meant to fit together to fulfill each other's dreams. My vision is to develop as a great guitarist, nothing more. Therefore I am not in his way, and he is not in my way."

"No, we never have," Rudolf responds, when asked if they have ever done Christmas dinner together. "The thing is, we are always on different sides of the planet. I have been living in America for 17 years, and before that in the UK. I left Germany when I was 17-and-a-half. On the other hand, we are living two different worlds—he is macrocosm and I am microcosm. We have been talking about Schenker Brothers over and over for all these years, and I asked him, 'Do you really think you would be happy with me in the band because we are both looking for two different things?' He is a rat, I am a horse, the complete opposites in the Chinese horoscopes. At this point in time I think we have left it far too long. The only thing that would be interesting and possible to do with my brother would be the ultimate Scorpions reunion. This would be a brand new studio release with music written by a combination of all the people, and then doing a world tour. When we do things like Wacken, we do that to help them, to fuel them with new ideas to get people back into it. That's all we have done. I have been doing this since 2009. I get a call, 'Michael, we need you!' The ultimate Scorpions reunion would be the original line-up from the Lovedrive album."

" I had told Rudolf that we would find another guitar player," says Herman, referring in fact to way back, when it was obvious Uli would be leaving quite soon. "We found Matthias Jabs, who I think is a fabulous guitar player, and more importantly, as discussed, a team player. At the time—and for the above stated reasons—Michael had already decided to start his own band, The Michael Schenker Group. But he did say, 'I am in Germany and if you want me to, I can put down some guitar parts.'"

"As a replacement for Uli, I thought about Matthias Jabs, who was a very good guitar player," recalls Francis Buchholz on his selection out of an audition process that apparently, by some accounts, looked at 170 applicants, including Paul Chapman who would soon wind up in UFO as Michael Schenker's replacement. "I knew him already because I had helped him with calculus mathematics. Herman's opinion was that Matthias was too young and inexperienced, so I placed an ad in Melody Maker: 'German rock band seeks lead guitar player.' We ended up auditioning more that a hundred players in a rehearsal studio in London which we had rented. We selected three players, but after we had done more work with them, we were not so convinced anymore, that one of these three would fit into the band. I suggested Matthias again and we gave him a chance. He was able to play all our songs immediately, and we took him to the studio recording the album Lovedrive. Unfortunately it took some time for him to get adjusted, so Michael helped out with some guitar work."

"I first started playing guitar when I was 13," says Matthias, explaining his roots to Hit Parader. "I liked music and had the feeling to pick up the guitar. I never had a lesson! I had a friend in school who could play a little, and he tried to teach me some chords, but he wasn't good enough. I got a book with chords in it, and I learned from listening to songs on the radio. It was very easy to learn to play the guitar. It's an easy instrument. So many people play guitar, it must be easy!"

"Johnny Winter was an early influence... "I learned mostly from him in the beginning. He had a fabulous live album in 1971. I also listened to Jeff Beck and Ritchie Blackmore, Deep Purple and Led Zeppelin. I also like the Rolling Stones, the Beatles and Jimi Hendrix. There were no German guitarists of note at that time to learn from. Radio is not the same in Germany as it is in the states. There are no FM stations that play rock 'n' roll all day. There's only two hours of rock music a day on the radio. The music you hear is from the records you buy, or tapes people bring into the country. There is very little good radio in Germany. It's all government-controlled. Today there are still only a few rock 'n' roll bands in Germany."

"They're still not into the music," says Matthias, concerning his parents. "When I decided to become a musician, they were very suspicious. They didn't support me in any way, but now they accept what I do. But they don't even want to talk about music—it's the opposite of support. My parents really wanted me to play piano. I fooled around with it, but it didn't feel right. As soon as I had a guitar in my hands, I knew it was the kind of thing I wanted to play. It's a different feeling than piano. As a boy, if you sit in front of the piano, there's not much you can do with it. But with a guitar, you can do much more."

Asked by Sam Dunn if Scorpions had given Germany their very first true heavy metal band, Matthias figures, "Well, I joined in '78 and I think the first time we went on tour in England in '79 together we were reading the term heavy metal. That's when it came up. But yes, we are the only German or international rock band coming out of Germany. Meanwhile there's a band called Rammstein, and they have some international success and they're very good, but not the way we played. We played the US and everywhere in the world. There'll be an exception with Germany still. No matter who else was coming out, there were a few bands like Accept, who at least made it to the States at some point. Other than that, there were some German bands... whenever we play Brazil, we meet German bands we have never heard about. So they, to a certain extent, are successful abroad from Germany's perspective. I think when I joined, before my time, Michael just played on the very first album, Lonesome Crow, and that didn't have really a distinctive sound. But the following albums where Uli played on, they always had mixed styles, because of his strong influence of Hendrix's music and guitar playing. So they were two different styles at the same time. When I joined with the album Lovedrive, it became more like the sound of a unit. I think with the following album, Animal Magnetism, in 1980, we enhanced that."

"In the '70s, when Uli was in the band, it was like Matthias said: two different styles," reiterates Rudolf. "And it's a style created more by composing because Klaus and me, we did it that way already in the Scorpions, composing like we're doing now, while Uli Jon Roth, he was more the Jimi Hendrix kind of guy. So what can we do to include this in the Scorpions sound? It was very difficult because the sound of the Scorpions and Jimi Hendrix is very weird, but for some people who like the Scorpions in the '70s, that was their focus. They say, 'Oh great, this is a band that has two different styles but somehow it fits together.' But then when Uli left, there was no composer any more. In this case I had the pressure to compose the whole album. In this case, with Klaus. So we now had the possibility to have one way of writing, and this was the first basic foundation of building up the signature Scorpions sound. When Matthias came in, we put all these things together and had one sound."

"The situation was, Matthias was really playing as a band member," said Rudolf, addressing the same subject from a 2011 vantage point. "Not as a solo guitar player. You can be a solo guitar player playing in a band, but not being a real band member music-wise. I think Matthias, Michael and also Uli are different in their technique. Matthias was the first guy who really started to see himself as part of the band, and tried to use the lead guitar very much focused to the songs. For him it was clear that the song is the most important part of the guitar. So in his case, when we started working together, especially also with Dieter Dierks, we were really a great team by really building the house of the Scorpions, the music of the Scorpions, in an intelligent, fearful and guitar-orientated way."

"Regarding the title Lovedrive," continues Francis, back to the first record with the new guitarist, "we were a little unsure if this word existed in the English language. But our German tour promoter, the famous Fritz Rau, who promoted the Rolling Stones at that time, liked the title and we decided to go for it. Lovedrive got us a record contract in Europe with EMI, in America with PolyGram—today it's Universal—and in Japan with RVC, or to put it in other words, Dieter Dierks got the contracts and we were signed to Dieter's label Breeze. With financial and promotional tour support from PolyGram, and contracts we signed with the agency DMA (Nick Caris and Dave Leone) from Detroit and with the famous New York management company CCC, which was David Krebs, Steve Leber, Peter Mensch and Cliff Burnstein. We got booked on a tour with Ted Nugent through big halls almost everywhere in North America. That tour was the start of our career in USA and Canada."

Essentially, Dierks' Breeze Music, executed by Dieter and his lawyer Marvin Katz, had signed long-term recording contracts with Mercury in the US and Canada, EMI Harvest in Europe, and RCA for Australia and Japan. Dieter then made the connection with Leber Krebs (later Contemporary Communications Corp., or CCC) who put the wheels in motion for the band's first US tour. It is also of note that Leber Krebs' Cliff Bernstein had been poached from Mercury Records, by David Krebs, with Bernstein eventually moving on to Q Prime, and David retaining management of Scorpions through 1988. Also, Herman says that the first contact made with the band was through Peter Mensch, now and for many years, Cliff's partner in Q Prime.

At the time, in the press, the band had expressed their dissatisfaction with RCA, grousing that they didn't promote Tokyo Tapes at all, and that the record was hard to find in the shops in the UK. Herman even remarked that fans were phoning up the label complaining and that whoever was on the other end of the line was drawing a blank on the band name Scorpions. For their part, RCA felt satisfied that they had included *Steamrock Fever* on a label compilation. Clearly, the relationship was breaking down.

Noted Rudolf, in conversation with Jeb Wright, the shuffling of the band's business corresponded with the modernisation of the band's sound. "Actually, my reason was in this direction, I wasn't sure if it could be possible. By building a band, and not only looking for good musicians, but also looking for people you could build a friendship with, made us have a team that was ready for adventure, and to be ready to build bridges, and to be ready to do something outstanding. I remember in the '70s telling the boss of RCA, who we were on at that time, 'I know we can make it in the United States. You need to put our records out in the United States.' He would say, 'Yeah, yeah, but you know the American market is not like you.' Our boss in America was Bob Summers. One summer Bob Summers came to Germany, to Hamburg, where our main office of RCA Germany was. The guy called me and said, 'Rudolf, the RCA boss from the worldwide division, Bob Summers is here.' I said, 'I am coming directly.' I spoke to the guy and I said, 'I know we can make it in the United States. It would be great if you can arrange that.' He said, 'First of all, you sell records and then you can play live over here.'"

With relations going nowhere with the staid and frankly non-rock RCA, Schenker came to the realisation that, "In this case, we had to change our record company from RCA to EMI in Europe. In America, we went with Mercury. The guy who signed us to Mercury was Cliff Burnstein. The guy who signed us for management for Leber Krebs was Peter Mensch. They were the two guys from Q Prime. They saw us playing in Hamburg in the music hall and it was a great concert. Cliff and Peter were so touched by the concert they wanted to sign us immediately. It was the beginning of our world career. America was our country and it still is. We have some very good memories from the American tours. I know on each tour, we mostly toured between four and eight months in America. It was great to go on the bus through the countryside. It was fantastic to see how beautiful the American countryside is."

"We never got the chance to come to America with the old label," says Klaus. "I'm sure things might have happened a lot sooner if we'd been able to tour here. RCA just didn't believe in the band. We didn't realise they were only a big label for people like Elvis and Dolly Parton and not for heavy rock acts. When an album came out, they'd tell us they were waiting until the next one before sending us to the States. It was a bad situation and they definitely blocked us for all those years."

"I was 27 when I joined the band," sighs Herman. " Klaus and Rudolf were a year older. We had a hard time getting to America. We were the first band ever from Germany to break out in America. We used to tell our record company that we wanted to play in America and they used to laugh at us. They used to say, 'You want to play in America? What, do you think they are just sitting around waiting for you?' We said, 'Of course they are waiting for us.' We proved them all wrong."

As for Francis' view of the band's business at this juncture... "Let me put it this way. 1979, okay, how many years ago. First time we came to America, Dieter Dierks arranged the contract with that Chicago-based label Mercury. Mercury later on was Polygram, which is now Universal Records. Somehow, the lawyer of Dieter Dierks contacted David Krebs, and the record company had somebody working for them called Cliff Burnstein. He discovered us somehow. He said, okay, let's get this band. Cliff Burnstein and Peter Mensch were friends, somehow. They came together with Leber and Krebs. Peter Mensch was the junior partner, or junior, manager at Leber and Krebs. This is how I understood it. We had a contract with David Krebs, but with this company, CCC, Contemporary Communications Corporation—David Krebs and Steve Leber. So Peter Mensch was doing the day-to-day business, and Cliff Burnstein would be the radioman. He had a great ear for music. He knows all the radio landscape, or he knew it. I don't know, I haven't seen him in years.

"So they were a great team," continues Francis, on the split in management that was soon to happen. "So one day, Peter said, okay, we're going to leave Leber and Krebs, and build up our own company, Q Prime. This means to me, very smart, very intelligent. Oh, great name, I thought, we all thought. But we were contracted, and positive. So we said to Peter, listen, we cannot leave David Krebs and Steve Leber only because you build up a new company. Because first of all we have this contract. Secondly, we had a handshake with David Krebs to stay with him, you know, and he wouldn't let us go. We had lots of trust in David Krebs. He was a very visionary person. So we have to make decisions. Peter was very unhappy that we didn't go with him. But we stuck with Leber and Krebs. I think contracts have to be fulfilled. If you don't fulfil or if you don't serve a contract, you know... Contracts need to be served. If you don't serve them, you end up in court, you end up in trouble, and that's no good. But in the end, we left David Krebs in the '80s, and that became a bigger problem, when we met up, and joined forces with Doc McGhee."

Asked about his memories around the new team, Herman recalls that, "David Krebs signed the band for management and Dieter Dierks, our producer, got us over to the states. He knew Marvin Katz, he knew David Krebs. That's how all of us got together. So we ended up at Leber and Krebs, who also had a new band called AC/DC, which was a Peter Mensch signing. I think, you know, we had done the honour to go out with AC/DC as an opening band, and second tour with AC/DC, we were in the middle, special guest, and an unknown band from England called Def Leppard was the opening band. Then we went out with Ted Nugent, and we went out as an opening act with Aerosmith. We learned a lot from both, how to present yourself on stage, how to entertain the audience. We would go to the side of the stage every night. Later on, when we took Jon Bon Jovi out as an opening act in 1984 Doc McGhee told them, go on stage, go on the side of the stage, copy everything they do. They did, and as you know, very successfully."

Fleshing out the story of already knowing Matthias, Francis adds, "When I started out, before I met the Scorpions, I played with Uli Jon Roth. We had a band in our small village, near Hannover Airport, that area; we had a rehearsal room. We had a keyboard player, and he was at a school—the keyboard player became a teacher... where they can make some money tutoring mathematics. I was very good at mathematics. And that's how I met with Matthias. So I taught him mathematics. But not too much, you know? We stopped this after ten lessons or something. He thought he could do it for himself. That's how I met him. When Uli Jon Roth left the band, I was very much in the management, so I placed an ad in the London newspaper to find a guitarist. But finally we went... I said to the band, 'I have this young kid. Listen to him.'

"We were trying to become more international sounding, you know, find our direction. It takes time. With Uli Jon Roth in the band, he was more one direction, and the other guys in the band wanted to go a different direction. So we were always in the studios trying to find the right balance between these directions. When I listen back to those records now, with a glass of red wine, it's great memories. I'm always surprised how well, everything was conceived; very together. It was hard work."

"Lovedrive was an amazing album because there was so much going on around the band in terms of breaking through internationally," continues Klaus, remembering, like Francis, the fortuitous career circumstances the record represented. "And having Michael Schenker back for a moment, on the Lovedrive sessions, where it looked like a family reunion, the happy family reunion for the moment, but at the end it wasn't. But there was a very creative part that came from Michael Schenker on songs like *Lovedrive* and *Holiday*. Well, there were so many, *Coast To Coast*; there was a lot of good stuff, and it was an exciting album to make. The sessions were very intense and we were fighting to survive all these guitar problems. Having Matthias in and out, and Michael in and out, and touring, it was an album where we were fighting hard to survive, all these problems. But at the same time we were very creative, great songs—the songs were amazing."

"That came from outside," laughs Herman, on Lovedrive's incendiary album cover, on which a society couple plays kinky games in the back of a limousine with a big wad of chewing gum. "We had a cover designer whose name was Storm Thorgerson, who was from the company Hipgnosis. Hipgnosis made, Pink Floyd, the Zeppelin covers, *Houses Of*

The Holy, all that stuff. I knew Storm from my days when I was living in England. We always got on well, and when we joined Scorpions, I phoned him up, I said, 'Look, I'm in a German band now,' and he goes, 'You fucking German cunt! You're back in the fatherland!' You know, Storm, fucking nuts. So I said, 'Yeah, come on, make us a cover. We need something really crazy.' We told him the title. He started with Lovedrive, with the chewing gum on the tits of this chick, which was banned in America. They put red vinyl around it at the time. But we still sold a half million copies. That was the first gold album in America."

"It was Elton's," confirms Rarebell on the limousine used for the cover shoot. "Storm had done work for everybody including Elton John. He just borrowed it. I remember when he flew from London to Cologne, to Dieter Dierks' studio and he showed us the covers he had made. He brought about ten different covers. As soon as he showed us the cover with the chewing gum we knew that was the one. He is the best when it comes to making album covers."

As qualification to Herman's assertion, Lovedrive would be the earliest album of the catalogue to be certified gold. Reaching that plateaus didn't take place, officially, until the formal certification on May 28th 1986, well after the band was already bringing home the heavy rock for later platters. At the time, the album stalled at No.55 in the US but hit No.11 in Germany and No.36 in the UK, where hard rock was starting to make a play for respectability. Herman's red vinyl story above is true. Mercury did indeed receive complaints from US rack-jobbers, some refusing to work with the album. The real fix was a complete redo of the cover for some issues, which simply featured the band's logo squatted upon by a blue scorpion, which became a popular shirt design for the band.

Fleshing out the tale, Herman explains that he had "worked with Storm before, in England; I met him with Vineyard, as their drummer. When we made Lovedrive, I said to the guys, 'don't take a German cover anymore from a German record company. We have really good music here; let's make an outstanding cover so people have something to talk about.' I said to them, 'One guy in the world who is really crazy is Storm; he made Wish You Were Here, he made the Led Zeppelin covers, you'll like this, let's do this.' So calls went over to London, and I said, 'Storm, come on, make us a really crazy cover.' As you know, when he came up with the Lovedrive cover with the chewing gum, everybody in the room said, 'Yes, that's it.' There were alternative pictures. I had a few of those covers; up to a few years ago, I had all the alternative covers. I was in one of my crazy moods and cleaned house and I said fuck this shit, and threw it away. But it was nothing spectacular, nothing to write about. This was the best one. It was very striking. He made that and we said, 'Wow, that's it.'"

Lovedrive opens with a bold dose of steamrock fever called *Loving You Sunday Morning*, not as sexual lyrically as it might sound. At the music end, it's a chugging riffster, all rhythm guitars, a wall of sound, very much a proto-hair metal track of a type we might hear from Dokken, Quite Riot, Ratt or Mötley Crüe come the early '80s, or for that matter, Judas Priest circa British Steel through Screaming For Vengeance, a blueprint toward *You've Got Another Thing Comin'*, as it were. One notices as well, that Klaus and his vocals are front and centre—this was a deliberate move suggested by Dieter to help commercialise the band's sound. Exuding the sense of class Scorpions always embodied, just when the song should be running out of steam, the band serve up new and intensified rock parts late in the sequence, turning the song from what could have been a minimally ambitious party rocker into a behemoth of the new accessible rock.

"First of all, I had a big say in the studio about sound," notes Herman. "I wanted my drums to be heard on the record. Before, the production was different. We wanted the mixes to sound more like a band. Before, you could hear Uli's guitar up front on everything. In those days, the band wanted to produce an American-orientated album. Back in 1978, we used to ask ourselves, 'How can we get to America?' For a German band, coming to America was a dream. As it ended up, we came along at the right time. Rock was big and we were lucky to sign with David Krebs and Steve Leber, who managed, at the time, Aerosmith, Ted Nugent, AC/DC and Def Leppard. We came over and were able to play with them on tour packages, which exposed us to greater audiences. Peter Mensch was the one who signed the Scorpions to Leber Krebs. We came over to America and we fitted right into this thing."

Then it's up and away to the grinding committed rock of *Another Piece Of Meat*, part pedal to the rock, part half time recline, all guns blazing, including Michael for one of his three cameos. "*Another Piece Of Meat* I wrote in Japan," says Herman, now beginning to flex his muscle as lyricist for the band. "After we first toured there, I went out with a Japanese girl who was totally into Japanese kickboxing, where you can fight with the feet and hands. Every time they were hitting each other, the blood was going all over the place, and they were screaming for more blood. She was out of her brain watching this. It was a culture shock for me. She got really excited about this fighting, and the longer I stood there, the more disgusted I got with the whole thing. Also in the end, you turn around, and you go, 'Oh, come on, it's just another piece of meat.' It was basically the headline for the song. I wrote it in Japan in ten minutes. I had the riff in my head immediately (sings it). I thought, it must be a very heavy, dirty, rocking riff. So I sung this to Rudolf and we sat down and we did the song in, I think, ten minutes."

Indeed, the story is accurate to the album credits—although Herman gets a lyric credit on this plus two others on the album, he features twice in this one's credit, sharing music with Rudolf.

"It was always the one who wrote the song, gets the publishing, gets the money," explains Herman. "If you see on the covers, all of the songs from the old days are usually Schenker, Meine, Rarebell, which means that, even if Klaus wrote only two words in the lyrics, I would share it with him. The same was with *Another Piece Of Meat*. I wrote the song complete, and Rudolf made one chord in it, and I share the music with him, because this was the attitude we had from the beginning. There were only three writers in the band. With Uli Roth, we had to experiment, play around with it, and then the song came out of it. So we split those ones four ways, as you see on the album. But usually Rudolf wrote the most songs, and therefore that's why his name is on all those songs; from *Make It Real* to *Blackout*—all those songs are Rudolf."

After the record's second clanger in two tracks, we're into a rote and largely forgotten power ballad *Always Somewhere*, the lyric of which reprises the theme of *Loving You Sunday Morning*, namely missing your woman because you are on a rock 'n' roll schedule, on tour, rockin', always somewhere. This one gives way to well-regarded instrumental jam *Coast To Coast*, which also features Michael.

"He was actually there the whole time, the same as me," explains Rarebell, asked about the extent of Michael's involvement on the record. "The way we usually work is that we put down rhythm guitar, bass and drums, so we have a foundation, and then Michael... in those days as you know, he split up with Phil Mogg from UFO, and at the time Matthias was already in the band. Don't forget, we made an audition in London. Peter Tolson was already coming from Pretty Things. We had some really good guitar players. But then Rudolf said no, we want to pick somebody from Hannover. It makes life less problematic. So we took a young guitar player by the name of Matthias Jabs, who could copy everything that Uli played before. But when we were in the studio, I had *Another Piece Of Meat*, and Michael was there to play the solo. I wrote with Klaus, *Loving You Sunday Morning*; I told him to play the solo on there and *Coast To Coast*. So he played those three songs. He would usually come in the morning, and buy a case of German beer and drink it until four in the afternoon, and he laid down two or three songs, you know? That's Michael."

"Then we started a short tour in France, and the first gig in Lyon, 6000 people, sold-out show, and he did not show up. He was already on his bike on the way to Spain. He did that two more times where he cancelled shows out of the blue. We said, 'Look Michael, we can't work like this. You have to be reliable, otherwise the promoters are not going to book us anymore.'

In the end, because of this, we decided to have Matthias. At this stage maybe he wasn't as good as Michael or Uli, but as you know, over the years he became fantastic. But he said also, 'Come on, I can't go in and do this all the time. You can't tell me tomorrow that you are taking Michael back.' So we stayed the same since those days."

Says Rudolf on the album's grinding, powerful instrumental, "First of all, *Coast To Coast*, you can see the people reacting very well. Especially when you've got four guitars, including the bass of course. When four guitars are standing in front and really making the guitar army, and the sound, especially for America and Canada, a heavy kind of groove... we always know that this song will have a very good reaction. It's also a good part for Klaus to have a rest from singing."

Flip to side two of Lovedrive, and immediately you're hit with another modern heavy rock classic in *Can't Get Enough*, a manic panic of a tribal rocker and an urgent performance from the drummer all the way up to Klaus who turns in one of his most powerful performances. This one's short lyric makes a half-hearted attempt to equate rocking out with sex, although Herman says, "*Can't Get Enough* is simply by the end of the show, that we couldn't get enough of the music and we wanted to continue. That's what the song's about. I think Klaus wrote some great lyrics there."

Then it's a reggae tune! Yes, *Is There Anybody There?* is pretty much that, albeit with a tight forward pulse and a few stacked power chords, the accompanying lyric very much in the band's traditional wheelhouse of love and loneliness. The track was floated (granted, in the UK) as a single, backed with *Another Piece Of Meat*. But this writer doesn't recall ever hearing it once on Canadian or American radio, even as *Loving You Sunday Morning*, *Another Piece Of Meat*, *Can't Get Enough*, *Lovedrive* and *Holiday all* were moderately regular spins on the deep track FM of the day—how's that for picking them?

Speaking of *Lovedrive*, a proto-power metal gallop serves as the bedrock of the album's slamming title track, on which Michael contributes. Lyrically, there's only two verses of nonsense about being in a hot car with a hot chick (albeit with lots of chorus repeats), a surprising dearth, much like the economy of words one fails to notice when pondering *The Sails Of Charon*. *Lovedrive* is nearly five minutes of wall-of-sound guitars, an example of the band's alchemical guitar weaves par excellence, in and through parts that studied metalheads found impressive, the root of which could only be the band's European, Teutonic sensibility, no?

Rudolf's in on the writing credits as he is with every song on the album. "I mean, they're great albums, no questions about this," begins Schenker, explaining the necessity of his pervasiveness. "They are fantastic. Lovedrive, I remember, was a very outstanding album for me as well, because after Uli Jon Roth left the band, I was the only guy who composed. So in the next moment I had to compose over 12, 14, 16 songs, from one day to the next. So it was a very hard thing to do in one week. But on the other hand not. Because I said to myself, okay, when Uli is doing his stuff, maybe that's a chance for us to create a complete Scorpions sound. Because when Uli was in the band, we were more or less a two-piece band—two-piece, I mean, two different style bands. One was very much Hendrix-influenced, and the other part was already the Scorpions sound, and it was Klaus and my compositions. So in this case, when I started to have to compose the whole album, I was really into it, to make an outstanding album, not by mistake, but to try it. Then my brother had his, what you would call honeymoon, and he came over to Germany to celebrate and called us in the studio. 'Okay guys, I'm here; can I listen to what you guys are doing?' We asked him, 'Hey, what do you think? Do you want to play something on this song or that song?' He did, and it was great. It was a fantastic album. With Lovedrive, we needed to present the real Scorpions sound to the fans, and because of my brother playing with the band, we got a very strong impact to the worldwide press, because everybody went and said, 'What? Michael Schenker is playing with the Scorpions?! That's unbelievable. I have to buy this album!' Immediately we were in the Top 50 in England, in the charts, and stuff like this. So Lovedrive is a very important step for the band."

Lovedrive closes with another Scorpions power ballad, *Holiday*, which has actually survived the ravages (and ridicule) of time to become the most popular of the old school light songs from the band. Notes Herman, "*Holiday* says it all: 'Let me take you far away; you need a holiday,' you know? Close your eyes and I will take you to a sunny spot. And everyone can imagine it in their heads. But for me, it was a great song because I could take a break and have a sip of wine and relax five minutes, and then continue with the show. That was the way I looked at it."

"*Holiday* is not a hit in the charts, but it is a hit by the fans," adds Rudolf. "Because the people, especially for the part 'longing for the sun,' the people enjoy it, and we always get good reaction on the Internet, and people love it like crazy. I mean, as we know, and that's a very important point, when we played Wacken exactly one year ago, with all the friends, my brother and Uli John Roth, we played there, and we had the set list made by the fans, we really got the information from the hardcore fans that this song, *Holiday*, is something special. I remember when we played back in '79, the first time we played for Lovedrive promotion in England, all the big theatres, and we started the first show at Newcastle or somewhere, the promoter came in and said, 'Hey guys, hey, what's that? Acoustic guitar? Hey, are you crazy? This is the beginning of heavy rock;

you'll get beaten up by the people when you play acoustic guitars.' We said, 'We don't think so.' So we played *Holiday* and the reaction was unbelievable. So the point is always, if you have the mixture, the mixture between really good heavy songs and then very beautiful ballads, the fans will have no problem with it. The problem is only if you give them a medium kind of thing. Then they are angry, because they want the kick-ass side of stuff."

Once the shenanigans with Michael were over, the band settled into touring the record with Matthias as their fast and firm guitarist. First was a headlining jaunt through England, mid-May '79, followed by Japan in June. Rudolf quipped at the time that fans in the north of England responded much better than the south, but that in Germany, the reverse was the case.

July 29th 1978 represents the band's first touch-down in America, where they played Cleveland as part of a festival date that included Journey, Thin Lizzy and AC/DC along with headliners Ted Nugent and Aerosmith, to an estimated crowd of 68,000 (although Herman says that when Scorpions actually went on, in the morning, it was more like 30,000). Into August, the band, along with AC/DC, supported Ted Nugent, with AC/DC getting replaced by Blackfoot mid-month as the tour hit that band's southern US home base. The tracks regularly played from the new album on this tour were *Lovedrive, Always Somewhere, Loving You Sunday Morning* and *Another Piece Of Meat*, with *Is There Anybody There?* and *Can't Get Enough* played about half as often.

"We got enough from advances to cover a lot of expenses," Rudolf told Jon Sutherland, "and we made a deal with the record company that if we couldn't break on the tour, we would be let out of our contract. We toured non-stop from February 1979 until November 1980 with no time off. Klaus was in danger of losing his voice. His vocal cords were like the fingers of a guitarist building up calluses on top of the strings."

Scorpions then jumped off to play the venerable Reading Rock fest in England, Saturday, August 25th, the middle day of three, as a last-minute replacement for Thin Lizzy, who were to headline. Ergo, in effect, Scorpions headlined, and in fact, they were famous enough to do so, partly because the acts weren't all that massive for Reading in '79, the other headliners being The Police and Peter Gabriel, with the seconds on long bills for each day being The Tourists, Steve Hackett and a very early days Whitesnake.

Reading was followed by the Nürnberg Open Air in Germany on September 1st. Headlined by The Who, the bill also included Cheap Trick, AC/DC, and the Steve Gibbons Band. Then it was back to the states for another ten dates, in Texas and along the east, to close out 1979 and all touring obligations for the record.

These things tend to go full circle, as Herman relates: "From a touring point of view, when we started in the beginning, we were opening act for Ted Nugent, and I remember Aerosmith. We played in front of AC/DC, Def Leppard opened for us, and we were special guest of AC/DC in the end. We were lucky, because it was the same management, so we were doing good... They gave us enough space on stage—if you call three-and-a-half yards deep enough to play on stage, it means that the drum riser was built up in the middle of the stage. Klaus could not run from one side to the next, because the drum riser was between. But it was enough space, and they gave us enough lights to perform our 30 minutes in front of all the people. Then after came AC/DC and Ted Nugent. It was a strong bill, and we learned a lot, but they gave us enough space and enough lights overhead—it was Leber Krebs who managed all three bands."

"Ted Nugent, at the beginning, was very arrogant to all of us," continues Rarebell, who says that he and Bon Scott were so close, they used to go out after the shows and sit in with local bands. "Ted wouldn't talk to any of the opening acts, so to speak. The only time he talked to me on the first tour, was because I fucked one of his girlfriends. He didn't like that, and he told me something. I said, 'Listen, leave it up to the woman.' I think he almost started a fight, but then he looked at my arms and he thought twice about it. I'm not easy with those things, as you know. I'm a peaceful man, but if somebody goes about me, I know how to handle myself. So I never had a fight with him, and I never fucked any of his other women (laughs). From that day on, we respected each other. Then one night he started talking, 'Are you into hunting?' I got to know the guy. We had different opinions about life, but we seemed to like each other, somehow. Maybe because of that. But I told him, I said, I don't like hunting, and I don't like animals to get killed. Probably no one ever told him that before."

As for Aerosmith... "Well, we have known them for a long time, because David Krebs, as you know, he was their manager, over two decades, and the first people actually that I met in the band were Brad and Steven. Joey I met several times, and then later on in life, as you know, one show in '81 they opened up for us in Phoenix. By that time they were split, the band was terrible, they played terrible, and the band was finished. As you know, Bruce Fairbairn brought them back to life. But I've known them for a long time and they know us. At one time, when Joey went away, they wanted to use Michael Schenker as a guitar player; I don't know if you know that. They auditioned him. But Michael and Aerosmith are like sun and moon, okay? It would've been really... he would've gotten killed. Really, for sure. You put one crazy guy in, then, okay. But five, that is very, very bad. Anyway, I've known them all for a long time, and because of them, we were introduced to Def Leppard, who are managed by Peter

Mensch. Peter Mensch actually found the band in Germany, turned David Krebs and Steve Leber on, and then in '79, they got us into Cleveland Jam to open up at 10 o'clock in the morning. That festival was with Thin Lizzy, AC/DC, Journey, Ted Nugent and Aerosmith. It was amazing, really amazing."

In tandem with the end of the Lovedrive tour, the band's previous label, RCA, issued Best Of, which, quite incredibly, was just that, featuring what are pretty much understood to be essentially the flashiest, heaviest, most accessible songs from the RCA years, closest thing to a ballad being *In Trance.* As a continuation of the band's career confusion with record wrappers, the album came in three different covers, a fairly racy one for Germany (we got this in Canada as well), an even racier one for Japan, and then the classy leather jacket version for the US reissue in '84. Made sense for RCA to do this, as touring Lovedrive in the US had helped put that album in the charts for fully 30 weeks. In 1982, RCA issued another compilation for Europe, Hot & Heavy, as part of their Take Off! series, with half the same tracks as Best Of, half a bit more obscure.

"We all thought that," says David Krebs, regarding his office's belief that the band had to concentrate its efforts in the US. "As a student of history, I told the Scorpions that the one thing we were gonna do, was not tour England. I said in my opinion, if I looked at England, they were an energy trap for anybody coming from the continent, because they felt rock 'n' roll was like, their thing. The Scorpions, for years, had been trying to crack through England to get to America. We came right to America. I think their first show was opening to 80,000 people in Cleveland, which was headlined by Aerosmith. They were great. I think that went against the grain of thinking, but it was perfect for them. The English had no great love to see... especially a German band to make it; there's no way."

"Lovedrive was my first album, in '78," reflects Matthias, in closing, articulating where it fits in his life. "There definitely are a few favourites and we're still playing those songs today, like *Loving You Sunday Morning* or *Holiday.* That is definitely good stuff.

And the quickest one—I mean, Lovedrive was relatively quick. But it's always the same. When the band starts out—it wasn't the Scorpions' first album, but with this line-up it was—the band starts out and things are fresh; you go for it. You don't think twice, or maybe you do, but not too many times. The longer you do it, the more albums you have on your back, the more you start thinking, and it gets harder and therefore... you see that sometimes with new bands. The first two albums are great and after that ugh, nothing new comes out. We still had something new to offer, something exciting. But obviously the Scorpions don't go in the studio and come out six weeks later and everything is mixed and mastered. But you also you have five world smash hits on there (laughs)."

Animal Magnetism

"Rare like uncooked meat"

New label and new management in place, plus some great new tour memories, Scorpions continued to build on the good tidings afforded Lovedrive by coming up with what was known as Animal Magnetism. In the doing, they kept on shedding all vestiges of the eccentric or even European in their sound. Animal Magnetism would contain one ballad, not two, no reggae tunes and no instrumentals, and this is with one more song than Lovedrive.

Ergo, the album was the band's most uniformly rocking to date, that sentiment underscored by a continued strategic move toward a simplicity of sound, an American sound, big riffs, big rhythms, more and more rhythm guitar occupying the mindspace and less lead.

The title of the record came from literary party drummer Herman, and then visually it was over to Hipgnosis again to stir up the controversy that was fully expected. Says Francis, "The album cover, again, was designed and photographed by crazy guy Storm, from London. I personally did not like the album cover so much, but it was the best to choose from."

"Like Lovedrive, one of my favourite album covers," counters Herman, "with the girl kneeling in front of the guy, with the dog. I wrote a lot of songs on that one, as you can see on the back cover. The title was from me also, and I believed in this animal magnetism. At the time, for me, it had a sexual meaning, and also the animal magnetism as attraction between two people who could respond on a telepathic level. So there were these meanings, and I'm still very interested in this nowadays. But this was the main point of the album, the philosophy: can we get this done, can we attract people with this magnetism in America? We did, you know?"

"That's ridiculous," scoffed Klaus, in 1984 asked about complaints from the religious right that the cover (which later inspired Spinal Tap!) depicted "an immoral act." "All that cover showed was a girl, a man and a dog. It was a sensual cover, but there was certainly nothing explicit about it. I heard that a number of people were saying that we were supposedly telling women to become whores, and for men to dominate their women. That's absolutely not true. Those are the same people who play records backwards looking for messages from the devil. Rock 'n' roll is a very sensual form, and we're a very sensual band (laughs). We don't do *all* those depraved things that you hear about. In fact, quite often we bring our families with us, so there's really not that much of a chance to get into big trouble. We seem to find a way to cause some problems, though. Rudy was arrested in Texas during the last tour for busting up a hotel bar, but other than that, we were pretty quiet. We enjoy having a few beers between shows (laughs). But we hold our beer very well—after all, we are from Germany."

Animal Magnetism, issued March 1st, 1980, opens with *Make It Real*, and it's obvious Matthias and Rudolf are arena rockers in the making, as is their rhythm section, as is consummate vocalist Klaus. Packed with galumphing guitars, it is also melodic in the extreme. The song is one of Herman's favourite of his lyrics ever. "It's my philosophy, you know, that if you really believe in something, you can turn it over. You have to have a lot of determination behind you. I think if you really want something and you really go after it badly then you will get it—if you are determined enough. Animal Magnetism was the first album to go platinum."

Partially true. It was the earliest album of the catalogue to go platinum, but that designation didn't happen until 1991, long after its gold certification in 1984. When it did go gold, it was the second Scorpions album ever to be certified, after its follow-up, Blackout had gone gold pretty much upon release. As a final fine point, Blackout received its platinum certification the same day, March 8th of 1984, as Animal Magnetism had reached gold.

Make It Real was launched as a single, backed with *Don't Make No Promises (Your Body Can't Keep)*. However, as in the past, the public decided that there were songs that captured their attention more forcefully, and it managed only a No.72 placement in the UK charts.

Speaking of *Don't Make No Promises*, that one chimed in at track two, announcing the rest of the record with a bang, rocking hard and fast like *Another Piece Of Meat*, but then similarly collapsing into a chunky verse at half the speed. "*Don't Make No Promises* is a song I wrote with Matthias," says Herman, and it's definitely a rare Jabs credit, and the only one on this album, against a sole author credit for Herman on *Falling In Love* and fully five additional lyric credits. The lyric is of a type that I'm sure would make Uli cringe, basically a short missive about picking up a girl who came to the show and then finding out she's piled on so much fake stuff (wig, padded bra), there wasn't much girl left. "That is another true story," laughs Herman. "I went to bed with a girl who unpacked her tits and there were no more tits. She wore a padded bra. That is why I said, 'Don't make no promises your body can't keep.' It is like the guy who says, 'I'm going to fuck you all night' and then he fucks her for two minutes and rolls over and falls asleep."

As for writing with Matthias, Herman says, "So he would sit there, and he would hum me the melody (sings it), and say, come on, put some words to this, what you think of this, oh, this is great, and continue on these lines. He's humming me everything and I'm writing the words to it."

"I write a lot of stuff and I'm getting better and better and better," noted Matthias, years later, asked about the dearth of credits for him early on. "In the first couple years I only concentrated on guitar playing, because that needed to be done. Over the years I've been writing more. I write for other people too. But for some reason, Klaus and Rudolf are such a team. In the old days, Herman wrote a lot of the lyrics, especially for Animal Magnetism. So those two were our team and that produces the Scorpions style people want to hear, with me playing the guitar in the way the Scorpions sound. So songwriting-wise, you know, you can't bend over backwards too much to make it sound like somebody else. So if you write songs, you write songs. Therefore, I think, time will come. I've been getting much better."

Back to the track sequence, things get progressively slower come *Hold Me Tight*, the first of three slow but mesmerizing heavy rock constructs on the album. Lyrically, this one's about a relationship breaking down, due to the nomadic life of a rocker. "I think the slow ones are the most difficult ones to play," reflects Herman, "because as a drummer, you always seem to go on the speed side; you want to play fast, and suddenly you have to half everything there and play in slow motion. Those things are really difficult to play, because you have to have total control with your laid-back feeling. Especially a song like *Still Loving You*. It was not easy to lay down, but it still has the quietness and the meditative mood in there."

"Dieter always made me play with a click track," continues Rarebell. "This way you had the opportunity to make a cut. In those days, you could not drop in and out digitally. You had to make the cut on the tape. So we used a click track so we could at least make an exact cut, you know? He was very tough, because in those days, you had the analogue tape. In other words, if you made a mistake in a song, you'd play the whole song again. Or an engineer would sit there for five hours and cut that huge tape. So I remember, especially as a drummer, I played many songs 50, 60 times, until I nearly dropped off the chair. Nowadays it's so easy. You know, you go in and record, and if you have a good verse or good chorus, you can repeat it; you can cut in and out wherever you want. It's a piece of cake, nowadays."

"Herman was always a bit different from the rest of the band," laughs Francis, on his partner in Scorpions' dependable, rock-solid rhythm section. "When we wore jeans and leather he would show up in a white suit. When everybody went to bed sleeping, Herman would party all night. Money did not last long in Herman's hands. When Klaus asked him once for some coins he said, 'I am generous, man; I carry no coins.' He liked to spend his money, liked to give large tips. On the other hand Herman always came up with great lyrics. I do not know how Herman and Klaus split their duties in this matter, but somehow they wrote good stuff."

"For Animal Magnetism, I remember that Dieter Dierks did the recordings with us in the small studio, called Studio 2," continues Francis. "For the Scorpions, all albums took a very long time to record. The contract with Dieter Dierks permitted us to spend lots of time and because it was Dieter's studio, he did not mind. It just took us time to get songs from scrap into their final form. The hassle was, that we—and Dieter as well—were never really happy with early results. We always wanted to continue working on the songs until the record company's deadline. But at a certain moment you have to stop playing with ideas and phrasings which may further improve the recordings. Then you have to start mixing what you have recorded. Herman always wanted to mix one song per day. But he used to leave the studio after the recording of his drum takes and came back five months later asking us, what we have done in the meantime. But many things had happened in the meantime, many ideas had been recorded, some of them already selected, others not. Recording is like putting a big puzzle together. Once you have the final picture, you do not care about all the small pieces anymore. Many times we ended up working a couple of days per song on the mixing alone, in order to get all the pieces in place."

Still, the band felt rushed with this album. It's the apocryphal strike while the iron is hot. Ticket sales are good, the offers are coming in, get an album written and recorded and get back out there. After all, it isn't going to last forever. Indeed, the band had just finished up tour dates in December of '79 and were into the studio the same month, finishing up the album in February of '80.

"This album, it's a very interesting album," muses Rudolf, in retrospect. "It's also one of the albums which is not finished. We came back from the fun of the Lovedrive tour which was over a year long. Then we went directly into the studio and we had a very short time, and went on an English tour. In the short time, I think we did a good job. I think a very important song off the album is *The Zoo*, which I like very much— it's a classic, no question about it. *Lady Starlight* I like very much. And *Make It Real*, maybe for the European market. *Animal Magnetism* is even a great song. It's a very heavy kind of song, but it is somehow an album in between. An album in between Lovedrive and Blackout. I know many people like the album very much, probably because it is rare. It's rare like uncooked meat. We didn't take the time to make something really, really precise. I think that's what some people like about it. But yes, Animal Magnetism was good, but not as good, as I thought it could be."

Next up was a bit of a forgotten, half-committed rocker with a funk edge, written by Rudolf and Klaus, called *Twentieth Century Man*. Lyrically, there's a bit more ambition than usual here, Klaus mourning the loss of human connection in the age of technology. *Twentieth Century Man*'s howling guitars and pulsating bass then gives way to the album's only ballad, *Lady Starlight*, to close the first side of the original vinyl, small string section as fancy adjunct. Klaus pens the words to this one as well, and it's classic Uli-era wordsmithing, with summer days and lonely winter nights, dreams, memories, lost love.

Onto side two, and we're into a chunky, rhythmic, irresistibly melodic arena rocker called *Falling In Love*, similarities to a future smash track called *Rock You Like A Hurricane* palpable. "A typical song of the road, *Falling In Love*," says Rarebell, the sole author of this grinding, groovy track, one with amusingly few words at all. Of note, it is interesting that when Herman wrote music, he did so on a piano or some other type of keyboard. Because he never had one on the road, where in fact lots of writing took place, he says that many good ideas were simply forgotten.

"Then *Animal Magnetism* same thing, *Only A Man*, same thing," continues Rarebell. "This is basically an album about, you know, being on the road, a musician totally crazy on the road. That's what we were in those days. But this is a song where I did both the words and music, where I would come to the band, and I would hum them the song. I would say, 'Yeah, I wrote this song called *Falling In Love*; this is how it goes (sings it). Can you write a riff to this?' Then they would start it, and I would go, yeah, that's it. I had the words already in my head and sometimes it would take only an hour to write a song, especially with *Falling In Love*. I had that riff in my head and I was singing it to Matthias and Rudolf, and they picked it up directly. I said, 'Yeah, that's exactly what I heard.' Then I was seeing the line and I told them the words and the whole song was done."

The big back beat continues through *Only A Man*, which features a circular, almost malevolent, squarely heavy rock verse of doom, softened by a melodic chorus. Comments Herman, "Rudolf comes to me and he plays *Only A Man* and he says, 'Yeah, write something dirty here. This is going to be a really hard-rocking riff here.' This is how we used to work." Rarebell obliges Rudolf's request, writing a fairly vivid jumble of words about groupie action on the road, tinged with a bit of the regret of what happens when a rocker returns to the fires waning at home.

Closing out the record are the album's two most famed tracks, *The Zoo* and *Animal Magnetism*. *The Zoo* is a concert classic for the ages, boogie of rhythm but nothing else, basically a simple, flat-headed heavy rock tank, but with parts that help maintain headbanger interest. An added frill is the talkbox, performed by Matthias.

"Yes, the album had two strong songs on it anyway," says Rudolf, dismissive of the rest, "especially *The Zoo*, which really became a strongly played song in Canada and United States, and of course *Animal Magnetism* which lately was showing up in the film The Wrestler with Mickey O'Rourke."

As for the lyric for *The Zoo*, Rudolf says, "I remember it was the first time as a rock band in America, and the management was based in New York, Leber Krebs, and they said to us, we have a good friend here, and he will show you the interesting parts of New York. He took us out and said, 'Here's this, and here's this, and this street here, this is The Zoo.' We said, 'What, The Zoo?!' ' 'Yeah, they call it The Zoo because it's crazy here.' This was something for us again, because I remember, I was sitting somewhere in the Midwest and picked up the guitar and it was one of the only songs which I wrote on the road. I was watching television and there was a warning, what do you call it, a twister, a tornado warning and I was like (sings the riff) and I made the whole thing in around 20 minutes. I came into the dressing room and said, 'Klaus, here, I have to play you something' and he said, 'Hey, you know what that reminds me a little bit of? The street, The Zoo.' We went back home and Klaus wrote the lyrics."

The Zoo is definitely one of the tracks on Animal Magnetism that Rudolf figures never quite got finished to his satisfaction, going so far as to say that it became finished over years and even decades, as the band played and transformed it in a live environment.

"Yes, of course, when we played the song live, the last 20 years and even longer, there were always things added to it. *The Zoo* was not like it is now from the first moment. As I can remember we didn't want to finish the album because Dieter Dierks said, 'Guys, we have to finish now because the record company is waiting for the master. Period' 'No, we want to change something there!' 'No, do it on the next album.' In this case, the song's not finished for our side as musicians, but we had to bring it out, because the record company was waiting. So of course you are using this possibility then live. You are editing things into it, and the song became a little bit different live. Maybe you don't notice so much, that when you have the possibility to listen on the album then, yeah, then you hear, very clear. But also, of course, when you re-record the songs, you want to say, 'Okay, let's see, what kind of idea I have there,' or the other guy there and there. So when something spontaneous comes to us, yeah, that's great, let's keep this, we did it. But it's very rare that it's something that anybody could be very angry at."

"Animal Magnetism was where we had just a taste of American success and worldwide success," adds Klaus. "With Animal Magnetism, I think the biggest song on that album was probably *The Zoo*, one of the songs we still play, and one of the all-time classics. Also, a great album, and a great moment in time, that we shared there in the Dierks Studios. But it was still in the middle of something where the band was on its way to the top. A couple of years later, Love At First Sting, it was a very powerful record, and all these records were leading up to Love At First Sting."

So this one was Klaus's handiwork, but I asked Herman who between them was indeed more motivated or excited to write lyrics. "Well, it was like this. You imagine, when you do a whole album, in the beginning, I was definitely the one coming out of England, so my English was the best in the band. So that was the obvious reason they asked me to write the lyrics in English, because my English is best, you know? Then next step was Klaus came to me and said, 'Listen, there are so many songs now; we have about 25 songs to choose from. You're going to have to help me out and write some lyrics too, you know, and we'll pick the best ones.' So that's how we used to do it."

Then finally the album closes (down) with its slowest song yet, the daring title track. Sure the riff moves ably and nimbly but Herman is asked to back it up with a tortuous crawl of a beat (and his lyrics are even more tortuous, if you notice them at all—credit due how cool the music is, one supposes). The fact that it worked and is a beloved Scorpions track is testimony to the talents and tones and performances of the band at hand. Before we close, it must also be mentioned that there's a tenth Animal Magnetism track on some issues, called *Hey You*. It's quite uncharacteristic of the album, and somewhat substandard, and it's yet another of Herman's.

Touring in support of Animal Magnetism begun in mid-April 1980, in Germany and France, always a Scorpions stronghold. "Which surprises me most because we are German; 'cause you know our fucking history," mused a perplexed Herman, doing press at the time, on why Scorpions are so big in France (as is AC/DC). "There was Hitler in the war screwing them up. The British bands come over here putting on German gear, it makes me laugh. What do they think they're doing bringing another Hitler back? It is interesting for them if they come from England and America. They come and play little Hitler because you have all that shit on English TV. You are polluted by those movies telling you Germans were all bad. Okay, there is a helluva lot of bad German people, but I tell you, six years I lived in England, I met a lot of bad people as well. I don't give a shit about borders because they don't exist. All we wanna do is play good music and give those people a good time. People who believe in borders don't get anywhere. Our planet is very small. Go out at night and look at the sky, then you know what's happening. There's a million planets out in the system and so why do we believe in our little countries, our little egos? What for? Rock 'n' roll is the international language. People know what you mean all over the world. Okay, we've got a bad past. It doesn't matter anymore. We were born behind that time. I tell you I couldn't give a shit about borders. We could be Europe as a nation, America as a nation—one day it will be the world as a nation."

By mid-May, the band briefly touched down in the UK, with Tygers Of Pan Tang as support. Later in the month, the band embarked upon a considerable North American leg, as sandwich act between openers Def Leppard and headliners Ted Nugent.

On August 16th, 1980, Scorpions played Monsters Of Rock in Donington, along with Touch, Riot, Saxon, April Wine, Judas Priest and Rainbow, who headlined. The show was commemorated as a live album, a single record, on which only Rainbow and Scorpions were represented by two tracks, Scorpions contributing *Loving You Sunday Morning* and *Another Piece Of Meat*. As importantly, the Donington showcase was considered a milestone event for rock in the UK, an ushering in of the New Wave Of British Heavy Metal, even if the only NWOBHM band proper on the bill was Saxon. The year was closed out with additional UK and mainland European dates. Little did they know, but Scorpions wouldn't be hitting the open road again until March of 1982.

"There was a certain vibe," muses Matthias, surveying the experience of the Animal Magnetism album as a whole. "We had just finished our first tour in the States supporting Ted Nugent, and AC/DC as a special guest for half a year. It was our first time ever in the States. It took us six months and we came back and the next tour was already booked, again with Ted Nugent. We weren't a special guest then and I don't remember who the opener was that time. So we had to do this album quickly. That was the quickest album we've done. I think it took us two months. Since the big studio was booked, we were in Studio 2 at Dierks again, and we were in a very small place, and there was a certain vibe. On there are the first impressions we made when we were in the States for the first time. So much to talk about, like the lyrics for *The Zoo*—you can tell we had been to New York. Stuff like that. We were very much influenced. It was a very unique working atmosphere, different from any other production we've done. It was a certain vibe. Song-wise, there are the ones you mentioned, but *Only A Man* was one of the songs, and there were other good ones too. To us, it was sometimes surprising that the album, in North America, including Canada, was received so well. It must be the vibe."

Blackout

Perhaps Lovedrive was the eye-opener, the record that suggested the wider possibility that the Scorpions could indeed break America big. Its follow-up Animal Magnetism was arguably the first realised, pan-world record for the band. Then there would be Blackout, a further step toward rock domination, a record with wilder mood swings than its predecessor, but more than anything, a professional, self-assured brightness. It would set up wonderfully the smash hit status of Love At First Sting with that record providing even further rock god gains. But what's more important, when all discussion of the financials melt away and legacy becomes the key concern, Blackout is firmly the fan favourite of the catalogue, a solid classic, one of those apex experiences in a long illustrious career with much exalted rock contribution, although much of it, disconcertingly, produced before Blackout than after.

"Also one of my titles, was Blackout," notes Herman, who explains the iconic cover art, featuring a screaming figure, head bandaged, forks in his eyes. "That was Gottfried Helnwein, Austrian painter, and that is not Rudolf on the cover, that's Gottfried. But, as I said, for me, Storm's the most crazy designer. I have no idea if he's still alive these days. The Blackout painting... to this day, Helnwein owns it. It's a self-portrait of himself. He doesn't want to sell it. He owns it himself. Everyone thought it was Rudolf. It's not Rudolf."

Blackout almost marked the end for Scorpions. "I remember the situation," begins Rudolf. "There was a problem with Klaus's voice. We had to wait. We recorded in France. We rented a mobile studio and recorded down near the Cote D'Azur, and worked on the album and then we found out that Klaus couldn't sing anymore and was getting worse and worse and worse. So we needed a break. Klaus in the first place, after the first operation, said, 'Guys, I can't make it. Look for a new singer.' I said to him, 'No, no, no, no, you have to try everything. When you've tried everything and we find out it's impossible, then we can think about it, but not before.' So he tried everything and he made it. But in between there was a big gap, because we started recording, I think in February, down there in France and then we stopped at the end of March."

"Before we recorded Blackout, Klaus Meine had lost his voice due to too much touring and not enough caring about his health," adds Francis. "He used to go on stage without any warm-up, going from zero to 100 in a minute. That almost killed his voice and thanks to doctors operating him, we did not end up in rough waters. The basic tracks for Blackout were recorded with Dierks' mobile studio in southern France, but being 'back home' to Dierks Studio, I played most of the bass again."

"My voice was gone!" recalls Klaus, speaking with Dmitry Epstein. "In the early '80s I lost my voice, I couldn't sing. I went straight to the hospital and had to have surgery on my vocal cords. I went to see a band at a local venue and, because I was not allowed to speak for a while it was hard to bring the voice back up. I was thinking, 'This is what I used to do. Can I ever do it again?' It was a very difficult time, during the recording of Blackout. But then Rudolf—and my family, of course, but in the band it was Rudolf—was a very strong support to take me through this thing. He said, 'You do everything for your voice, and we'll wait for you. We don't want another singer, but you have to work hard on yourself to make it happen.' It took me six or seven months, and then my voice was back. What kind of future would I have had if it wasn't? I don't know. Maybe I would have been a writer, maybe a music journalist. I never thought about it! But probably I would've gone to do something allowing me to stay in the music business: producing young bands or something like that."

Specifically, the band had begun recording in early 1981 at Villa San Pecaire, Saint Jacques, Grasse, France, main reason being the desire to record in a large, boomy room and not a typical cramped studio. But Klaus's woes had come to a head upon the return to Cologne, where overdubs and his vocal work were to take place. Instead, Klaus found himself under the care of the Cologne University Hospital, where sessions were scrubbed and he was duly operated on. After the operation, it was thought Klaus was in good shape, but then nodules were found on his cords, and into May of '81, work was still on hold.

"I said to myself, 'okay, I'll go on vacation,'" continues Schenker. "I went to the Philippines, and I had some great experiences because I didn't know before, that we were a big band in Asia, because nobody told us. Of course in these days there was a pretty big black market, pirate stuff, no charts or anything. I remember the first time I went to Manila, in the airport and I hear *Holiday* playing. I figured, what's that? Is the record company picking me up? Maybe they surprise me. There was nobody. I went to the national airport and again, they played *Holiday*, and I said, 'I can't believe this, there must be somebody involved.' Then I heard from the guy who was at the place where I have my vacation, and he was the same age, and exactly the same birthday. He mentioned to me that

Holiday is the biggest song in this area. I had this great place there and I started writing. I wrote two songs for the album, *China White* and *Dynamite* in the Philippines. I think we started working in the studio again around September or October. I tell you one thing, it was a really hard thing for Klaus. But now he knows how to train his voice, warm his voice up, which is very important."

So Klaus wound up getting the job done, with a little help from his friends. Don Dokken, who had been making music in Germany through circuitous circumstances, shared interpreters with Scorpions, and it was through this Niko, that Don made the acquaintance of Dieter Dierks.

"Yes, Niko had also been the interpreter for Scorpions for their first tour of America," explains Don. "He knew their producer and he told him, 'Hey, you should check out this band and this guy named Don Dokken.' So Dieter Dierks said, 'Well, I'm going to be in Hamburg, I'm flying to America, I got an hour-and-a-half to spare, I'll come see him at this club on this day.' But we weren't booked that day and I said, 'Hey man, I want to have Dieter Dierks see us play,' so I booked myself in a club that held about 50 people just to have him come see me play. He came into the club, saw me play and said, 'I don't like your band.' I went, 'okay.' That was the end of it. He said, 'I don't like your band but I like you. I think you're a good singer and you're a good guitar player and you sound a lot like Klaus Meine.' Then about six months later he called me up and said Klaus had surgery on his voice and he can't sing right now but we need somebody to do background vocals on the Blackout album.' He said, 'I'll fly you to Germany if you want to sing on the Scorpions album.' I said, 'Shit, yeah, man!' I flew to Germany and he said if you sing the background vocals and help with the lyrics, you know, Americanise them, I'll let you use the studio for a week to do a demo. I did that, and the band Accept was in there also recording. Their manager, whose name was Gaby Hauke, who ended up marrying the guitar player Wolf Hoffman, took that tape to the record company Carrere and I got my record deal."

"But yeah, I just sang on *No One Like You, Dynamite, You Give Me All I Need*; I did all the high shit. I did a lot of grunt work like, 'Try this note,' 'Try this note,' just so Klaus didn't have to burn his vocal cords out. I was young, I was 26, my voice was super-high. I was green, I was a virgin. I don't even know... I listen to those songs, and they all became big hits, but I can't tell, I can't even hear my vocal. Because I think Klaus went in and did a lot of stuff over. I just did a lot of the grunt work so he didn't have to blow his cords out. I can hear me in a couple really, really high spots. That's what happened."

As to any thoughts of Dokken joining the band... "No, that was all bullshit. I mean, I heard those stories. 'Don's going to be the singer.' I've known Klaus now for a long time, and we've talked about this over the years..."

"Certainly," recalls Klaus, asked if he thought his career might have been close to kaput. "Yes, there was a point, after months and months, after six months or something, after surgery twice on my vocal cords. I knew the material on the Blackout album, and feeling like it was a mountain I would never climb again. I simply gave up on it. I saw a band performing and I watched the lead singer, and I had a feeling. I remember this very well; it's like, man, this is exactly what I used to do, and this is what I enjoyed, until now in my life, and now it's gone. That's how it felt, for a moment, until Rudolf got me back on track and said, 'No way, man. Do any therapy or whatever you need to do, and things will turn out fine.'"

As for Herman's recollection of this difficult time, "Well in '82, when we did Blackout, Klaus lost his vocal cords. He couldn't reach the high notes anymore; it was like this, 'Ack, ack!' So he got a specialist in Vienna who operated on him and the training on the vocal cords, and after nine months he was okay again. He could sing. But in those days, we waited nine months for him. We wrote more songs and just waited simply until he was recovered. We started renting a house near, in the South of France, where we recorded all the basic tracks. But then his voice went, so we simply waited until he was recovered. It was start at the top."

All told, Scorpions consider 1981 somewhat of a lost year for the band, most gratingly because of the complete lack of touring. Eventually, however, they did get the Blackout album out of it, albeit in fits and starts and not until early into 1982, with the record not emerging until March 29th. What's almost comical is that Herman, managed to get a solo album out, called Nip In The Bud, issued by Harvest in Europe and RCA in Japan, i.e. same arrangement as Scorpions, but without the North American release. Recorded with a small band of unknowns, the album is nonetheless competent party rock, with classy but cheeky cover art to boot, definitely in the spirit of Herman's mischievous main band. The album was re-recorded and re-released as Herman Ze German And Friends in 1986, featuring some of his new friends made since 1981.

The aforementioned *Dynamite* and *China White* are, of course, two of the sturdy rock anchors of the Blackout album, the former being a tight, taut, Priest-style speed metaller, modern for its day, the latter being a lumbering, sinister, atmospheric composition with a gut-wrenching, Zeppelin-fried Sabbath riff.

"*Dynamite* is a typical live song," figures Herman. "'Kick your ass to heaven,' you know, 'let's get tight tonight;' all that stuff is typical live material. It's a great riff; I love the song. Same with *Now!*. Those are typical live songs, which really had their basis in the live performance, being on the road. Then of course you have songs where you have love and pain in your heart, like *You Give Me All I Need*. At the time we were all young and we went through our love problems with marriage and divorces and all that stuff, and this is definitely reflected in those songs. This is the Blackout period, which was living on the road, and it's basically what the album talks about. Especially *Can't Live Without You*—that's a song about the audience."

Rudolf couldn't decide which guitar solo he liked best on *China White*, so there's a different one depending if you get the US or the European issue. On both versions, of course, you get a lyric that relates in no way to the title of the song, for *China White*, Klaus writing and then delivering with an impassioned roar a cry for the triumph of good over evil. Says Herman, somewhat dubiously, "*China White* is one of my favourite songs because it's so heavy. The song was basically... China White is, as you know, a heroin addict's special thing. So it was about this chemical." Either Herman is remembering it wrong, or the lyric is extremely veiled.

But the centrepiece of the album is the title track, with its smooth, melodic verse and fierce, hard-charging riff come chorus time, a perfect rock anthem to kick off what would be four very good years for rock spanning roughly '82 to '85.

"When we were putting the album together, we wanted everything to fit together just right," said Schenker, mid-tour for the album. "We had some fast songs and some slow ones to balance them out. All people have two directions. Most people, especially rock people, only want to show you one direction. I myself show two directions. They are danger and quiet. *Dynamite* and *Blackout* are dangerous. *Always Somewhere* and *Holiday* are quiet. In the music of the Scorpions, you will see both of these directions."

"That's a good story," laughs Rudolf on the dead brain cells that inspired *Blackout*. "I remember we had a party with K.K. and Glenn from Judas Priest and there were also the guys there, for a while, from Def Leppard. We were having a party with K.K. and Glenn and they gave me a drink, and it was beer, and I was, 'No, no, you have to have the right mix: whiskey, beer and wine on top of it.' They are like, 'What!?' I was, 'Yes, come on.' We were getting heavily drunk and we had a good time. I think K.K. had the idea, 'Hey, let's go to the Def Leppard guys.' Because we were in Cleveland, the Cleveland Hall, and next door was the hotel. So we went to the Def Leppard guys and they were watching television. They were very young in these days. This was 1980 I think. We were playing together, Def Leppard, Judas Priest and Scorpions in Cleveland. So I saw them watching TV and I put my drink into the television (laughs). The whole television went 'poof!' This was the situation and I said, 'okay, we have to leave, we have to go now.' But anyway, it became so crazy, and the next morning I wake up in my hotel room. I said, 'What's happening?' I went to Herman and he wasn't there, he wasn't at the party, and I said to Herman, 'Hey, I'll tell you what, it was crazy last night. I remember to this point and this point' and he said, 'You know what you had? You had a blackout.' I said, 'Blackout?' Then he said, 'Hey, you know, that's a great title for an album.' Because of this kind of special party, I went back home and said I think I have to write a song, the music, because Klaus was writing most of the lyrics. So I sat at home and made the song and then went to Klaus and he came up with the lyrics and then we had it."

Rudolf must have been blacked out, because Herman remembers the story quite differently. In one telling, Rarebell says the night's hijinx began with Rudolf running around the parking lot of the band's Dubuque, Iowa hotel claiming to be lost, with the local cops trying to figure out if they wanted to arrest him or not. After Herman sweet-talked them into turning the drunk German over to him, the two proceeded into the hotel, where there was... not so much a bar, but a lounge area, where you could at least get a beer. Herman says Rudolf then grabbed a glass of beer off of a kindly patron's table and then dumped it into the TV. Rarebell doesn't remember the TV as going 'poof' but he does confirm a couple of Priest and Def Leppard guys were there to witness Schenker's continuing meltdown.

"This is a very true story," is the way Herman began his telling of the tale to me on a different occasion; a recounting that evokes a nice mix of the two versions above. "This was the time when Judas Priest played before us, as the special guest on this tour. It was somewhere in the Midwest, I forgot where. Anyway Rudolf got really drunk after the show, and I was sitting in the room with Glenn Tipton, with the singer, and the other guitar player. He came in the middle of the night, two in the morning, completely drunk out of his brain. He was watching TV, and he throws the rest of the fucking bottle of beer into the fucking TV. There was steam coming out of it, and everybody was pissed off. The next day he couldn't remember any of it. He couldn't even remember that he nearly got arrested in a supermarket. He was standing there in the supermarket; the police thought he was breaking in there. They told him to stop it or drop it, and his wife was frightened to death; poor thing couldn't speak English at all. The next day he couldn't remember anything of this and I said to him, 'You had a blackout.' The minute I said that, I said, 'This is the title of the album and it's the title song.'"

"But yeah, he saw the TV, he took his beer, threw the complete beer in the TV until the fucking thing was smoking, and then he left the fucking room without saying a word. Couldn't even remember the next day, when we told him. In his opinion, he was never in that room. You see what I mean? A real blackout, so it really fit."

"We were with them that night, as I told you, and we would be together on tour," continues Rarebell, transitioning into other memories of camaraderie on the road. "Another one is Adrian from Iron Maiden, and Bruce Dickinson, who I spent many nights with in those cheap motels on the road, because I lived for six years in England, so we had lots to talk about. But never a problem. Of course, on stage, everybody tried to kill each other; everybody wanted to be the best. But in private, actually, I had a very good feeling with them. Same with AC/DC. I got on tremendously good with Angus and his brother Malcolm. In fact, in the beginning when we played England, and we played the Hammersmith Odeon, or if we played Manchester, they always came to our show, you know. We've been best friends since '79. Don't forget, we had a four-month tour with them, special guests of Ted Nugent, and in those days when Bon Scott was still alive we got on really well, because we were both party animals, and after every show we went to the clubs. We smuggled in Rick Allen, the drummer from Def Leppard because he was only 16 then. We'd say, 'Oh, he forgot his passport; come on, let him in, he's with us,' or something like this and we got him in. Rick Allen—when you speak to him to this day, ask him about what I said. Very funny."

In any event, while *Blackout* is considered a weighty, significant, authentic number (trivia note: Herman got some help tightening up the song's lyric from his girlfriend, Sonya), *No One Like You* was the album's smash single, ushering in a string of blueprinted and idiosyncratic power ballads for the band. Still, the track contains some direct, pointed, memorable power chords, as well as a gorgeous twin lead solo that cuts through to the memory circuits and once embedded, never leaves.

When asked, years after the fact, about his biggest contribution to the band, Jabs goes right back to this most famous of solos. "I think that the most important part is that when I joined, my sound like in *No One Like You*, the double harmony leads in the intro or solo, is something that I was already doing prior to joining the band. I did this in the local bands that I played in before joining the Scorpions. So I brought this into the band in addition to what they already had. I think that since I joined, the band sounds like a unit, one band. Then all of a sudden, we started becoming very successful. To this day, I use my leads to just enhance the songs, not to over-play and show off. I think that that's the most important part. The job of a lead guitarist is to keep the level of the song, not play something that doesn't belong there. I'm always trying to enhance the song with whatever I do. That why, I think style-wise, we sound much more cohesive since I joined."

"*No One Like You* is also a very interesting story because I composed the song four years before it was released," says Schenker. "I always played it to the guys and I never got the reactions until one time I played it for Matthias and he was saying, 'Hey, that's great,' and I said 'I know, but you have to convince Klaus,' who always said, 'Yes, it's good, not bad.' But he started to write lyrics and then we went into the studio and we created this arrangement. In the '70s, and then especially in the '80s, my whole day was creating. I would make breakfast and then compose and then eat lunch and go back to composing. I wrote a lot of songs that had to wait for years to really become a record song. This happened with *No One Like You*. Like I say, I wrote that years before it was recorded on Blackout. Klaus was not so sure of that song. The rest of the band said, 'Rudolf, we have to do this song.' *No One Like You* became the most played radio song in 1982."

"I got to spend the night at Alcatraz and that was really exciting," recalls Klaus, Alcatraz being the filming location of the song's production video, the band's first true MTV-era clip. "There were Japanese tourists there in the morning taking pictures of the electric chair because they thought that was where Al Capone was killed." Filming of the clip took so long that the guys had to stay overnight, freezing cold as they tried to get some sleep. The next day, on the boat back to San Francisco on the mainland, it was discovered they had forgotten Francis. Herman confirms the story, noting that, "It was cool, although *No One Like You* was really low budget. As you say, we shot it on Alcatraz, which was great and I am glad I went there. We were there overnight and we locked in our bass player. Maybe we should have never let him out. He fell asleep. With one bar you could close all of the gates in the hallway for all of the cells. Nobody knew he was sleeping in one of those cells. We found him eventually. That was a very good experience."

"That was a very unusual experience," recalled Klaus, speaking with Hank Thompson back in the fall of '83. "We wanted to do something different, and our management somehow was able to get us the use of the Alcatraz prison facility for our video. We went over to the island one evening and filmed all night. It was a most unique feeling—especially when the history of the place was told to us. We even had the electric chair brought over with us. Evidently, Alcatraz never had one, so the people who were filming our video had one made. Of course, it wasn't a working model. But it was real enough to make me feel very scared. We had to spend a long time in the prison. We had to film certain parts of the video over and over again. The funniest part was when Francis fell asleep in one of the cells and was accidentally locked in. He woke up and was screaming to be let out. Francis had been getting in the way. So we decided to let him stay in there a while and cool out. It was the first taste of prison for most of us, and we didn't like it. We all decided to try and do our best to avoid places like that in the near future—unless we were making another video."

Give Me All I Need is a similar track, almost a bookend to *No One Like You* and was also a bit of a hit in some territories. Rudolf notes that the track was written "when I came back from the vacation in the Philippines; that was one of the last songs." All told, the tune sports the rounded pop rock edges applied to most of the Love At First Sting songs, while, given its earlier vintage than that, it's in possession of at least a modicum of Euro rock gravitas.

Another late addition to the album was *Arizona*, perhaps a follow-up to *The Zoo* in that it is a picture postcard of a slice of American life. "Arizona, they somehow have this very easy way of living there," reflects Rudolf. "The song also has this kind of easiness in it. One roadie told us about this interesting experience he had, and Klaus put that into the song. There's nothing special about it. It's only because Arizona has this easy way of living and the song has the same special blend."

Of note, Herman, quite convincingly, swears that the story scratched out in *Arizona* is something that happened to him, that he was whisked away by a lady in a black limo for some backseat fun out in the desert under the stars. "Well, I wrote *Arizona* lyrics, as you know," says Rarebell. "It was a true story. It was after a show one night, and I stood there in the warm Arizona night, and one of those girls picked me up on the street and took me in the mountains and fucked my brains out and then took me back in the morning again (laughs). This is what *Arizona* is all about. It's all a true story again."

Continues Schenker, "And *Now!*, I remember when we recorded the album, and Dieter Dierks said we need one more fast song. I went in my hotel room and started working and came up with the riff, and then I went to Herman and said, 'Here, give me a great beat,' and then *Now!* was there. Klaus wrote the lyrics and everything was fine. That was the last song written for the album."

Now! is not really up to the band's magical riff-mad standard, perhaps sounding a bit forced, perhaps presaging the writer's block the band would have with respect to faster songs throughout the next three studio albums. The intelligence quotient embedded within the guitar riff is sadly reduced versus past rave-ups, especially when compared to *Virgin Killer*, *Speedy's Coming* or even this record's nimble, visceral *Dynamite*. Also, much like paired speedster on the record, *Dynamite*, the *Now!* lyric is a bit of tossed-off nonsense, both being a hot mess of sex, rocking out and partying, Klaus's and Herman's English as second language not given much of a polish if any. Asked about *Dynamite*, Herman adds, "I've always played double bass, now and even in the Scorpions, which you can hear in *Dynamite*, stuff like this, and *Coming Home*. This is all double bass stuff. Remember I had the two huge double bass drums on stage."

In terms of pure power ballads, Scorpions offered up *When The Smoke Is Going Down*, pretty much the least visited track on Blackout amongst hardcore fans or indeed radio programmers. "That is an interesting thing," explains Rudy. "I remember we were sitting there in France in a nice house, a very spiritual house. I came with the song and Herman said, 'Rudolf, it's not as strong as *Holiday*.' I said, 'okay, it's not as strong as *Holiday*, but what can I do?' (laughs). But then somehow Klaus came up with a very good idea. We always somehow include the crowd in our songs, and this one, when the concert is done, the vibe that is still in the hall has something that is very intense. So he came up with the idea and everybody liked it. Some people think we're talking about marijuana (laughs)."

Rounding out the album is a true harbinger of things to come, a faceless happy-go-rock hummer called *Can't Live Without You*, featuring a hooky unison chorus somewhat redeemed by an axe-alchemical pocket rocket of a verse. "That was a good thing," recalls Rudolf. "I was watching television, and somehow, the riff… I always have my guitar with me, and I did that lick and I thought that's very good. When you have a person like Klaus, he immediately picks up on it, and he made it as another song for our audience." Lyrically, the song was galvanizing for devotees of the band and for fans of rock in general, given that contrary to the literary logic of the band, it wasn't about being on the road and missing some bird (proceed to *No One Like You*), but about the band's relationship with their fans.

Can't Live Without You was launched as a single, backed with *Always Somewhere*. Its No.47 showing on Billboard's Hot Mainstream Rock Tracks chart signalled that the band was bubbling up from the underground, whereas its No.63 placement on the UK chart signalled nothing more than business as usual. However, *No One Like You* vaulted to No.1 on Hot Mainstream, translating to a No.65 placement on the penultimate Billboard Hot 100 chart. This one was also a No.40 charting single in Germany and a No.49 in Canada, a country that has always been on the side of the Scorpions. More impressively, the album as a whole rose to No.10 on Billboard, vaulting it to near instant gold status, marking the first award designation for the band, and then platinum status a little over a month before the next record would arrive and explode.

Back on a creative tack, Blackout offered a myriad of twists and turns not evident on the rounder, more even-keeled Animal Magnetism album. The hits were hookier, the middle more mainstream, the rock edgier and the soft stuff quieter. But a constant theme was the brightness, the slashing clarity of the guitars. It was an album full of events, sequenced well, confident, ready to take on America, the band having paid its dues, emerging as experts in the exploding field of heavy rock.

"Blackout, it's a complete album," reflects Rudolf. "With everything in it. If you see the album as a rainbow, it's a complete rainbow."

"The Scorpions' Blackout is better suited to the heavy-rock fan who likes nasty noises and isn't particularly concerned if they've been done better elsewhere," wrote Rolling Stone's J.D. Considine, reviewing the album. "Guitarist Matthias Jabs may borrow liberally from Eddie Van Halen's arsenal of guitar tricks, and singer Klaus Meine does bellow like Judas Priest's Rob Halford, but the overall effect is so audaciously over-the-top that it works anyway. Part of the credit goes to producer Dieter Dierks, who provides the band with a dense but meticulously detailed sound that keeps the music from bogging down. Mostly, though, it's just a matter of good ensemble playing fronted by a singer who knows how to wring the last ounce of impact from each song."

Added tastemaker Jon Sutherland, in the well-regarded but briefly in-print Record Review, "It's been two years since the Scorpions came over to lay Kraut Metal on willing headbangers and the matter has come to pass with Blackout. It's a bruiser that picks up two steps ahead of where Animal Magnetism left off. The Scorpions have always been better at creating melodies than their most direct competitors (i.e. Iron Maiden, Saxon, Def Leppard). The band has the ability to mesh melody and rock with the best. It's difficult to predict the success of this album and its ability to test time, but from the initial few listens, there is no doubt in my mind that this album is a killer. How this album, so much better than many already good Scorpions albums, can't end up as one of the great heavy rock albums, I don't know, because I think it is."

"Blackout is undeniably the best hard rock album I've heard in ages," pronounced Kerrang!'s Steve Gett, in an even more favourable notice. "The two-year wait since their last LP has definitely been worthwhile. Words can't really describe the power evidenced on the record— beg, steal, borrow, or better, buy a copy at all costs. You will not be disappointed. The action commences with the effervescent title track during which the Scorps race ahead at full steam. The drums are rock solid, the guitars loud 'n' proud, and the vocals are brilliant. Indeed, it's hard to believe that Klaus Meine has actually had any problems with his throat! Both Rudolph Schenker and Matthias Jabs deliver a red-hot lead break— I'm in ecstasy. An over-the-top review, I'll admit... But then again, Blackout is a totally over-the-top rock 'n roll album."

Scorpions hit the road immediately upon release of the evidently impressive album in late March, beginning with a few warm-up dates in continental Europe before executing a complete blanketing of the UK. Klaus now had on tour what he called an electronic device that could zap and dissolve any nodes that might develop in his throat. After a few more European stops, it was into North America, where into July of '82 they played mostly with Girlschool and Iron Maiden, into September and October.

As was typical of the manic times for the band, having just played

Seattle with Iron Maiden on July 16th, the band found out they had the chance to squeeze in a major gig in LA the very next night. What was supposed to be a typical outdoor concert featuring Loverboy and Foreigner was turned into the Anaheim Summer Strut, with the addition of a couple more acts. Recalls Rudolf, "We got back to the hotel at 2:30 in the morning, and had to be up at 5:30 to catch the airplane for Los Angeles. This is rock 'n' roll and I love it. It was so great out there today. The feelings were so good and strong. We are all very glad to come and play."

The band got to showcase Blackout to 75,000 people, having somehow got their gear a thousand miles down the coast overnight—and there was a show booked the next night again, halfway back up the coast in Oakland.

"My voice is holding up very well," said Klaus, interviewed by Jon Sutherland in Anaheim. "I went back to Vienna during a break in the tour and saw the doctors. They did some tests and said that I was healthier than ever before. I still do exercises and take therapy for it to be safe."

Rudolf, amusingly contrasting Scorpions with Maiden told Circus, "We have very hard songs, very slow songs and very fearful songs. In 1982, when Iron Maiden toured with us, normally the male fans would say, 'I want to go hear Iron Maiden.' Then even the girls who liked Scorpions would say, 'Iron Maiden is not my music. I don't want to go.' Now, when they come to hear Scorpions, the girls tend to like *Always Somewhere* and *Holiday*, and the guys growl, 'Oh yeah, I can't get enough!' So they're both happy. We can build up our atmosphere."

At the band's St. Louis stop on July 9th, a fan threw a glass jar with a few live scorpions in it, onto the stage. The jar shattered and the scorpions took cover under and behind the amps, giving the road crew a more stressful than usual tear-down at the end of the night.

A month later, August 11th, Rudolf got himself into a bit of typical rock 'n' roll trouble in Corpus Christi, Texas. "I still can't understand what happened. I was just sitting around, having a few drinks. Maybe I was throwing a few things around, but I wasn't hurting anybody. Then the hotel manager came up to me and said, 'You must leave.' I told him I was staying in the hotel, but he didn't seem to care. He asked me to come to his office for a minute, and the next thing I knew I was in handcuffs! When the police arrived, they were told that they better be careful because I was a very dangerous individual. They took me away to jail and I ended up spending quite a while in there before I was able to get out. It was my first time in an American jail, and it wasn't very enjoyable. They treat you like a criminal (laughs). Once our road manager came down and explained everything, they were only too happy to drop the charges and let me go. The funny thing was that as I was leaving, one of the officers who arrested me actually asked me for my autograph and some albums.

I was happy to give him the autograph, but there was no way I was about to give him any free albums after the trouble they put me through."

Early '83 was spent on writing and early recording sessions for what was to become the band's next album. More on this later, but briefly, into April of 1983, the band went to Sweden to record at Abba's Polar Studios, featuring some intriguing personnel changes, i.e. a possible dropping out of the rhythm section, namely Francis and Herman. These recordings would be scrubbed, and the band would not return to Sweden come time to resume recording.

On May 29, 1983, Scorpions played Steve Wozniak's gargantuan US Festival, on the much lauded "heavy metal day" of the four day party. Without getting ahead of the story, the milestone gig re-affirmed the band's commitment to each other, with the classic line-up back in place. On the day, they played second to the headliner, Van Halen, following Quiet Riot, Mötley Crüe, Ozzy Osbourne, Judas Priest and Triumph. The band was flown in by a helicopter, transferred to a limo... by all accounts, they were floored by the magnitude of it all.

"Without a doubt," answers the US Festival's Michael Frisch, when asked if it might be perceived that Scorpions won the day. "Everybody over the years has said that Scorpions blew Van Halen away. It was probably Scorpions' best performance. Still to this day, they said that the US Festival performance was one of their best."

Indeed the band was on fire, running all over the stage, Rudolf doing Pete Townshend windmill chords, the penultimate being a famous Scorpions dogpile to close out the night, winding up a ridiculously accelerated *Can't Get Enough* with a wall of thrashing sound.

The full set list for the stand consisted of *Blackout, Don't Make No Promises (Your Body Can't Keep), Loving You Sunday Morning, Make It Real, Lovedrive, Coast To Coast, Always Somewhere, No One Like You, Can't Live Without You, He's A Woman - She's A Man, Another Piece Of Meat, Dynamite, The Zoo* and then finally the manic *Can't Get Enough.* It was a defiantly recent and modern batch of songs, crafted perfectly for the stage, for slamming rhythm guitars in lockstep, for a studied band of strategists designed to work like a machine.

But the real significance of the US Festival was its symbolism as a coming out party for metal in America, all of these bands on a swift, determined rise, save for the headliner who had already arrived, and Triumph who would stall. To be sure, the press and attention would be on the LA metal scene, but big metal bands from all over the map would do brisk business in the ensuing six, seven years as well, with Scorpions just about to break it big with Love At First Sting.

"Pretty good performance," says Bob Crosby, also an US Festival VIP. "But they all seemed to be fine. You would think that heavy metal day would have been a little more rowdy, but the talent were probably more behaved than some of the other days (laughs). But it was so big that it was somewhat intimidating to a lot of people. Judas Priest was very confident in their role, and their playing, and where they were at. They came off mature, as much more of a mature group than Mötley Crüe, who were more like the little guys just getting there. You know, jumping around. I have to say, being a bit of an older guy, it was a new sound of music that was coming on strong—I really wasn't doing heavy metal shows. But you just couldn't deny it. It was really coming on so strong, that you couldn't ignore it. So yeah, in that sense it was probably the biggest platform of popular support, of at least anything I ever knew of at the time. US Festival stood out over several decades. Not only was it mass people, but it was sophisticated production, state-of-the-art at the time."

There were definite sentiments being voiced from the stage that indicated an awareness that metal was on the rise. "There were," says Bob. "Every one of them felt that their time has come. That it was not a new rekindled sound or style of music, that it had come, that it had reached its acceptance, that it was now relevant. You could say that about country and classic rock, and now you could say it about heavy metal. It was its own genre, whereas leading up to that, you had punk and all these different versions of it that were short-lived, or weren't really piqued to where you would classify them with country and classic rock. But heavy metal seemed to do that."

"There were so many people there," recalls Judas Priest's Rob Halford. "There were like 350,000 people there. Wasn't that the biggest crowd ever? For that day? It was a three-day event. One was new wave, one was country, and one was metal, and metal walked in and just exploded. I think it was a unifying moment in America for a lot of people. It was almost like our Woodstock. That US Festival was our Woodstock in terms of that metal day. There was us, Van Halen, Scorpions, Triumph, Quiet Riot—how great was that? It was an absolutely sensational day out. Just everything was in the right place at the right time. It was a tremendous line-up, the bill with all those acts being together. Such a diversity as well, when you think about it. What a great mix. Yet the overall push of that whole experience was definitely geared towards a metal moment."

"Now, more than ever," continues the Metal God, "it is becoming our Woodstock because it's 20-something years and they've recently put out a DVD to celebrate it. I thought they lost that footage. The people that produced it sent us three songs just to get the band's approval, and it was like a time machine. An absolute time machine. I remember it vividly because we flew in by helicopter, and the first thing we saw was 250,000 vehicles parked. We went into that amphitheatre with all those people. My God, it was unbelievable. But it could have happened anywhere. As it was, it was on the west coast, California. Looking at the way America works and the influence of the east coast and the west coast, just like the Haight-Ashbury did its thing in the '60s, I'm sure the US Festival... because people still talk about it. Go anywhere across America to a generation, and they'll go, yeah, I was either there or I remember that. There's some kind of timeline that connects that together. It was absolutely remarkable. It was one of the biggest shows ever. You've got Mötley Crüe with their glam look, you've got Priest with their metal look, you've got David and Van Halen with their look. It was a real smorgasbord, visually. You think back in time how everybody was looking with their appearance. It was like a larger-than-life microcosm of the metal scene on one stage."

Love At First Sting

"There was a baby boom in France"

Survey the years, and it becomes obviously exhausting and exhaustingly obvious that the Scorpions' rise to fame and fortune was gradual and long in coming. From the band's birthing in '65 to a first record seven years later, through another four or five records still in the wilderness, we are now at 13 years rocking with the rapt attention of merely a small fanbase—but with much goodly music to the goodly band's brand. Then Lovedrive makes some waves and Animal Magnetism makes a few more. A crack American management team leads to a triumphant US tour and then... the lost year, 1981 and the crack in Klaus's voice. In 1982 Blackout arrives and then so does the band, as seasoned pros on the worldwide rock scene, and for those in the know, wise veterans who deserve the same respect as Priest, breaking at the same time, and more experienced than Maiden, also breaking at the same time.

Then Love At First Sting is upon us, its first single *Rock You Like A Hurricane* arriving as a single in advance of the album's March 27th, 1984 launching, sending expectations sky-high, given its exotic, half-sour melody, its sense of drama, its production heft. "To be in a cage with all those girls around us in *Rock You Like A Hurricane* was very cool," says Klaus, who recalls the shooting of the video for the track as his favourite filming experience, with Matthias adding, "*Rock You Like A Hurricane* was also interesting as we had real black panthers and real leopards." Indeed the clip (creatively pretty dull, actually, despite the live props) was in heavy rotation on MTV, helping vault the album toward platinum status but quick.

Unfortunately the rest of the album wouldn't, in total, live up to the billing, weighing in lighter and simpler than its predecessor Blackout, but nonetheless widening further the band's base, to the point of quickly going gold and then platinum and then double platinum by the end of 1984, eventually cresting at triple platinum with a designation at that hallowed ground up into 1995.

Try as they might, Scorpions couldn't entirely escape controversy with their record wrappers. One would think the black and white photo, of a man and woman in embrace, a bit of breast exposed, the man, intriguingly giving her a tattoo... shouldn't be a problem. However Walmart voiced an objection and so an alternative cover was whipped up, featuring the band shot from the inner sleeve, frankly one of the best photos of the band ever taken, all leather pants and determination with a palpable trace of rock 'n' roll malnutrition.

"Helmut Newton is a German who lived in Berlin and later moved on to Monte Carlo," notes Herman, on the photographer who arranged the sleeve shot. "It was Rudolf's idea to use Newton. He said, 'We need to use him to make an outstanding cover.' The cover made a lot of noise. We reached a lot of different people that we had not reached before. We got spots in Time magazine and other huge magazines because all the intellectuals accepted Newton. They have a clique between themselves because Helmut was hip. Since he did that with the Scorpions then we too became hip."

Love At First Sting opened on an acceptable but not overwhelmingly impressive note with one of the band's simple power chord rockers called *Bad Boys Running Wild*, that title alone being enough to rankle and wrinkle the nose of those fans steeped in the Uli era.

"I was more like the rocker in the band," says Herman, writer of the song's lyric. "On the road, having fun, sex, drugs and rock 'n' roll, and always writing to the hard aspects of the songs, the rock stuff like *Bad Boys Running Wild, Hurricane, Blackout, Dynamite, Make It Real*, you know the songs. And then Klaus was the one who wrote more on the romantic side. He wrote songs like *Still Loving You, Wind Of Change*. For most of the ballads, the lyrics were done by him, because he could associate more with this kind of feeling and I could associate more with the feeling on the road. I was always the one being out on the road every night being the party animal."

Bad Boys Running Wild definitely comes from that side of the band, indeed, fitting in with the whole idea of party rock taking the music industry by storm, much of it being generated by LA bands, but Herman doing his part to keep up the German side. His gamesmanship continues for *Rock You Like A Hurricane*, which very well might be the band's biggest song ever. At least in America—you'd have to give the title from a global perspective to *Wind Of Change*, still years away at this point.

Notes Rudolf, on *Hurricane*, "I remember composing the song and coming to the rehearsal room and I played the song and we played around with it. The melody was there, everything was there, and Klaus came up and said, 'Rock you like a hurricane' and I said immediately, 'Yes, oh great, that's a great line.' People said, 'No, hurricane isn't strong enough; it has to be even faster!' And we said, 'No, no, it's the perfect situation. I'll tell you one thing, the music and even "Rock you like a hurricane" goes together. You can't do it better.' You could easily throw it out because you don't think it fits together. Some people have different minds about the hurricane. Some people think it must be faster, some people think it has to be more crazy. But I think the lyrics, especially the little bit of, what do you call, double meaning lyrics, give the whole thing a kind of sexual hurricane."

"Those lyrics were very easy to write," says Herman. "I woke up early in the morning after fucking and doing cocaine all night and I opened up the curtains. 'It's early morning, the sun comes out. Last night was shaking and pretty loud. My cat is purring and she scratches my skin...' She had scratched my back during our lovemaking. I just sat down and wrote it right then and there. It was five in the morning and the girl was still in bed as I was sitting there writing it. The next day I said to Rudolf, 'I have some great lyrics for that riff you have.' That song is still one of the most played songs in the entire world."

"This album was the best balance we ever had between the rock songs and the ballads," continues Schenker. "To be the perfect thing was *Rock You Like A Hurricane* on the rock side and *Still Loving You* on the slow side. But I think Love At First Sting would have sounded much better if we didn't go right to digital. Because we were one of the first bands to use digital. We made a mistake by going digital to digital to digital. Sometimes the guitar sound is very thin. We didn't use the compression of the tape. Somehow we didn't get a really big guitar sound. We had to record on digital, but it wasn't the best because it was one of the first machines, a 3M or something. and we had to go to analogue to get the compression and then back to digital. I'm not very happy with it."

"Our management in particular told us that we were going to have to write more radio-friendly, because we want airplay and we want solo tours," concedes Herman, who does admit that the album is a little on the commercial side. "So think about something commercial. But we didn't think about the commercial aspect when we wrote *Rock You Like A Hurricane*. This was a song that was heard by the record company and they said to us, 'Ah, that's a great song.' We thought they were going more in the direction of *Bad Boys Running Wild*. That's why we put it song one on the album. But whatever, that was the one that made it big. We wanted to go more commercial for American radio, because we were listening to Foreigner and all the bands who were out there at the time on the radio. So we thought, okay, we have to make the songs in this direction, that we will get play. But we thought the other commercial songs maybe would have hit much faster, on the American radio, so we were pleasantly surprised when one of our favourite rockers, *Rock You Like A Hurricane*, actually made it. I'm very proud of *Rock You Like A Hurricane*. I wrote all the words there, and that makes me happy. The other thing, *Bad Boys Running Wild...* each of those two songs basically, I'm very proud of. At the time, don't forget, there was a hell of a lot of touring going on with the band. The whole time, you can actually say we were touring."

Another one of these commercial songs Herman is referring to comes next. *I'm Leaving You* begins riffy and even Germanic enough, but then that all falls away for gentle strumming and proto-hair metal vocal melodies come verse time. All of a sudden—and I remember this distinctly from the time, at university in Victoria, BC—a spreading and surly dissatisfaction was at hand within the ranks of loyal, long-time Scorpions fans.

"Blackout and Love At First Sting are very successful albums from the early '80s," explains Matthias, attempting to articulate the shift in the Scorpions sound. "I think that's when we finalised the Scorpions' signature sound, and we became famous due to that music and that sound. So I think it took some time. It had to do, also, with our visits to the US, the first couple tours. I think they were very strong influences. We learned a lot from supporting other bands like AC/DC, Ted Nugent at the time, and we were touring with other bands like Sammy Hagar, Pat Travers and we just learned a lot. You know, songs from Animal Magnetism, like *The Zoo*—42nd Street, New York; I mean here's this young German band coming for the first time to America being impressed by all the skyscrapers in New York City, Manhattan, and that's when you start writing songs about this. It went into the music and that made us sound more international than other German bands."

"Of course, we were the first," continues Jabs. "So we were the ones that were able to open doors for others. But Scorpions are more diversified, if that's the correct word, than just heavy metal. We are beyond heavy metal. We have other qualities too. Like the power ballad, very melodic songs. Some of these other bands concentrated more on the hard and heavy side while we have more variety, and that helped also to open doors for us in other countries in other parts of the world. Like in Asia, the Japanese love their hard and fast music, at least in the '70s, '80s, '90s. But in other parts, the Golden Triangle—Singapore, Thailand, Malaysia— where we play everywhere, they are very much into the ballads. So because we have this variety, we were growing faster and bigger than a heavy metal band, which is, to a certain extent, limited to their sound and therefore the audiences also. You only talk to a certain type of audience, while we had a radio hit here and there. But it's also reaching out for the mainstream audience, too."

"As you said," reiterates Rudolf, "we opened a door for other German bands to open the door to find the trick how to open it. Scorpions, when we started to play in Europe in the early '70s, we really were a gang. Bang

bang, rocker with a gang. And we really were a gang because we're coming from Germany. When we're out of Germany, we were foreigners. As a band, we were always driving in one car. Five guys in one car, 700 or 900 kilometers, and we were talking and making plans and stuff. Being a gang and finding our way to really find the keyhole where we go into the world and play our music. I think that was the way we opened the door. Other people following us, they never thought we already were thinking and trying to make a planned vision to get out of there."

"So young bands, they came in and said, 'Oh, we made it now in America.' Accept is in a German magazine. Wolf Hoffman, he said, 'Oh, no problem, we made it in America, we are big; we are becoming bigger than the Scorpions.' They never know when you make it in America that you really have to follow up with some really strong things. Like him with one record, saying, 'Okay, now everything is set up.' That's different with Scorpions. When we came with Lovedrive into the Top 50 in the United States, we said now we want to do it better. With Animal Magnetism we were a little bit better. But with Blackout we gave a whole kick because we said we really want to make an amazing album. Then Love At First Sting, we wanted to always get better and better. But the young German bands, they always said when they had a chance to play in America, then they're already big and that's the misunderstanding."

Something that didn't really snowball until years later was any level of controversy over who was playing bass and drums on the Love At First Sting album. "I was good friends with the Scorpions, all of them, but Rudolf Schenker in particular," says Bobby Rondinelli, New Yorker, and drummer for Rainbow at the time, who was told about the idea of playing with the band on the phone by Rudolf in the morning, and then informed that a flight had been booked for him that afternoon. "I'm still very friendly with them. I spoke to them when I was in Germany, on The Lizards' tour. I was inviting them to the show, but he was in the States at the time. But I'm good friends with Rudolf."

"Yeah, that's me on there," continues Bobby. The whole album? "Yeah." Who is the bass player on the album? "Jimmy Bain. We were there the whole time, doing the whole record. Jimmy was over there for a couple weeks before I was, and they called me in and I was there for two weeks. We had a good time. Jimmy's a great guy; I loved Jimmy to death."

It seems that Jimmy's main memory from his brief time with the Scorpions was getting to hear one of his Dio songs finished!

"*Stand Up And Shout*, I had written that song, the music for it anyway; I had written it about a year or two before I got into the Dio band. So I recorded with the band, the backing track, and we went and did all the other backing tracks. Ronnie had some vocals done, but he didn't have anything for *Stand Up And Shout*. He had done everything but *Stand Up*

And Shout. He hadn't recorded them yet, but he had written them. I went off to do the Scorpions, Love At First Sting, in Europe. So I went off to Germany, then to Sweden. Then about a month and half later, when I was over there, thinking how I was going to wind this up and about coming back, I got tapes sent over from Ronnie, with the vocal on it. Which was just totally mind-blowing, to have a song that opens your first album with the band that was just so powerful like that. I couldn't wait to get down to rehearsals and play it to Rudolf and the guys, 'Hey, check this out!' So that was funny. I've got another one. The Scorpions, every day we'd go to the studio in Stockholm, they would play the rough mixes of Holy Diver before they started recording. We'd have to listen to it from end to end, which was really, really cool, that they would get a lot of inspiration from that. They were really into the album."

But a correction to the tale comes first from Francis. "The first attempt to record the album Love At First Sting was made by Dieter Dierks with 'hired guns' to play bass and drums in a recording studio in Sweden. I thought he did that because I had renegotiated the contract between Scorpions and Dierks, giving more rights to the band. But those Swedish recordings got erased. We came together again and the album was recorded in Dierks Studio. It turned out to become one of the best selling albums of the Scorpions."

Why Sweden? Klaus at the time, said, "We had looked everywhere for a studio that would give us all the latest recording features. We wanted a state-of-the-art facility. We had grown a bit tired of using the studios in Germany and France and a friend told us about this incredible place called Polar Studios, which Abba had built a few years back. We check the place out and instantly fell in love with it! It had everything we had ever dreamed of. We really tested our talents this time, and we knew we had to have a studio that would give us a free reign with our musical ideas. It's still very much a traditional Scorpions hard rock album, but we brought some new elements into our sound. Things were worked out in more detail while recording this record. There wasn't the 'let's go in and jam' attitude."

"Everybody thinks it was Jimmy Bain playing the bass guitar and Rondinelli playing the drums," clarifies Herman. "What actually happened in those days was that nobody was happy with Francis' bass playing. So we said, okay, we'll try out another bass player. So I phoned Jimmy Bain who I knew from England, and I said, 'Jimmy, would you like to come to Hannover? We're rehearsing, and you'll play the bass on the next Scorpions album.' Jimmy said, 'Great, I'll do that.' So what happened, in the production, when we were in Sweden, basically I left for a two-week holiday, and behind my back they phoned up Rondinelli who came in to the studio to play on a few songs, which, thank God, it never worked out and it never made it on the album. I found out about it many years after, that they did this, and I wasn't very happy with it, because it's kind of a mistrust or betrayal, or however you want to look at it. But the bass, same thing, Jimmy's bass was excellent, but it was not the Scorpions chemistry anymore. Which was typical of the playing with Francis. So at the end, every track is Francis playing on the album and every track is me playing the drums."

That two-week holiday Herman alludes to... at the time, the story had oscillated between Herman being "very sick" while recording the album and not up to the task physically, along with rumours that he was quitting the band. But absolutely, if the official credits of the album can be believed, nothing from the April '83 sessions in Sweden was used. Polar Studios is not mentioned, instead, the official credit going to Dierks Studios and "32-track digital recording & mastering," which supports Rudolf's contention of, essentially, too much digital.

"In '84, I had a big alcoholic problem," says Herman, coming clean in the telling of the story on a different occasion. "So I went in a clinic in Stockholm, and they flew in Bobby Rondinelli, who played on the complete Love At First Sting album, and then we took the album to Cologne, and it didn't sound like Scorpions anymore. It was very busy; it didn't groove anymore. It wasn't played to the point. In other words, it didn't fit. So then they had to wait for me another two months, erased everything again in Cologne, and I played all the drums again there."

Indeed, there's an early version of *Bad Boys Running Wild*, provisionally titled *Heartbreaker* or *Heartbreaking Awards*—same music, completely different lyrics—that demonstrates what Herman is talking about, namely a drum part from Bobby that doesn't quite flow with the arena rock vibe Herman brings to the table. Rondinelli's *Coming Home*, same thing, although to be fair, he would have smoothed it out for a true LP version and then again, what's wrong with showing a few chops? Actually, the cool thing about the *Coming Home* demo is the additional chord changes. The track would have been worse for it, less metal, more pedestrian, but there's a soul to the rehearsal version that is nice. *Leaving You, Big City Nights, Still Loving You*... these are played a little more straight but no question, the main difference from the final versions is the performance at the percussion end.   "Love At First Sting, we had other things that were keeping us busy," says Rudolf, remembering the musical chairs, comparing it to the Klaus issue that had slowed the band's progress on Blackout. "This situation was where we went to Stockholm to record the album, and then Herman found out that he had a problem with health and stuff like this and he had to go to the clinic. In this case we were working at this time with Rondinelli. We had some very hard times to keep up the high level of what we were looking for. It was not easy; we had a very hard time to really get this thing done. Then we went to the US Festival, which we played, and Herman was ready, the whole band, but we also had problems with Francis, who wasn't coming up with the right bass and stuff like this. But, when we played the US Festival, the tour we did, somehow everybody gets so motivated that we recorded in Cologne the whole album again, and this time it took us three months and the album was done. I remember we mixed the last song. We ended up the album around the 14th January '84, and we mixed the last song around 8 o'clock in the morning, and our plane was leaving at 9:40 to Birmingham, where our Love At First Sting world tour was starting. I mean, it was very hard work and it took the same time as Blackout, but in a different way."

"Jimmy Bain was involved too," confirms Rudolf. Of note, we probably wouldn't have caught wind of all this at all if the band hadn't made the mistake of inviting the UK music press up to the Swedish sessions. "Both of them, because of the situation where we loved the band very much, both guys, they were ready to do everything to make the album good. We could hear that everybody was working very, very hard but in the end, we got the result we were looking for and we didn't need anybody else. But sometimes you have to go with the hard way to get the people... you know how some people work. Some people think that there's an easy way to get something very special out of you, and you have to convince them in a hard way. Really, our hearts were bleeding by getting other people into the game, but in the end, it worked out. The other guys, they really were working hard, and it was either living or dying, and they made the decision for living."

Receiving the US Festival offer, while the band was holed up in Sweden trying to make Love At First Sting, also played a role in getting Herman back to the fold. "Herman was in horrible shape," says Meine. "I don't know if it was too many drugs or too much fucking, but he just had a total breakdown while we were in the studio in Stockholm. He couldn't function at all. It was a very bad situation for Herman, and for the band as well. That's when we called Bobby. Bobby has been a good friend of ours for a long time. At that moment, we didn't know how quickly Herman would improve, so we didn't know if Bobby was joining permanently or temporarily. Luckily we received the offer from the US Festival soon after Herman had his breakdown. So we took some time off and agreed that we'd all meet in California and see how everything was going. By the time of the festival, Herman's health was very good. It was obvious that he had straightened himself out and was ready to resume his duties with the band. Bobby Rondinelli did a great job for us, and he proved to be a real friend, but Herman is the drummer for the Scorpions and Bobby understands that."

Back to the record that would smash open doors for Scorpions, next we get *Coming Home*, which opens like a dreary ballad but then cuts into rocking quickly. Still, despite the fact that, really, commerciality seems to not be the major concern with this one, the riff is quite simple, and the verse even simpler.

"We love what we're doing too much to even consider giving it up," said Klaus back in '84. "That's what the song *Coming Home* on the new album is all about. Most people would assume it's about returning home after being on the road for six or seven months. Actually, it's just the opposite. The song's about coming home to the road where we truly feel we belong. When we go on tour we all get in a frame of mind where everything revolves around the shows. The travel, the hotels, the hours of waiting are all rewarded by the two hours we get to share with the fans every night."

Adds Rudolf, "*Coming Home* actually is the story about the time when we had success worldwide with Lovedrive, and we went on a worldwide tour including Japan and Asia. Especially, the first time we played in America, we felt so happy. Our dream came true. We played in Canada. Our dream came true that we could play there, because this market, especially America and Canada, was our dream to go. For us those places were pure rock 'n' roll. In '82, our first headline tour we did in America, we started with Rainbow as a special guest. And with Rainbow, we played through the Canadian markets. I remember very much that after two or three gigs we did in Québec, in Montreal, Ritchie Blackmore said, 'Hey guys, I wanted you to headline because it's your crowd.' We said, 'No, we don't do that; you guys are the headliner—we keep it this way.' We had great success, and then we did the headline tour; we were headlining. Iron Maiden first for special guests, then Girlschool. Then we came to the US Festival and this was the idea, *Coming Home*. The stage became our home. It was actually a story about being back on stage: here we are, coming home. I think that was actually the story behind it. We really enjoy playing from one arena to the next one. The crowd is a very important part of the whole thing."

Then, inexplicably, there's another fast one, *The Same Thrill*, with very much the same structure, a sort of two-note riff of briskness but boredom, which falls away come verse time. However, given their heaviness, and the sterling sound of the record, and the performances, both tracks are of headbanging use, packed with guitars, Klaus singing fine. "I remember we started recording this in Stockholm," says Rudolf, "and we tried to have a song that had the same energy as *Now!*, which was on Blackout. We tried to create the same vibe and that was the situation, actually. I can't remember the lyrics, but we were trying to get a song down that really had a great attitude and was very powerful, very rock 'n' roll, vocals and guitars."

Big City Nights is very much of a pair with *Bad Boys Running Wild*, both hummable hard rockers, both similarly sized hits, both of a second tier behind *Rock You Like A Hurricane* and *Still Loving You*. It is interesting that Klaus wrote the lyrics to this Herman-like song, and in fact all of the lyrics past the first two tracks on the album.

"I think it happened because we started touring America," considers Klaus, on the band writing these simpler, more direct, arguably more pedestrian songs. "When we came over to America the first time, in '79, we started as an opening act, special guests, and then with Blackout, headliner, touring the states, months and months and months every other year. So many songs, from *The Zoo* to *Rock You Like A Hurricane* were inspired by seeing America through the windows of a tour bus. To live this crazy rock 'n' roll dream, every big arena, rock stage, every night, five nights a week... so I think by Love At First Sting, it's interesting, every time we went back to Germany to Dieter Dierks' small studio in Cologne, in Germany, for us, we toured all over the world, especially America, it gave us the inspiration to write all of the songs that became big rock anthems. We became, in a way, well, an American band. If we would've moved to America in the mid-'80s, I don't know if it would've been a good idea. But we had our whole business, manager, record company, everything was focused between New York City and LA. The whole band, people working around us and stuff, the videos we were doing, everything was based in the United States."

"The video for *Rock You Like A Hurricane* was a great deal of fun," recalls Klaus. "We used David Mallet to direct it, and he's a big fan of our music, so he came up with a storyline that fit in very well with the song. We had nearly $100,000 to spend and we used over 250 female extras while filming. All those girls were just camera-crazy, and watching them scratch and claw outside the cage we used in the video was incredibly funny. We had to do a number of takes before we could stop laughing at what was going on."

Says Rudolf, concerning *Big City Nights*, "The inspiration came... I remember we played in '82 in Tokyo, and we came back from a party that finished around four or five o'clock in the morning, in our hotel, and I remember before I went into bed, I was closing the curtain and I saw this amazing sunrise. It was in Tokyo and we had a special kind of hotel, a really high floor of a big hotel, which, there are not so many of them in Tokyo. I could see Tokyo and I could see the sun coming up, a red fiery sky, and I called Klaus immediately and said, 'Klaus, you have to see this skyline!' He went somehow and had the idea about the lyrics. As well, *Big City Nights* was inspired by touring. It was a very important point for us, especially in the early years, when we did big rock tours around the world, that we were so much into playing live. But that is where the most inspiration came to us from."

"We wanted to be radio-friendly," admits Francis, on the simplicity of songs like *Big City Nights*. "Because we knew that we could conquer, quote unquote, America, the United States, only with radio. We did that great on the Love At First Sting album, because we had radio hits on that. So whether or not we did things right, with the next album, you try. You know, you have a great album, and then you're back to the studio and start from scratch again. You have songs, and then you record them and try to make them sound good. What direction do you want to go? Do you want to go more melodic? Do you want to go more bluesy? It's decisions you make, and then sometimes the people, the fans say, oh, no, it's too poppy. But while you're in the process, you're so close to the picture that sometimes you don't know. Is it good, is it not good? You just try. But of course, the radio helps. It helps everybody—everybody! I mean, if radio would play, nowadays, more rock, you know, rock would be larger. But times are changing."

Next up were two of a pair, *As Soon As The Good Times Roll* and *Crossfire* adding hue and dimension to the album, the band using all of their guitar faculties but neither in a rote heavy metal context nor in a radio-friendly hard rock context. Both use atmospherics, both hold back, both belie a sense of maturity and creative bravery, the former framed around a reggae beat, the latter, a military march, appropriately ironic for Klaus's anti-war sentiments. It is right here, the middle of side two, where an uncompromising metalhead could conceivably locate and ascribe respect for the album, despite its lack of metal.

Noted Klaus on *Crossfire*, speaking with Malcolm Dome, "It's a comment on the escalation of nuclear weapons. People have this idea that we only write lyrics about sex 'n' drugs 'n' rock 'n' roll. Certainly, the bulk of our material leans in that direction, but we do have other interests. *Crossfire* is a plea for peace. That's especially relevant for me, because Germany is caught somewhat between the superpowers. We are in the crossfire. Strangely enough, *China White* has a similar thing, but because of its title, everyone assumed it was a drug song. Consequently, it got ignored."

More contentious would be album closer *Still Loving You*, as fully rote a power ballad as one could draw up, and a massive smash hit for the band, much to the chagrin of the traditional Scorpions fan.

"That was the same situation as *No One Like You*," says Rudolf, of the massive hit's penning. "It was composed seven years before it came out and I always tried to get the guys into it. I never forced the band to play one of my songs, but I noticed that when the time is right, then the song will appear. I never pushed and said that we had to do a song because I believed it would be very good. I had to wait. In 1983, I remember the day, we were in the personal studio, and I again started to play the song, because I was believing so much in it. Sometimes people don't hear the special thing about it at any specific time, so I started playing it and Matthias started locking in and put his guitar in it, and Klaus always liked the song too. But as a band we couldn't play it and then we found the right link in it and the whole thing became very strong. I remember Klaus told me the story about how he put his lyrics together. Because you know how special the song is. He went out once in the winter time and there was snow, and he was walking in the park and there was a snowstorm, and he was walking into it, and he came up with it in his mind without writing the lyrics on the paper. He put the lyrics together, went home and wrote it down."

"This song was unbelievably big in France," continues Rudolf. "We sold 1.8 million singles with just that song. Hey, and I'll tell you one thing, this is a good story. I remember we did four or five years ago a TV show in France; that was the best live show in Europe. The concept was that they always had two or three different bands. There was always a spot where the DJ or the guy who was running the show did an interview part, and he was sitting there, Klaus and me and the guy, and he told us, 'You know, you guys, that in 1985 there was a baby boom in France.' We said, 'What, a baby boom in France?' He said, 'You know why?' and we said no. He said, 'Because of *Still Loving You*.' Everybody made love to this song (laughs). The interesting thing is, two years later, we met this guy and this woman and they came up to us and said they were big fans and they said, 'We named our daughter Sly' and we said, 'Sly, why?' 'Because of *Still Loving You*, SLY.'"

"They did well in France," confirms David Krebs. "First of all, *Still Loving You* was a No.1 hit everywhere but here. That was a major song for them. So yeah, Scorpions were big there. Scorpions at one time were the biggest band in Russia. They still may be the biggest band in Russia."

"He was married, disciplined on the road, and he wanted to save his voice," laughs Herman, on why the band could always count on Klaus to write serious, romantic songs like *Still Loving You*. "No drinking or smoking or taking any drugs, because the next night, he thought about his fans, and I have high respect for this. He just retired and saved his voice for the next gig."

"Well, you know, it's like the combination of the two," figures Klaus, "Herman and myself, that brought out such great songs like *Blackout* and *Rock You Like A Hurricane*. When I came up with a powerful hook line like *Rock You Like A Hurricane*, Herman was the guy who would come up with those dirty, nitty-gritty kind of lyrics. 'The bitch is hungry,' and all that. So it's a combination of the two of us, which was perfect. It was just brilliant."

Doing press at the time of release and somewhat playing up what people expected of him, Klaus said, "One of my favourite cuts is *Rock You Like A Hurricane*, which is the story of going out on the road and looking for a little love—especially at first sting! It tells of what life on tour is like for us. It's strange waking up in some strange city with a new 'cat' lying next to you every day. But it's something that we've gotten used to."

Now that we've retired the album's track list, again, no Matthias Jabs in the writing credits. Comments Herman, "I think, you know, Rudolf is, and always will be, the Scorpions songwriter. He is the backbone of the band. He composes all those great typical Scorpions riffs, whereas Matthias is more the fast lead guitar, and Rudolf is more the foundation, rhythmical player. I was more the heart and soul in the whole thing, you know? So basically this is how I see the characters in the band."

"I would say that I am, more than 90%, the lead guitar player, the guy that comes up with the riffs and the melodies," reflects Matthias. "Rudolf, he's a great songwriter, first of all, and you know, today you don't have that anymore (laughs). But he calls himself more like the rhythm guitar player, the one that plays the odd, tiny little melody or solo in a ballad here and there. But together, we work great as a team. So he plays all the basic stuff and I do most of the overdubs for example, all the solos anyway. When it comes to twin leads, I do it all myself. In a few songs, we try to do it with two guitar players, but then again the harmoniser is more precise, if you know what I mean."

Once the band hits the stage, this is the era of songs that Matthias prefers, even after 30 years of bringing it to the masses. "Oh yeah, I definitely like to play *No One Like You* for example and *Rock You Like A Hurricane*. I also like some of the ballads. *Still Loving You* is nice for example. But I prefer maybe the up-tempo songs, so I would say *No One Like You* is my favourite. From Animal Magnetism, *The Zoo*. We're still playing that today and that's one of my favourites. *Blackout*—I have many favourites—*No One Like You, Dynamite* and *When The Smoke Is Going Down*, a nice little ballad. Love At First Sting is, I think, overall, my favourite album. It has all the songs. With every album, we put in everything we have at that particular time and we have nothing to regret. It's something to be proud of."

Specifically on the tour tip, however, the Love At First Sting campaign got off to a shaky start—especially in the UK.

In conversation with Kerrang!'s Malcolm Dome, Klaus groused, "We had a number of difficulties organizing the tour. Firstly, work on the album took so long that we only had time for a couple of days' rehearsal before the first date at the Birmingham Odeon. Therefore, we couldn't work out any movements, having barely had time to rehearse the songs.

So all we were able to do was go onstage and let the strength of the material speak for itself. On top of that, our new stage that was still being built in America, and it wasn't ready for the beginning of the tour. Then, when it finally did arrive, we were so unhappy with it (Malcolm: the design was based on the giant scorpion and the whole thing is said to have cost some £20,000 pounds) that it had to be scrapped. Light & Sound Design in England, then put together a new concept, which wasn't ready until Hammersmith Odeon."

"So just to cap everything, we had to play our London gigs in an unfamiliar setting, not having found time to work out how best to use it! The whole tour was terrible. We weren't at all happy with what was going on and never really generated enough enthusiasm for our performances. With hindsight, maybe we'd have been better off cancelling our British gigs. Such an option was open to us, but we rejected it in order not to disappoint the fans. I'm not sure if that was a wise decision. On top of all this, our album came out late, and consequently didn't do as well as we hoped in the UK. Almost everywhere else, however, it's proved to be our best seller yet. Mind you, I have often wondered why our record sales in your country remain so low (Malcolm: around 30,000). Our tours always sell out, so are EMI doing their job properly? It must be significant that in parts of the world like Mexico, where the Scorpions don't appear live, we can shift 100,000 copies of an LP. Something must be wrong in Britain!"

"I don't think there's much difference there," says Herman, not sympathising with my assertion and disappointment that Love At First Sting is a Scorpions dumbed-down from the band that regally riffed its way through Blackout. "I think both albums had great rock songs. It was a continuous story, actually. Coming back off the road after the Animal Magnetism tour, we were full of crazy rock 'n' roll times in America, and we were licking blood, so to speak, and Blackout is just a continuation. Maybe a little bit better album, a bit more sophisticated, better songs, whatever, but as you know, it became platinum immediately. And the same with Love At First Sting. This was the real Scorpions. Those albums are the real Scorpions: Lovedrive, Animal Magnetism, Blackout, Love At First Sting. You know, that for me is the real Scorpions era and the real Scorpions albums."

"You know, we argued all the time, particularly about music," continues Herman about the band's method for coming up with the batch at hand. "Everybody has his own ideas about music, but in the end it was very good, because if there was really a song on the album that nobody liked, and only one guy liked it, you could be sure that the other four talked so long on this one guy, that he forgot the song in the end (laughs). 'Take this awful fucking shitty song off the album!' I think the disadvantage is, if you look at Scorpions now, there are only three original members there. That means only three people have a say. The other two, the new drummer and the new bass player, have nothing to say. So for example, if there is a song that is not so great, and one guy thinks it is great, then he has only the other two against him. He only has to make one friend, and the song is on the album (laughs)."

"Love At First Sting was a change in our recording situation, because this is our first album that we recorded completely digital," figures Rudolf, summing up the record that would become the band's career high point. "We recorded it digital and we did the mastering digitally. The whole thing was completely digital. Which was a mistake, somehow, I think, because these days you always go from digital then to mastering analogue to get the tape compression. We didn't do that. That's the reason the guitars are little bit thinner on that album. The guitars on Blackout are much more powerful. So this was a mistake, but many people didn't hear it as a mistake. But I think the compositions on Love At First Sting are excellent, especially songs like *Hurricane* and *Still Loving You*, no question about this. We had two very, very strong songs. On the ballad side, there's *Still Loving You*, which was a mega mega hit in France. So amazing. And *Rock You Like A Hurricane* was on the rock side, and in America, a Top 20 hit, went around the world, and still I think is the biggest rock hit we ever had. Of course we had songs like *Big City Nights* and *Bad Boys Running Wild*... it was really the right time, and I think this album sold in America over four million and worldwide also very much. Somehow we came back from the big festival, the US Festival, with this big feeling. We went into the studio again and were playing like crazy to make an album full of emotions and attitude. I think even when we recorded everything in digital, we're not so happy about the sound, but the emotion and the spirit came across and made this album very successful."

"But it's their best-selling album," defends Krebs, when confronted with the opinion that the band had eased back on the rock pedal making Love At First Sting. "It didn't go as far as Def Leppard in terms of lightening. There's a line where... who knows where it really is until you go over it? (laughs). And where the audience wakes up and says, 'You went too far.'"

World Wide Live

"We went on stage knowing we would win"

The time definitely seemed right 'n' ripe for another Scorpions live album, and it was the massive victory lap of the Love At First Sting tour that would provide the material. Beginning in Birmingham, January 23rd, 1984, Scorpions would promote the album through England and then mainland Europe until February 29th, Irish meat-and-potatoes rockers Mama's Boys as support. The last date of this leg, in the band's Paris stronghold, would represent the earliest material on the upcoming record, to be called World Wide Live, issued June 20th, 1985.

March 17th, the band begun a massive North American swing, with Jon Butcher Axis supporting—Meine remarked at the time how much Butcher reminded him of Uli—through April 22nd and Bon Jovi taking over up until July 18th. A cluster of California dates at the end of April would cough up the lion's share of the material for the record.

May '84 found the band in Chicago, set to play what is now called Allstate Arena—for three nights runnin'. "You know, it's funny because this really is the city where everything started for Scorpions in America," said Klaus, doing press in the Windy City, incidentally a stronghold for UFO as well. "When our debut Lonesome Crow album came out in Germany way back in 1971, it was picked up over here by a small Chicago-based label called Billingsgate. That led to a kind of underground cult following for the band. Then when we came here in 1979, on our first visit to the states, we played at the Chicago Fest, which was like a huge city party on Lake Michigan. There were loads of different bands and we performed on a platform stretching out on the water. There must've been about 10,000 people watching and there was so much pushing, a lot of fans ended up falling in the water. It was very crazy."

"A few weeks later we were back, playing a club called B'Ginnings in the suburbs," continues Meine, this Schaumburg, Illinois show also including Sammy Hagar and Pat Travers. "People were camping outside the place at seven in the morning. On the next trip, we did two nights at the Aragon Ballroom, where Al Capone used to go dancing, and sold them out. With the success of Blackout, we returned to Chicago in 1982 and packed out a 10,000 seat hall. Later we decided to play the Rosemont Horizon and after the first night sold out in just 25 minutes, we were forced to add two extra nights."

A short Japanese tour in early August would see the band playing with Whitesnake, Michael Schenker Group and Bon Jovi. At one point, it looked like MSG might have been support for much more of the Love At First Sting campaign. "Perhaps it worked out for the best," said Klaus, when this fell through. "It would have been fun to tour with Michael. Of course, our roots go way back—he was, as I hope everyone knows, the original lead guitarist in Scorpions. But he has his career now and we have ours. We're still very close, and in fact, Rudolf and I showed up and jammed at one of his British gigs late last year. But perhaps Rudolf would have had his attention taken away from our tour. He may have felt the need to watch out for Michael every now and then. Right now, we don't want any distractions."

"I realised having Michael along would be a big distraction for me," agrees Rudolf. "When we are together, I feel very protective of him. I have one eye out for him all the time. Michael's a brilliant musician, and he will be a big star in America some day, but he's going to have to do it on his own."

Upon return, there'd be a second North American leg, mostly supported by Fastway. Then into late October, it was back to Europe, where support would come from Joan Jett. The Sporthalle, Cologne, Germany show on November 17th '84 would provide some source material for the album. But a bonafide live milestone would take place in January of 1985, with the band's first Rock In Rio.

"Rock in Rio was a fantastic thing," recalls Rarebell. "If you go to YouTube, there is a drum solo there from Rock In Rio. With all the 400,000 people clapping along. It's my best drum solo. When we arrived in Rio, it was January 5th and the concert was on the 19th. So we had two weeks off, and I think all we did there was just fuck and sleep and party. There was nothing else to do there. I was in the same hotel on Copacabana Beach with Roger Taylor from Queen, and Chris Squire from Yes was there. The others, all the family people had a different hotel on another beach. But Brazil is just crazy. I mean, in those days, party, don't forget, Ozzy was on the bill, Queen, AC/DC, Scorpions, and Yes and Rob Stewart—do I have to say more? It was a great festival."

Then it was straight to Japan yet again, followed by triumphant festival dates through the summer, including Knebworth and Donington. Knebworth would reunite Klaus with his old friend Ritchie Blackmore, who was headlining the show as part of a reformed Deep Purple. "Come on, the guy's really great, but not such a good soccer player," said Meine weeks before the show. "He takes his soccer seriously though. We always play Ritchie whenever we can. When we played with Rainbow last, we hammered them 5-1. I don't think Ritchie was impressed. We always said we'd give him his chance to extract revenge and Knebworth offered the opportunities. I really hope Ritchie's prepared. We're really in the mood to stuff him and Purple." Backing off, Meine offered an olive branch. "It's not a competition. We're all just there to play good rock 'n' roll for everybody. It's pure press nonsense to suggest that we are in any way annoyed. Look at it this way, Purple are a legend to us."

Every track utilised through its four sides of vinyl hailed from the Matthias Jab era and no earlier, i.e. Lovedrive forward. Matthias even got his own showcase, a solo jam called *Six String Sting* (omitted along with *Another Piece Of Meat* and *Can't Get Enough* from the earliest CD issue but restored for the 2001 remaster). Through 19 tracks, there were only two ballads, the persistent *Holiday* and the effortlessly massive *Still Loving You*, with much of the harder rock sped up in the marching powdered manner indicative of the era, Klaus fading away on articulating his words, Herman pounding the whole thing into crazy submission.

"I was never pretty drunk or coked-out or smoked-out," explains Herman, asked how medicated the band might have been while playing live. "I tried to play all the songs totally sober. When the concert was over, of course, I had a bottle of Dom Perignon waiting in my dressing room , so I drank a few glasses of champagne, smoked a joint, but that was about as far as it went. I never got very high on coke. First, it lasted only ten seconds with me, so I said to myself, what is the point? Then my dick became about one centimetre big so I said to myself, what is the point? You know, I cannot fuck because I cannot get a hard-on. I have a headache after ten minutes. I thought, always, stupid drug, I smoked instead and had a few glasses of champagne. But I was always very disciplined with that. When somebody pays $25, $30, he should get his money's worth."

As for the hewers of wire and wood in front of his drum riser... "Well, Francis, he was a heavy Chivas Regal with Coca-Cola guy. You could literally see on stage which glass he was on. Between the songs he would always have a nip, and by the end of the show, he always had about a half a bottle empty, so he was pretty plastered. But it made no difference in the playing. Rudolf, same sort of thing. Klaus, in the beginning would drink whiskey to get loose, but in the end, when the tours were very long, he stayed fit. He drank water, fruit juice, stuff like this. I worked out before every tour, in a fitness studio running, getting conditioned. But during the tour there was mostly no time. In the hotel, you could go downstairs to the fitness centre and run a bit and do a bit there. But it was never a proper workout like you could do at home. But to this day, I keep fit."

As mentioned, really the only extra bit of material on World Wide

Live (aside some different chords in *Dynamite*), was Matthias' painful, screeching, full-on rock guitar solo *Six String Sting*. "I get embarrassed when people call me a great guitarist," noted Matthias back in '85. "I'm glad they appreciate my talent, but I don't consider myself great. The most important thing for any musician is to fit into the framework of a band. I can't go off soloing and leave the band wondering when I'm going to stop. That wouldn't be fair. There are many guitarists who do just that. But the Scorpions are a band, and our egos are satisfied by the cheering crowds when we finish a song, not by playing a long solo."

As for his weapon of choice... "I favour Gibson guitars over Fenders. I like the way they sound. There's a control you have over a Gibson that you don't have if you're playing a Stratocaster. I play both on stage, and I love both, but there is something I find very appealing about the Gibson."

"I take a dozen guitars with me on the road," adds Rudolf, same subject. "I have 18 Flying Vs in my collection, but I don't see any reason to take them all with me. I have a V from virtually every year they were manufactured, and I'm always on the lookout for ones I'm missing. It's a wonderful hobby. They each have a different sound and feel—there's a distinct quality about each."

"It's not as easy as it may seem," explained Rudolf, when asked about picking the songs that would go on the album. "We recorded almost all of the shows on our last tour, and I figured I'd just sit down and listen to them for a few days when we got home. Well, the fact is that the tapes sat around for a long time before I had the nerve to start listening to them. I began to realise what a tremendous job I had chosen to take on. The tapes seemed endless. I love our music more than anyone, but by the 20th time you've heard *Blackout* in one day, you begin to lose your sense of reality."

"Rudy was the one who insisted on picking the tracks that appear on the album," laughed Klaus. "He couldn't understand why everyone else in the band said, 'Sure, if you want to do it, the job's all yours.'"

The choice of what compositions should go on the album had, however, been made pretty easy through the band's intensifying conviction over the years that everything the band writes should translate live. "Absolutely," agrees Schenker. "For the Scorpions, we feel if a song will sound good on stage, it should sound good in the studio as well. We've always shied away from making records with a lot of extra frills on them because we know we won't be able to reproduce that sound on stage. When I sit down to write new tunes, I always try to picture myself on stage playing them. If I get a feeling of excitement from the riff I'm playing, then I know that song is worth exploring. I'm building a studio in my home in Hannover. I realise I'm not there that much, but now when I am home, I can really make some interesting tapes for the band. I don't think we'll actually record any albums at my place, but I've always wanted to have a professional quality studio at my disposal, and now I'll have one."

This deliberate strategy of crafting songs that are devoid of ego and thus translate live reaches its extremity with a band like AC/DC, tour mates of the Scorpions, but it is also part and parcel of the Ted Nugent and Def Leppard catalogues, both of those bands sharing stages with Scorpions as well. And then internally, quite graphically, it becomes obvious that the slabs of four-on-the-floor sound written in the Matthias Jabs era had indeed lacked by design that texture and detail found all over the songs written when Uli Jon Roth was in the band. Driving audiences wild, live in concert, is key to any heavy rock band's success. And Scorpions, armed with all these songs that could cut through the mud of hockey barn acoustics, did indeed put on a show that drove audiences wild—including the girls, of course, who lapped up the power ballads while their boyfriends went for beer.

"We have had some very strong LPs come out since the last live album, and we changed our record company, so we don't see any reason to play the old songs," remarked Klaus, back in late '84, when it was only likely the next record would be a live one. "Also, Matthias wasn't in the band at the time, so he naturally feels more comfortable playing the songs he recorded originally. We feel we're at our best on stage. There's a freedom of expression there that you just can't have in the recording studio. We have the best of both worlds. We spend days and days trying to get a song to sound perfect in the studio, and then when we get on stage it sounds better than ever."

"When Scorpions made Love At First Sting, we knew it was an album we couldn't rush through," explained Rudolf, writing a special column for Circus magazine on the subject of assembling World Wide Live. "But on tour, you get a different kind of feeling from the one you get playing in the studio. When we decided to make World Wide Live, the band thought, 'No problem! We'll do the whole thing in a month-and-a-half, and it's finished.' Of course you can't really do that. Some people thought the album was late, but the band had just been too optimistic at first. I told them, 'No, we can't do it that way.' We recorded in many places: London, Brussels, Paris, San Diego, Los Angeles, Costa Mesa, New York, Hannover, Stuttgart, Cologne, and Hamburg. The London concerts were at the beginning of 1984, Paris was at the end of February, and we kept recording all through the year. It was truly World Wide Live, because we wanted a documentary album of Scorpions live, and we wanted to get our best."

"Madison Square Garden in New York looked like it would be a pressure point," continued Schenker. "At Madison Square, we knew it could go one of two ways: we could be very good, or we could be very bad. When we played the tape back, it was not very bad, but it wasn't good enough—not as good as the performances from Los Angeles, Costa Mesa and San

Diego. So you can see the Madison Square Garden show in our film instead. You ought to be able to; we had eight or nine cameras there. But nothing on the record was taken from the New York concert. Madison Square Garden is a special place—a *very* special place—and everybody was nervous. Because everybody knows that New York is the hardest place to make it."

"Back in Germany, we pored over many tapes," continued Schenker. "We did lists at home, with everyone noting down his favourite tracks. And when we got together in the studio, with the exception of two songs, everybody had the same opinion. It was a problem for us to get a good sound throughout the album. But by listening together in the studio, you have a much better chance of getting what you want, because the studio is like a microscope focused on your music. Maybe the rough mixes we'd heard at home were not so good, but once we had a good mix, we could tell the difference between takes that were just all right and takes that were really good. That's because, when you're listening in the studio, you're hearing 100%."

"We knew we wouldn't get a No.1 hit with World Wide Live. But when I look back, I see that Lovedrive has sold maybe 500,000 albums, while Love At First Sting is 2.5 million at the moment. So there were two million listeners who didn't know *Holiday*, *Loving You Sunday Morning* or *The Zoo*. We thought they'd like those songs. People who didn't know us so well would be able to hear what was happening on stage with Scorpions, and could see the visual side of the show from our film. They could find out other things about Scorpions too—like seeing me drive my Mercedes at racing speed on a normal street in Europe!"

"But mainly they get to see and hear us as a live band. For them, a live album is something extra. It's my feeling that most of the songs come over better on the live album than they do in the studio versions. The songs are much more to the point—they have more tension. You can feel the communication between the audience and the group. Having that tension is important, not just in our songs, but in life. Tension makes your life interesting."

"Take a contract between the band and a producer or a manager," says Rudolf, transitioning to something he wanted to get off his chest, namely that things might not be going so well with Dieter on the progress of the next album, which would emerge much later than anybody expected. "In order to progress, it's very important for everybody to be afraid that he may lose the other person. Then the producer or manager will work that much harder and the band will be happier, so the band will work harder as well. Contracts tend mostly to destroy that whole situation. When we knew in our hearts that this combination of people was working very well for us, we decided not to do long-term contracts ever again. Maybe we'd sign for one year, then re-examine the situation. I think Dieter has always worked hard… But with managers and producers, the best way is to work step-by-step."

"The Scorpions were able to go out on any stage, play great and drive the audience wild," says Francis, back to the Scorps as a live act, affirming the power of the band's energy and ability to throw cool heavy rock shapes live. "The strength of the band was that we were able to fight through our music. Especially on festivals with many bands, we were fighting to be the best. We went on stage knowing we would win, and we were always truthful to our fans. The Scorpions were a winning team! In the studio we worked very hard to get the best result possible. Our weaknesses were internal disagreements between the band and management. The sound was the combination of the instruments and voices. Each band member had his own sound and precise ideas how the sound of the band should be. The album World Wide Live was fun for me, because when selecting the tracks we wanted to use for the album, it turned out that I had played to my absolute satisfaction on all the recordings. I was surprised, because we did quite a lot of show during the concerts."

"There are so many dynamic personalities in this band," said Francis back in '85. "I'm satisfied to play my bass and lead the spotlight to the others. I get my share of attention. I don't stand in the shadows like some bassists. I have my chance to dash around the stage. But I have the responsibility of maintaining the rhythm of the song, and I take my job very seriously."

It perhaps takes the video version of World Wide Live to provide a full-bodied impression of what Scorpions were like at this high point in their career. I mean, not only is the production and mix of World Wide Live LP a bit midrangely and lifeless, on the positive, the video shows what an energetic bunch of rock 'n' roll athletes the guys became once they hit the stage.

"We do what we feel we have to do, which is basically give everything and a bit more," ponders Jabs. "We could never stand still onstage, like lots of bands do. They appear kind of introverted, like looking down on the fret board, playing the music, and we were never like this. We want to not only give all the power we have through the music, but also with the physical movement, the running around. Our tour manager said, in the '80s, 'You guys need traffic lights onstage' because sometimes an accident happened or we collided or whatever. You're running up and down the ramps… That's how we express ourselves, trying to give the public the most maximum power, and we still do it."

"Let's say it this way," adds Rudolf. "First you're playing only music, then you feel it's like talking. You know, my hand's moving always and I'm creating something, and if you watch other people when they talk, some people are talking like this (puts his hands on his lap) and telling everything, and other people have to move. When we started playing music or playing in front of more people and became more of a band, we really... it's like improvisation of instruments. I remember the first time when my brother went to UFO and I called Uli because we had to do one more concert to fulfill the contract. I said, 'Uli, what's happening? Can you play this gig?' He said, 'No problem, I'm coming.' So we rehearsed together and did the concert. I tell you one thing, I was already in this kind of rocking onstage, and Klaus also. We've always had this feeling we want to do more than other bands are doing. I remember Uli Jon Roth and me, sitting on our knees and playing guitar, and Klaus comes from behind and takes our heads and pushes them together. Only after the show he came and said, 'Hey, what's this? I was scared!'"

"I remember the first show in Japan, and we start *All Night Long* and because all the photographers were in front of the stage, Klaus—what he didn't notice was the stage was very slippery. Klaus came from behind and wanted to go to the microphone, running, tried to stop and he couldn't. He goes immediately into the photographers. We always thought when using the stage there was no limit; that was our situation. When we went onstage we didn't know what could be happening. When it was something very outstanding, we went backstage and we said, 'Hey, that was great; let's do it again.' Then we start to do this more, and more perfect, and more powerful. That was Scorpions: not 100%, 150. In the end, we were jumping over each other and we tried crazy things. That was a part of the pyramid, first three guys then five guys. It's all because of what fun it was, to play onstage. It's music but also to do something which people go and say, 'Hey, you have seen this?! It was great!' So that was the whole picture."

As regards the pyramid, Herman recalls that, "the idea came one night when we were standing on stage, and Klaus came from behind and he jumped between the two legs. He said, 'oh come let me jump between the two legs, yeah?' and then I don't know who said it, but maybe it was Rudolf, who said, 'Hey, why don't we make a pyramid?' That came together in a normal rehearsal. Just a momentarily inspiration. We were rehearsing, on stage or doing a soundcheck, and he said, 'Hey, why don't I jump between you two? It was first the three and then we make it five now. So we rehearsed it. Because it's difficult when you're on the bottom— you have to carry the whole weight. I was always the one who was at the bottom, as you know. So that was quite difficult. I had black and blue spots on my legs, believe me, especially in the beginning."

It behoved Rolling Stone yet again to review a Scorpions album only as part of a metal round-up. "Coming from Deutschland makes Scorpions, in their own way, truly *über alles*," wrote Tim Holmes, chucking the band in with the likes of AC/DC. Yngwie Malmsteen, Quiet Riot, Ratt and

Mötley Crüe. "World Wide Live, four solid sides of raw, adrenalin-injected metal, is a "best of" live compendium of their last four records, with a couple of lengthy in-concert axe scrapings thrown in. The songs twist around the sex-party axis in the pidgin-English argot that only recognises the most banal slogans in the collective rock unconscious. Fond they are, these Scorpions, of the rich metaphoric turf available in the verb *to sting*. Two of these guys have been ringing their heavy chord changes for nearly 15 years, which makes them their own spiritual forefathers."

Remarked Kerrang!'s esteemed Malcolm Dome, "Every one of the 16 songs delivered herein has been volcanically improved way beyond the unnatural constraints of the studio originals, busting forth like the Incredible Hulk forced to don Dicksonian glitter clothes. In essence, this is a tribute to the crustacea in the band, but let's also give a special mention to producer Dieter Dierks, a man who's come in for some savage and graceless criticisms in the past but who has done both himself and the band proud right here and now. The Scorpions' UK tour early last year was a disappointment. But World Wide Live should wipe out that unfortunate experience and underscore just why the Scorps stand loud 'n' bold as one of the best rock acts revolving on the planet. In a year which has already seen some excellent LP releases (from the likes of Springfield, George, Fogerty, Uli Roth and Accept), the Scorpions have chosen the right time to serve up a monster raving loony party."

World Wide Live would reach gold almost immediately upon release (remember that each piece of vinyl is counted, so it tallies two at a time) and then platinum September 4th '86, with the video version of it reaching gold shortly thereafter in December (of note, initial plans were for the band to release the album with something closer to a documentary as its visual companion). Not nearly as beloved or revered as Tokyo Tapes, the record was the work of a band operating fully in the corporate world. In other words, the album was treated as so much product, like Judas Priest's Priest....Live!, but unlike, say, the also concurrent Live After Death from Iron Maiden, which got a boost with the fans because it was the first full-on live record from the band.

"The Scorpions are a live band, and we try to re-create that energy wherever we go," said Klaus at the time, after a bit of trash-taking at the current breed, namely Ratt, Quiet Riot and Mötley Crüe. "Kids want to feel energy from their rock 'n' roll. They don't want to sit around lethargically. The Scorpions always offer that to their audiences; we are always trying to ensure that our records have the same feeling about them. The last album, we invited some kids into the studio to add their voices to a couple of numbers; not too prominently, just enough to give it that live feel. That, essentially, is what we are always striving for. You will never hear an overproduced Scorpions album for that simple reason."

Savage Amusement

"Everybody tried to stay four years"

To opine that the Scorpions found themselves bogged down after the end of the ebullient Love At First Sting tour would be a gross understatement. It would be more than two years until the band would pump out the all-important follow-up to their smash breakthrough. Now, with most bands, when that happens in and around this kind of career triumph, it's usually because they're cleaning up, touring for three years straight. Not in this case. Scorpions would play a handful of European festival dates in 1986, but then do nothing but fret over their next record for all of 1987.

The highlight from 1986 would undoubtedly have to be the annual Monsters Of Rock at Donington, August 16th, where the band billed above Warlock, Bad News and Def Leppard, second on the ticket to Ozzy Osbourne.

Sounds' Steve Double, however, didn't quite see it as any sort of a highlight, writing that, "As Ozzy Osbourne will be supporting the Scorpions later this month in Europe, they were one band who could be sure of a good sound throughout. The Scorpions are the biggest rock band ever to emerge from West Germany. It's not hard to see why. They're reliable workmanlike rock commotion reflects the very essence of latter-day heavy rock without ever approaching the shining beauty at its core. Uniformly relentless and one dimensionally brutal, the Scorpions are both depressing and rather pathetic. Their ham-fisted sexism—tattooed across their foreheads by album titles such as Virgin Killer and Taken By Force, and by artwork like the chewing gum molestation on the Lovedrive cover—fits clenched fist in iron gauntlet within the base framework of the form. Despite their obvious power, the Scorpions could only plough a dour and unforgiving furrow through a set not too dissimilar in blueprint to the one which preceded it. But where Def Leppard's precisely structured rock soars with an effortless beauty borne out of natural talent, the Scorps have built their success upon science, upon Heavy Metal By Numbers."

Donington aside, if 1981 was a lost year, check out 1986 or indeed

1987, 'cos to add insult to injury, what would be issued as Savage Amusement the following year was considered a sizeable letdown, maybe the band's first not great album since... well, it depends on your acceptance level of the Uli Jon Roth era and the band's ball of eccentricities. Indeed, underscoring the sense of second-guessing the guys had been going through, the band had considered the album—the title Passion Ruler was being thrown around—to be pretty much finished as early as September of 1986. Little did they know the hand-wringing still to come.

"It was our mistake," explains Rudolf. "Not... I don't want to say it was a mistake of the producer, Dieter Dierks, but it was the days of, if you remember, Mutt Lange and Def Leppard, the Def Leppard sound. It was a great sound, no question about this, but we don't have to forget that the sound came also because they had to use a rhythm machine because the drummer, Rick was an invalid. So he couldn't play real drums, because he was missing one arm. So in this case they used a drum machine, very strong, and worked with sound and stuff, and Dieter was very much into the same thing. In this case, Savage Amusement has great songs on it, but the songs are a little bit stiff because of programming. And programming of drums, in these days, wasn't so easy to do. It was too stiff, and the human touch was not in it. There was also this kind of digital thing. Everything came together, but anyway..."

In a separate interview I had with Rudolf, he actually called Savage Amusement the low point of the band's career, at least in terms of record-making. "Yes, because the production wasn't as good as it could have been. Somehow that was one album too much for Dieter. Because we were very much of the team in the early days, and somehow Dieter had different ideas for Savage Amusement. He wanted to be the second Mutt Lange, with more production and computer drums and stuff like that. We were not so happy about that, but we found a way to finish it. For us it was always important to work as a team, but on that record it was more like a dictatorship. But he now sees the situation in the same way, because we met up a few days ago at a concert in Cologne, and he sees it the same way now that we have some distance. In this world you can't do everything 100% right. There are always things going wrong and all you can do is repair them."

Back in '86, after cryptically letting it be known that they wouldn't be working with Dieter forever, Rudolf also signalled a change in the songwriting process. "I'm working to complete my own studio in the basement of my new house," explained Schenker, setting in motion a chain of events that would affect many records to come. "It's very important for me, because if Scorpions have work to do on a basic track, I can take my tape home under my arm and play the overdubs at my house. I have my special atmosphere there. When I can play at home, I have much better ideas than I get anywhere else. Sitting there, I'm in a natural atmosphere, which is very important to a musician

After a long time on the road, it's good, too, to be in a quiet place. It's the opposite of being on tour. At home, it's just me, my wife Margret and my son Marcel. We can see only one neighbour. In the Mercedes, it's 30 minutes from our place to Hannover, but past the forest land there's a small town about five minutes away. Of the band members, Klaus lives the closest. He lives 15 minutes away from us, and Matthias is now just three minutes from Klaus's house. We're all starting to live in the same area. Francis lives the farthest from me, and even he's only 45 minutes away—if I drive fast." Notes Matthias, looking back at the process 20 years down the line, "I can tell you, the one that took the most time, and wasn't that great anyway, was Savage Amusement. That took forever. It had also to do with the producer trying to be Mutt Lange. When Def Leppard took, I think it was four years with Hysteria, everybody tried to stay four years (laughs). It was like the battle of the producers and we were unfortunately in the middle of it. And songwriting-wise, it wasn't a great album, and production-wise it wasn't great anyway. It was okay, but definitely not one of the better Scorpions albums and it took us like two-and-a-half years. I mean, we worked in the studio the whole time but we wasted so much time I don't even want to remember it."

Savage Amusement, issued April 16, 1988, is full of clichés and forced music, but really, the enormous work and thought that went into it helped make it an album not without its worthy moments. The record opens with *Don't Stop At The Top* and instantly we get an example of what will become the record's main virtue, the alchemical weave of guitars constructed my Rudolf, Matthias and of course indefatigable Dieter. It's something talked about as the overt skill of the Rolling Stones and it's something talked about as the secret weapon of AC/DC, an effect you barely detect. Within the Scorpions, it's a thing of heavy rock beauty, even applied to songs that here, add up to what is a record that spends much of its breadth and girth chasing hair metal. Still, *Don't Stop At The Top*, even as it does that, most notably through its pre-chorus but also through its chorus, it is within its regal verse that we hear that mesmerising blend of the European and the American evoked so richly during the classic Matthias era... which had by this point passed.

Next up is *Rhythm Of Love*, and the sequencing of it here imbues the album with a palpable letdown, underscored by its meandering start. Still, the song's chorus (featuring Canadian "rock queen" Lee Aaron on backing vocals) makes it catchy and worthy of its semi-hit status (No.75 on Billboard). The production video for the track is a favourite of Herman's: "If you are just talking about fun then it would have to be *Rhythm Of Love*, which was filmed in Hollywood; those days were a lot of fun."

Herman was indeed living in LA at the time and there is nothing more hair metal 'n' Hollywood than this. The clip's a mix of sci-fi, hot chicks in compromising positions and Scorpions miming live in their finest almost-hair metal clothes and poofed 'dos. As a trivia note, the main sex interest in the video was model and actress Joan Severance, who would go on to star in two Black Scorpion movies.

Some consolation can be taken from the fact that Scorpions took the tsunami phenomenon of California glam only part way, like Priest, like Aerosmith. Outside of Kiss, who were born to vamp, there seemed to be a tacit agreement that old men in neon, pink and too much fringe would send too blatant a message of pandering, as if punters couldn't pick up the pandered vibe from videos like this.

"No, we didn't go too far," laughs Herman. "But of course we went through the bullshit in the '80s, spiky hair and a lot of hair spray. We all did that, remember? But we didn't get as bad as Poison or Quiet Riot or any of those typical '80s hair bands. Management said, 'We'll get you a tailor' and guys came in, and then another guy put the band into elastic and plastic. We tried it all. I think you have to go on stage in something that you think fits you. You can't put a guy who is used to jeans and T-shirt suddenly in a Kiss outfit thing."

"I mean, they'd been going for a long time," says label exec Derek Shulman, high up at Polygram at the time and intimate with the Scorpions file, along with that of Bon Jovi. "They were around before the hair band era, and effectively was hastened... again, there are lots of little things that you would have to put together, but MTV was the catalyst in making the hair band era, the advent of hair bands, grabbing onto whatever videos were made, and record companies making videos of bands with big hair at the time (laughs). It almost became this coming together of various forces. Scorpions were around long before the hair era, but the fact that they were a band that had a very, very strong fan base all over the world and sold lots of tickets, but never sold huge amounts of albums... even though they did quite well, they were only helped by rock being accepted into the mainstream by MTV accepting these bands who were hair bands who were playing rock music. So they were healthy in that respect, but I don't think they were part of the hair band era at all."

"Dumbing down?" responds Shulman to that phrase floated. "Yes and no. They wanted... I mean, yeah, I was there for Blackout, and that was great straight-ahead hard rock; they were a rock band. But again, if you see them play, they're an entertaining band. They're not Pantera, let's put it that way. Pantera was a purist hard rock band, where there was a 'fuck you' attitude. Scorpions never had the 'fuck you' attitude about them. So they wanted hits as well. And it was their idea to do *Rock You Like A*

Hurricane and *Wind Of Change* and *Big City Nights.* Yeah, they wanted that."

The business paradigm had changed, says manager Krebs, and Savage Amusement might have been over-thunk because of it. "Martin, listen to me," exhorts David. "You're missing the reason for that. For Aerosmith and Bon Jovi and Def Leppard... if you're dealing with the '70s, the philosophy that we had was, we want one hit single every two albums. That was what we tried to do; not consciously, but we didn't want four hits. Now, with Aerosmith signed to Geffen, and I'm at the point where we're getting ten million an album. They want five hits. If you don't have five hits, it'll never come out. I think Bon Jovi was in the same position. Everybody saw, oh, we can do ten million with this kind of music. Nobody had ever thought that before. I would think that Rocks probably did three million. Now you get into Pyromania and you get into Bon Jovi... what's interesting, by the way, is, Toys In The Attic and Rocks, now, sell more than the Geffen records, not by a lot, but still more."

"But now hit singles was pretty was the whole game," continues Krebs. "The label saw that this was suddenly an amazing cash cow, so if we could get four hits and do four great Marty Callner videos, we can do big profits. That was the way they looked at it."

This explosion toward a diamond album never happened for Scorpions the way it did for the aforementioned Contemporary Communications Corporation artists, as well as Whitesnake, Bon Jovi, ZZ Top and Guns N' Roses. "But Love At First Sting could be ten million worldwide," notes Krebs. "Scorpions were a very well developed group outside of America. Other groups weren't. When you're looking... Aerosmith may have headlined Madison Square Garden before they ever did their first trip to Europe. They ended up going from great facilities into playing little theatres in England. I don't know if you've ever seen them, but at least at that time, they were not very pleasant, in terms of the amenities. The group said, 'Why the fuck do I want to go over there and suffer?' That kind of thinking. If I recall, when Aerosmith toured Europe in '77, we had to hire a private plane; otherwise they weren't going to do it. No, but there's a big difference between the philosophy of the '70s and the '80s, where you had MTV and hit singles and $10 million advances. That may be why you like those records less. Because they homogenized music in order to sell those kinds of units. But if you go to the shows of these bands, more than half the music for these bands is the '70s stuff."

"*Passion Rules The Game* is a song I wrote with Klaus Meine," explains Herman, back on topic and onto Savage Amusement's next track, another half-hair, half classic commercial Scorps track that was launched as both a single and a video. "This is a great drumming song. It's my favourite song of all time that I wrote for the band, and one of my favourite drum tracks, because it's very funky. I think it's a very underestimated song and it could've been a great single. We made a very great video, which we filmed in Wichita, and it was one of the best stage sets we ever had. I think the song is totally underestimated. Savage Amusement, for me, I like the drums on *Rhythm Of Love, Passion Rules The Game, Don't Stop At The Top*—great drum parts and sounds. But Savage Amusement was a lot of work, because after the World Wide Live release in 1985, we started to write lots of songs, '86, beginning of '87. We went to Dieter's studio and played him all the songs, and that was very disappointing for us to hear that we had composed a bunch of shit, you know? That's what he thought, and he said you all have to go back now and write some decent stuff for the next album. So this was a big psychological shock, and we were, 'Fuck you, I'm not going to go back now.' So it took another six months before everybody got back together and we finally started writing the Savage Amusement album."

"Well, I tell you what," says Rarebell, asked about the discarded material. "I was listening to it the other day, and I thought there was still a lot of good stuff there. To this day, I can't understand why it hasn't been used. There are a lot of Scorpions compositions that have not been heard by the public, but I still believe that there's a lot of great stuff there." One of these tracks was likely *Rock My Car*, which the band played live in 1986, a track that would have made a toughening addition to the record, given its almost NWOBHM gallop and wall-of-guitars critical mass.

Dieter's hard-charging attitude can be heard on *Media Overkill*, which begins with layers of studio effects, plus the return of the talkbox, before converting into a stomping riff 'n' rhythm that again, rides the line between traditional rock and the melodic hard rock going multi-platinum all around Scorpions and the older guard but pointedly not for them specifically.

"I mean, we didn't know any other way," sighs Klaus, asked about the endless hours put in going toe-to-toe with Dierks. "It was difficult and fun at the same time. Typically, we worked the whole day, and we went to dinner, and went to some pubs and get some drinks, and get some more drinks, and then past midnight. Dieter would be like, 'Come on guys! Now that we're in the mood, let's go cut another track!' We would go back to the studio and everybody was pretty much smashed and we would work till five o'clock in the morning to figure out the next day that it was all rubbish (laughs). Sometimes, you know, there were moments that were just magic. But it was the times, it was the songs, and of course Dieter put in a lot of passion. He was a very passionate guy. He never gave up, and he worked me very hard. He worked everybody very hard. In those days technology was totally different. It was more like, you know, if you want to record a song, it's the whole band in there playing the song again and again and again, and if it's not good enough, tomorrow we do something else. We come back to this track later. Until we get it right. It was totally different."

"Savage Amusement was the last album we recorded with Dieter Dierks as producer," explains Buchholz. "I think it is a very good album and we recorded it in the new Studio 3 of Dierks Studios, which is a big room originally designed as a TV or film studio. There was a large SSL mixing console and every tool you wanted as an internationally successful artist. Guitar overdubs and vocals were also recorded in the large Studio 1 and the small Studio 2, which means, that we were spread out all over the place in the studio."

Explained Dierks, in conversation with Metal Hammer's Pete Makowski, "I heard their first songs for this album two years ago. I got the cassette on November 15, 1985. When I got the first 14 tracks, I only liked two! So I went over to Hannover and told them that. After a while, they came up with new material and they started to hate the other songs as well. It is difficult to criticize them when they believe in the songs, but honesty is a must. If you are not honest with the people that you work with, it would be a waste of time. I could never produce and arrange a song which I don't like unless they make me feel confident with the song and we have discussed it. I can't do it."

Asked about the importance of being able to motivate the band, Dieter says, "I don't know how other producers handled the situation, but in the Scorpions, Klaus always comes up with the ideas and then the lyrics grow. It takes some time to improve on them and come up with new ideas. The words normally take longer than the song. I think it would be good now if they worked with another producer on the next album. After such a long time together, it would be good if they had a different experience. It is like a marriage when you know how the other one will react, you can push him more. It is something hard to communicate with one another because you know exactly how to hurt the person. I think that part of the producer's thing is that if you want a real aggressive guitar, you have to make the guy aggressive. It is all part of the psychological game you have to play to put the musicians in the mood or give him the last kick if he's tired. You have to push the band to their personal best. That is what makes work between the producer and musician valuable. This is my philosophy. Until the record is pressed, we work as hard as possible to get the maximum out of everything, the music, the lyrics, the arrangement, the feeling you create in the studio, the mix and finally the mastering. I have co-arranged and changed arrangements but that is part of the job. It helps having been a musician because then you can communicate with the band. It makes it easier for them to understand what you want."

Dierks admits to some degree of tension working on Savage Amusement, given that both band and producer knew their time together was up. "Yes. Like in marriage, there is happiness and tension. It is not just because the contract is over; every contract comes to an end. This has been one of the longest contracts ever between a producer and a band."

But Dieter was looking forward... "Savage Amusement took over one-and-a-half years, including pre-production, so this didn't leave me much time to work with anyone else. Now I am working with Accept, and we have also signed up a band from California called Joshua. I'm also signing a band from Cologne called No Excuse, and I've also had an offer from Robert Palmer who wants me to do some work with him. I think that every producer wants to be big with every band he produces. The Scorpions were my baby. It is like having children who have to leave their mother after a while. I have a lot of confidence in Accept. This band is similar to the Scorpions. Hard-working, very straightforward and professional, which I think is as important as talent. Talent alone is not everything today. The whole scene is more complicated and you have to keep your head together and Accept are very intelligent people. They are the next German band who will make it big. I have already done one album with them. The direction I tried to go with them was not possible with Udo. He is not a commercial singer. He is an outstanding rock singer. His way is unique and there was a conflict material-wise between the singer and the band."

"First of all, I think there must be confidence from the beginning," reflects Dieter on picking projects. "A lot of bands have asked me to produce them. They've heard the records I have worked on and liked them. I pick up on the vibes of the musician very fast. I can analyse the psychological structure of a person very quickly; maybe it is one of my talents. When I talk to someone, it doesn't take me long to understand how he feels, how he reacts and where his strong points are. We all have our egos. I have my ego, but I try to keep it down. I use my ego to push everyone to their maximum. I never have any real serious problems. You have discussions, mutual fights and I think that is important when musicians disagree with you sometimes. Argument is important. Also the musician has the right to push the producer and say I don't understand or this is not my scene. You have to respect that. If you don't have any personality, I don't think you stand a chance in this business."

The computer technology that defined the Savage Amusement sessions... Dieter figured it was here to stay. "I think it is a must if you want to stay in the business. If you work with young bands, for them it is totally normal to use all the equipment. If you stop learning, you don't have a long way to go. There will be a gap in producers. The ones who can afford the new equipment and the ones who still work the old-fashioned way.

Both will work up to a point. It is a mistake to try and work like a robot. In my opinion, there are too many clinical producers around."

Back to this clinical album, side one closes with *Walking On The Edge*, which is the band's first of two predictable stabs at a predictable power ballad. Still, count on Scorpions to at least turn in one high rent melody somewhere, and in the verse this time, not so much the chorus. Nonetheless it's better than Aerosmith's *Angel*, and it's better perhaps because the song doctors hadn't gotten involved yet.

Over to side two, and *We Let It Rock... You Let It Roll*, despite its pointless lyric, is arguably the album's best track, putting aside discussion of hit potential, thinking in squarely heavy rock terms. All told, it's a malevolent, rumbling rocker, again sent rich and dimensional by the band's penchant for interesting twin rhythm guitar parts. *Every Minute Every Day* continues in this manner, and grouping these two with *Don't Stop At The Top* and maybe even *Media Overkill* anchors the album with a consistency, the band and Dieter crafting a sort of hair metal with gravitas, very much like McAuley Schenker Group from around this time. But it all goes to pot with *Love On The Run*, the album's heaviest, speediest, thrashiest track, but arguably the worst song on the album— it's disconcerting in the extreme when a band that used to write such top flight extreme heavy rock now fumbles its way blindly through the style. But then again, the cracks were beginning to show with respect to this on both Blackout and Love At First Sting.

Savage Amusement winds down with its second power ballad, *Believe In Love*, and to be sure, all that fussy, obsessive work resulted in no real hits, no songs that are universally beloved by the base after many years passed. The album went gold immediately, however, but how could it not? Simply due to pent-up demand for a new Scorpions record alone, fully on the back of Love At First Sting, it was destined for big numbers, not to mention the fact that the late '80s was a huge sales period for heavy rock in general, led by the likes of Guns N' Roses, Poison, Def Leppard, Aerosmith, Whitesnake and Bon Jovi. Savage Amusement was certified platinum in 1995, but you'd have to say that once more it got a boost from another Scorpions album, this time, the surprise second wind afforded the band come Crazy World.

The tour itinerary for Savage Amusement was manic, as Scorpions tried to stay on top against a new generation of bands playing this vicious game, including a whole new heavier flank led by Anthrax, Slayer, Megadeth and Metallica. The campaign opened the day after the record hit the shops, with a ten-day stand at the Sport-And-Concert Complex in Leningrad, Russia, support coming from local heroes Gorky Park. "Maybe a 4000-seater," says Krebs, "so they did 40,000 people or something like that." From there it was over to the US in late May with Scorpions playing (in broad daylight) on a mammoth package with Kingdom Come, Dokken and Metallica, with Van Halen as headliners, through to late July.

"I had really liked the first Van Halen album," remarks Rudolf, a fan from way back. "I think it is still their best, and I have always liked how they went from a small club band to one of the biggest bands in the world. One day, when I first met Eddie, he introduced himself by coming over, singing the guitar part of *Speedy's Coming*, and saying, 'Man, we used to play that song all the time, and every time we did it, the people went mad.' Later, when we met David Lee Roth, he said they used to do *Catch A Train* all the time and that he really dug the band."

"If the Scorpions had come out with the album after Love At First Sting, in '86, instead of 88, they would've been one of the top five hard rock bands in the world," reflects David Krebs, the band's manager of nine years at this point, now looking at his German charges as a support act. "Next we came out with World Wide Live, which we had shot as a movie, but because they were touring; we toured the movie, to back the double live album. So that's '85. And everything was primed for them to come back in '86. But if you come back in '88, you've blown your timing."

"This is where they paid the price not coming back in '86," continues Krebs. "By the time they were ready to come back in '88, what *seemed* to make sense, which I felt was not the case, was for them to support Van Halen on that Monsters Of Rock tour. It got down to a very interesting thing with the manager of Van Halen, that, I said, you're making a mistake. The Scorpions are a giant act; you're paying them a lot of money. You should let them perform from dusk into darkness, with lights. He said, 'Take it or leave it.' I said, if the Scorpions play during the day, it will enhance how old they are. Because they were not... just lighting is magical; I know you know what I mean. Without lighting, I think that it hurt them. I don't know if you saw that tour, but I saw one show and I knew that we had made a mistake."

The North American tour continued on through 1988 with label mates Kingdom Come supporting for the first swing, Winger to close things out into October. Label mates again, Cinderella, supported the band for much of the continental European tour, November of '88 through February of '89, with the band closing out the campaign in the UK, February and March, supported by House Of Lords. From that list of high-hair rockers, it becomes obvious Scorpions were being pushed to compete in that market, much like Judas Priest for Turbo, not to mention Kiss, Krokus and Y&T during this time. But rock 'n' roll is a young man's game...

"I think the favourite albums, for me personally, are really Lovedrive and Taken By Force," reflects Rarebell, summing up the winding road 'til this point. "That one because of *Sails Of Charon*, with Uli Roth. Then of course Animal Magnetism, great album. Not because I wrote nearly anything on it, but because I just think it's a great album. But there's Blackout and Love At First Sting, and then it ends for me. I mean, in '88, Savage Amusement, which was also my title, that was really too polished for me. Which came because in those days, all those bands like Def Leppard, they made all those productions with Mutt Lange, as you remember, with the snare drum on the computer and all that. So Dieter tried this of course, to polish his stuff. That album took three years in the making. Everybody wasn't happy with the songs in the beginning, so we wrote all new songs, but still, in the end, the fire was out. That's what I feel."

Crazy World

"Do you have fibreglass in this studio?"

The ramp up to the Scorpions' next album becoming the worldwide smash hit album that it was, begins, as Herman Rarebell explains, way back at the beginning of the Savage Amusement tour...

"When we arrived in Russia in '88, we were virtually the first big western band to play there. Nobody ever played there before. It was just shortly before the first of May parade, Day Of Work in Moscow, and they were afraid that revolution would happen in their country. Then I remember a year later, August '89, we did the Moscow Music Peace Festival, Mötley Crüe, Ozzy Osbourne, Gorky Park and us and Jon Bon Jovi. And then we got invited by Mikhail Gorbachev on December 4th, 1989, and Gorbachev said to me, 'The biggest mistake that America did was when they let in the Beatles in 1964, and the biggest mistake I did in my country was when I let in you guys in 1988.' I swear that's what he said. Then as you know, three days later he was out of power, the Berlin Wall falls around the same time, November 9th—all those things happened."

"I must say that David Krebs was, in my opinion, the best manager we had," continues Herman, who credits much of the band's international success to Krebs, actually out of the picture just before the Crazy World era would take hold. "He took the band to America. He always let us fulfill our artistic fire. We could musically do what we want. Of course, he would say, 'Try to write me a commercial song for the radio.' Every manager would say that and every record company. They all want that done. Basically he had good ideas. He came up with suggestions, 'Let's make this festival,' 'Let's go to Russia,' 'I think we should go to this country,' 'We should go to Rock In Rio.' All those things were David Krebs. He made the suggestion to make the band known internationally. He brought us up to that level. But musically he would never say, 'From tomorrow on, I want you guys to play punk.'" Rudolf Schenker recognises that the band's association with the fall of communism was an extension of the band's identification with Germany, as ambassadors for German rock.

"Yes, with the history of the Scorpions and of Germany, we always had the feeling when we went to different countries that we want to show the people that there's a new generation coming from Germany. Not coming with tanks, coming with guitars and bringing love. That was also the reason we went to Russia. We wanted to show the Russian people... we noticed when we start to plan in 1986, Monsters Of Rock in Hungary, already with a promoter there that we have a big hit, *Still Loving You*, already in Russia. We told the promoter, we said we want to go to Russia. He said, 'No problem, there's a new man called Mikhail Gorbachev there for us; he can make it possible.' So he made it possible, we played there, and for us this was a very important part to really show the Russian people that there is a new generation coming and they're making music. We were very happy that our music was received so very well in Russia that we, in the end, were also invited by Mikhail Gorbachev to the Kremlin, the only ever rock band ever even playing in his office, and that's something very different."

"I think that's what I said before," continues Schenker, "that we became more and more a band to build bridges between generations, between religions and between continents and countries, and I think that's in part because we were coming from Germany outside the normal scene. And as an example, we played the Music Peace Festival in Moscow in '89— we came back. The song *Wind Of Change* was done because we noticed when away that there is something changing; there will be a big change happening. The other guys, Mötley Crüe, Bon Jovi, Cinderella and Ozzy Osbourne, they went back home and said, 'Oh, we kicked the Russians' asses.' But we had much more a feeling to feel what's happening there, what will be different or what is different now. I think that's what makes the Scorpions different to maybe other bands from America and England. Also until the late '70s we were managing ourselves because management was not allowed in Germany. In this case we had a very good feeling what's good for us and what's not good for us. The manager never came to us and said to us you have to do this and this and this. We did everything until the late '70s ourselves, until we met Peter Mensch and Cliff Burnstein and then we became a part of the big organization, and then everything else is history."

As to his reaction seeing all this happen to the band, Matthias Jabs told Kerrang!'s Don Kaye, "It's basically not a surprise to me because I think we are very open-minded, but at the same time we send out this positive atmosphere. I think people take us for real; they know and feel that what we say is what we mean, and therefore we probably appear more trustworthy than somebody who might have a job as a politician. I think we have a better chance to cross over borders and turn music into an international language which everybody understands. You can't expect things like this to happen, but if you're alert and the chance comes up, you just grab it, which is what we've done."

"We never dreamed of doing anything like this, ever," continues Matthias. "But we have always tried to know what's going on in the world instead of just hanging around watching things drift by. So if something happens, some great event, that's probably why we've been there first and have had a chance to play at these historic shows. Roger Waters called us up and asked if we would like to join him and his Bleeding Heart Band to perform The Wall—us and other musicians. We said, yeah, and it's a great idea—it was something we've never done before, to play someone else's music on stage. It was the perfect place to play that show. Actually, being there was the greatest thrill, since we never had a chance in our whole lifetime to go to this part of East Berlin. It was right behind the wall, the bit they called the Death Zone, no man's land, and right on that no man's land, they set up the biggest stage in rock history."

"Me and the generation I grew up in always accepted that there were two Germanys. Maybe my parents' generation remember how it had been one country once, but I never thought that way, because I grew up thinking Germany was two separate places. Especially since we couldn't go there and those people could come to our country, we somehow blocked it off. It seems to be farther away than the moon somehow. We feel like international people anyway. I was born in Germany, I grew up in Germany, but since then, I've been travelling around the world and I probably have a different perspective on things than someone who just lives in Germany all the time."

"We were happy to be part of the event," said Francis in 1990, the Scorpions being the only heavy rock band at the big concert at the wall, "especially since it was so significant an event. We had to play to this click track through headphones because the production was so huge and all had to be synced up. It wasn't easy for us to hear each other, but it was okay."

Without getting ahead of ourselves, the above events would indeed become celebrated in a hit song from the forthcoming album, Crazy World, issued on November 6th, 1990, and Scorpions would forever be linked to the fall of the USSR, the fall of the wall, and the rise of power ballads with whistling on them.

But first the band had to get their confidence back. No question, Savage Amusement was not received well by critics, or the record-buying public, really, having stalled at gold in the US as the boys tried to get their head around making their next record. But it wasn't like the band was suffering in aggregate. Much of 1988 was spent caught within a blizzard of big concerts, one after another, knocking them down. As is typically the case with rock careers, the whiplash effect of a big record is felt through at least a couple touring cycles. In effect, it could be viewed that Scorpions were still out celebrating Love At First Sting as they worked toward hitting the brakes in time for their next appointment with record-making.

Then there was the band's first compilation of their successful period with Polygram. English as a second language, inexplicably, showed up for the titling of it, Best Of Rockers 'n' Ballads seeing issue on November 14, 1989 and going gold inside of three months, platinum on October 21, 1993. That is indeed the true measure of a band's commercial depth chart. Most significantly besides this, the album went gold in Germany, for sales of over 250,000 units, but also in Canada, Finland and Switzerland. The track list comprised, essentially, the hits from the Matthias Jabs era, but also the nondescript Animal Magnetism rarity *Hey You* and the band's unremarkable cover of The Who's *I Can't Explain*, recorded for the anti-drug Make A Difference Foundation and a various artists record made up of bands who played the Moscow Music Peace Festival. So yes, aside from the record that left a bad taste in everybody's mouth, especially Dieter's, given that his contract with the band was now over and out, Scorpions were on a world-beating roll.

"Crazy World was the first album without Dierks," explains Francis Buchholz. "His chair was occupied with Keith Olsen as producer for these recordings. Keith had a very good reputation in the music business. We met him at the initiative of PolyGram New York, and decided to go for it. Recording in Los Angeles, at Goodnight LA Studios, most of the album, I remember having a great time in the summer driving around with a rental car. When for example Keith recorded guitar riffs, the rest of the band was free having a day off, only coming back to the studio in the evening to listen to the new recordings. At that time I was thinking about moving to LA. But my son Sebastian was just born and my wife, parents and sisters were still based in Germany. I decided to stay where my roots are. The rest of the album was recorded and mixed in Hilversum, Netherlands, in a wonderful studio named Wisseloord, which was owned by PolyGram. The recordings for Crazy World were very expensive. As I say, initially we went to Los Angeles recording everything in Goodnight LA, co-producing with Keith Olsen. The sound was great and everything worked out fine until we decided to just keep the drums and bass takes from LA and to record almost all the guitars and vocals in Hilversum, Netherlands, again. We had to fly our instruments and equipment from Germany to LA and then to Netherlands. As monitor loudspeakers we used my little Tannoys, which are still placed on my desk now. At least we saved on those costs (laughs)."

You want more laughs? Then belly up to the bar and reminisce with Keith Olsen about working with the Scorpions, complete with hilarious impersonations when appropriate...

"Geez, 'This is Klaus Meine calling. My wife Ina and I have been skiing. We would like to ask a question about the demo?' Oh man, the Scorps. Oh geez, it's been a long and arduous road with them. I am, I think closer with Matthias than I am with Klaus or Rudolf. Rudolf has a great sense of humour, especially now that they've gone through all the crap that they've been through. They realise that they're not God's gift to rock 'n' roll, so he's much better now."

More humble? "Yes, yes, he was being a rock star. You know, they had done *Rock You Like A Hurricane*, and then they did a couple of the really weak albums, and they got a new manager, Doc McGhee, who is a really active and energetic manager, you know, Bon Jovi. Doc McGhee! This is big-time. So they got this guy, and they decided to do a worldly album. So they thought about working with Bruce Fairbairn, and they were getting ready to go there, and they had shipped all their stuff, I think, up to Vancouver, and then something happened. I don't know what. I think it has to do with something with an album by Aerosmith, where the Scorpions were dropped on the curb. I don't know anything else, and I was not made privy to it and I don't want to know. I just thought that Bruce was just such an amazing producer and arranger and everything was fabulous. That man was brilliant."

"When we started with Crazy World," clarifies Herman, "the first producer that we approached, after we worked with Dieter Dierks, was Bruce Fairbairn, in Vancouver. Because we liked his work very much, and he said then to us, 'Well, I cannot do this right now. I'm working with Van Halen, and after that I have to do AC/DC.' So then we thought, well, who's another great producer? After Dieter Dierks, where can we go? And we came to Keith Olsen, because we liked the production he did for Whitesnake, the famous album with Aynsley Dunbar and *Here I Go Again*, all that stuff. We thought this was the right guy."

"All I know," continues Olsen, "is that I got this emergency phone call from my manager, Michael. 'Keith, what are you doing?' 'Well, I'm just finishing up this album.' 'Can you be ready to do another one in three days?' 'What?! Okay, I'll tell my wife.' I told my wife, and my wife got on a plane and went to France. Because I was supposed to take her on vacation, and she went, I didn't. I went into the rehearsal studio and started rehearsing to see where all the songs were and where everything was. While we were waiting for gear to arrive, you know, to be driven down from Canada, anyway, I signed a deal to do this album, and we started working on it, on the rehearsal."

"Then the 18-wheeler arrived, in my parking lot in LA. Which was big enough to hold an 18-wheeler and three cars, period. They started unloading gear, into my poor little studio. You know, do you really need to bring 15 4 x 12 cabinets? I think they had 50 guitars, ten or 12 basses, every pedal you can possibly imagine, and an entire Anvil case full of guitar cords. So, needless to say, we packed it all into the studio and then rented a huge facility next door, just to store all the stuff we didn't use, and ended up using a Marshall head and a Hi-watt head and two 4 x 12 cabinets, one for Matthias and one for Rudolf, and half a set of drums that Herman Ze German used, and a half rented set, some DW drums I'd been using."

"We cut those tracks in I think about a week, week and a half. Then started doing all the guitar overdubs and Matthias was fabulous! Just nailed these rhythm parts. His timing was spectacular. Then Rudolf started doing his guitars, and his parts, getting them done was arduous, because it had to be absolutely perfect."

"Then he said... and then I'll never forget, this is six weeks into the record, they've been in America or Canada for three weeks before that, and so it's been nine weeks. You know, they have their wives and their families, they've been out of town for nine weeks. Then Klaus walks up to me and grabs his Adam's apple and coughs, and goes (funny Klaus accent, hacking away), 'Do you have fibreglass in this studio? You know (coughs), you know I'm allergic to fibreglass.' I look at him, and the only words that came out of my mouth, being the sarcastic SOB that I am, I said, 'Have you ever considered a career change?' Have you ever known a studio anywhere in the world that doesn't have fibreglass? Of course not. It's like the universal thing that is in any studio anywhere. In fact, it was in his home studio in his home in Hannover. You know, he couldn't just come to me and say, 'Keith, we need to move everything to Düsseldorf,' or Holland, which is close to Hannover, so I can see my wife."

"So anyway, halfway into it, six weeks into it, we pack up an 18-wheeler, it gets put into in a 40-foot container, and it gets, I think, trucked to New York and shipped probably over to Amsterdam. In the meantime, we flew over, took a week to get used to everything, and then started setting up the stuff that they had in their homes, that we were able to bring over to this studio and started doing vocals. So we did the first ten days of vocals and backgrounds, doing other stuff. But Rudolf wanted me to make sure that I brought my acoustic guitar, and my two electric guitars that he fell in love with, and so here I am going into Amsterdam carrying three guitars. 'What are you going to do?' 'Oh, you know, just on vacation.' Well, 'Yeah, right sir' (laughs). So anyway..."

But what about the songs? "Yeah, there were some really good songs. The lyrics, they were really terrible. They're Germans. I call it Germo-English. They use simple rhyme schemes, 'Tease me please me before I gotta go?!' Herman wrote some, but there were a couple of songs... who was the keyboard player with Bryan Adams, Jim Vallance? Thank you. He wrote some of the songs with them, wrote some lyrics, wrote some great melodies here and there (sings *Send Me An Angel*). He wrote a bunch of that. He wrote parts for a bunch of songs. Maybe if it's only 10%, they took him off, or bought him off. Herman was fun. Herman Ze German, I don't know, not a month goes by before I don't get my half-hour call with him. But Herman wrote some of the lyrics, because he's pretty good at that, because he's the only one who had a decent vocabulary in English. The rest of them, they probably had 2,500 words."

"We never want to waste any time," noted Matthias, talking about Dieter Dierks with Don Kaye at the time. "It's just that the last time, when we did Savage Amusement, we had so many difficulties with our producer. This was the last album with him; we were basically stuck with him for more than ten years and it turned out to be no fun anymore. Since he knew that this was the last album he would do with us, I don't know why, but he set things up in a way that it just turned out to be a pain in the ass making that album. We were so happy to finish it, we got to the point where we were so happy that it was over that we didn't care if it was great or not."

"Of course we tried our best, but this time there's a whole new motivation to this band. We had freedom of choice for the producer, which made recording fun again, plus writing songs was fun again with the input from Jim (Vallance) and also, for the very first time, everybody in the band wrote songs and lyrics."

"He never even tried to write a song before, but this time he said, 'Why shouldn't I try?" says Jabs, with respect to the band's quiet bassist Francis Buchholz. "He came up with three pretty good songs and we used one of them. It's a real good song. There's a togetherness in the band now which we had maybe ten, 12 years ago. Now we have the feeling back; it's been really fun to make this album and we've had the best time recording. It's definitely harder. It's just wilder and crazier. It reminds me of the Blackout days but I think we have even better songs now. We have two ballads as well, so there's a nice variety, with a lot of edge. When we did the last album, after we did the demos, Dieter went with us into the studio and he recorded everything separately, trying to make, I don't know, a Def Leppard album or something. All of a sudden, we were dealing with the computer. Everything took so long and after a while all the spontaneity and emotion was gone."

"I was always happy to have good writers in the band," muses Francis, offering a glimpse as to how he saw his role within the framework of the band. "With the Scorpions, I was more interested in getting the management of the band into place, coordinating tours and logistics. To me it does not matter so much if I have a say in the composition process. When I work on a great song—but yet an unfinished recording—I can contribute in so many other ways. Most of the songs you hear on the radio have come a long way from a couple of chords and some vocal idea to a finished hit record. I like contributing with arrangement ideas and fine-tuning of the compositions. Of course, I do write my own bass lines, but I have never asked to get a writing credit for that and for my other contributions."

As for his favourite bass parts applied to Scorpions songs, Francis is essentially unconcerned. "In order to answer this questions properly I would have to listen to all the songs we have recorded. I do not have the time. There are many bass parts I could be proud of, but I am not that type of a guy, who is carrying his achievements around with him all the time. A bass part is to me very important, as long as we have not finished the final recording of it. Once it is recorded to my satisfaction, I do not care about it anymore. I even tend to forget what I have played, and I have to learn it again, when I want to play it live!"

"Furthermore, I must say that I am a lucky man," reflects Buchholz. "I have such a long list of moments and highlights, that it is impossible to put them in order. I visited friends in Frankfurt and their children showed to me a live performance of the Scorpions at the US Festival, Los Angeles in 1983, which they had taken from YouTube. I listened to my bass lines and discovered I had played them exactly the way they should have been played. Watching this live recording, I felt the positive power which came across those days, the unity we were able to create live on stage. Seeing that on TV was a proud moment after all these years. But every album from the catalogue is a favourite to me because I have always put so much heart and blood into the recordings. When I get asked a question like that, I think about my three children. Whom do I like most? The answer is simple: I love every child for its own personality. The same applies to the Scorpions albums."

For all its ensuing commercial success, Crazy World is not that different an album in aggregate style from Savage Amusement—it's just longer, more ambitious, better more often. This is in the spirit of Aerosmith and Mötley Crüe at the time, Bon Jovi, Metallica, and AC/DC with The Razors Edge. Bruce Fairbairn, Jim Vallance, Bob Rock, Vancouver... it was a little place and pocket in time in which these bands decided to buckle down and try real hard, mostly with positive creative and commercial results. Had Scorpions stayed in Vancouver, would it have made a difference? Probably not, for they got that sort of record with Keith, and also chalked up pretty robust record sales in the process, especially when worldwide numbers are included in the tallies.

As we begin examining the record, opening track *Tease Me Please Me* is a thick, leaden hair metal stomper that doesn't break any new ground, other than having the staffers at the band's label perform the back-up vocals. "Matthias, as you know, only started to write really late with songs like *Tease Me Please Me*," notes Herman, "when we got involved in the Jim Vallance era. I wrote the lyrics with Jimmy and with Klaus for all the Matthias riffs." Jabs' only other credit on the album is for *Money And Fame*; clearly his long-defined role in the band was not changing any time soon.

Recalling the production video for the track, Matthias says, "I remember being in Los Angeles and we were ready to shoot *Tease Me Please Me* and I said, We have to organize this as nobody wants to be waiting around.' Everyone shows up early in the morning and then they do your makeup and by the time you do your first scene it's eight hours later and the makeup is dry and you're drunk. I remember *Rhythm Of Love* we shot the scenes that people would be watching in their homes at like four in the morning. I said, 'What's the fucking point? We look tired. We are tired. We are drunk and we are tired and this is what you want the people to see?' You get organised. The difference between *Tease Me Please Me* was that we were organised. I didn't want to sit around and eat a bagel and drink a beer in the morning because I am waiting around. The first day they shoot all of the shit that we don't even need to be there for. Why should we be there watching them working? It is a natural process where you learn while you're going through it. At first you do everything they tell you and then, as you continue to make videos, you realise things can be improved and you organize it yourselves."

Don't Believe Her is next, and it's the closest Scorpions ever came to emulating the baby Scorpions, namely Accept, this one sounding a bit like *Princess Of The Dawn* grafted to any number of churning Balls To The Wall classics (of note, that band's bassist Peter Baltes had a short guest vocal on the last album's *Every Minute Every Day*). *To Be With You In Heaven* is another successful composition, obscure of atmospheric construct, reminding one of *Crossfire* or *As Soon As The Good Times Roll*, from Love At First Sting, i.e. slow to pay off, in no hurry to impress, in a word, classy.

Then there's *Wind Of Change*, which became the band's biggest anthem of all time, worldwide smash, world anthem even (take that, Frank Marino), yet not much more than an average power ballad but again, somewhat interesting of melody, uniquely political, and textured with some nice, bluesy guitar from Matthias.

"Well, of course, it's got to be *Wind Of Change*," says Klaus, about his favourite recorded moment of the entire Scorpions catalogue. "First, I wrote that song; second, it became the soundtrack to historical changes in the world. I mean, it was a No.1 hit in so many countries. That's one thing, but the other side is so much heavier. The song became so much bigger than just a No.1 hit. Because it's a reflection of that moment in time. It's an anthem to historical changes. Here in our country, when the Berlin Wall came down, so many people, in the East and West, so many people consider it the soundtrack to this very historical moment. So that's a very important song."

"We saw it change people when we played in Russia in the '80s," continues Meine, consistent within his character as the band member most looking for something more substantial from his lot in life. "*Wind Of Change* was the soundtrack for the end of communism and the bringing down of the Berlin Wall. We saw that rock music had a huge effect on the younger generation of Russians. They were tired of the whole communist system. They were tired of being behind the Iron Curtain. We were breaking through the Iron Curtain with Scorpions' music. We talked to young people back then and they told us that the time of the Cold War would be over soon. As a generation they didn't want it anymore. I am not saying rock music did that, but it was a part of it."

"With *Love At First Sting* we were on top of the game," reflects Meine, "with double-platinum albums in America and lots and lots of success, arena success all over the world, but then there was another chapter: Russia. We went to Russia—in 1988 to Leningrad, in 1989 to the legendary Moscow Peace Festival. Maybe this was because we were a German band! As much as we played in America and we always loved it and still love it, for us it was much more important emotionally to play in Russia than probably for any American band, because we wanted to see the other side of the world, we wanted to see this side of planet, this side of culture, since we are in the middle between East and West and, with the Berlin Wall, between the superpowers, Russia and America. We wanted to go there, and it was amazing, it was so emotional and it gave us a new spirit and a lot of inspiration. I think to go to Russia back then, after all the success we went through, was very important—especially with the success of alternative music. Because when Nirvana and all these bands came up, for many hard rock bands it was the end of the road. But for us it was a time when we opened a new book, a new chapter and, in return, had a world hit with *Wind Of Change*. Then the Berlin Wall came down, and this song became the anthem for the coming down of the Wall. In the East, like in Russia, the fans connect this song with the coming down of the Communism. But the '90s were not so easy to survive also for The Scorpions."

Placing the song in rock history, Klaus offers that, "*Still Loving You* is like a big power rock ballad; the words 'power rock ballad' are for songs like *Stairway To Heaven*; *Still Loving You* belongs there—it's a big, big song for us. *Wind Of Change*, of course, became a bigger-than-life hit, because it has this political background. This is so Zeitgeist. This is not only a strong song or a hit single, there's so much around this song that made it bigger than us. Our mission is to have a chance to reach out with music, to build a bridge between countries, cultures, religions. Whether we play in Europe or Asia, in all those different places people react to music very, very much the same. And going there and making the connection with people, we can have our share in world peace."

"*Wind Of Change* was of course the national anthem to all that," agrees Rarebell. "So we had tremendous luck that our song was falling exactly in this time of wind of change. Because of course in Europe, everybody played that song. People by the millions came over to Germany, and that's why we are now in the last place in Europe (laughs). You know, we have demonstrations, people demonstrating, put the wall back ten metres higher (laughs). I love that. But this is funny, how the Germans feel, because after that, of course, everybody had to pay much more in taxes. The solidarity tax was 7.5% more, and it became ridiculous. So now here we are, the East is completely rebuilt and the West is fucked-up. But then, in those days, you know, this was the natural hymn in Europe, that song. At the same time, in Germany, especially in Eastern Europe, everything changed from communism to capitalism. The wall came down and we carried along with the perfect song. It was like the film track song to the live picture, so to speak. So we met Gorbachev, the wall came down, we were in the middle of this and it was the biggest year for us."

"But of course that made a big change in Klaus's life," sighs Herman, "and I think that made a change in us. The band didn't want to play the song. We thought it was too commercial and too soft—but it became the biggest hit. And Klaus then said of course, hey, if I can write one hit, I can write ten. From that day, as I said, he refused to do something I wrote."

Remarked Rudolf to Drew Masters in 1990, before the politics of *Wind Of Change* would change his band's life, "When we travel around the world, we have a close contact with the people, and we have discovered that we're all the same, and that there should be no reason for borders or hate or fighting. We have to all learn to live together. It's very inspirational. When you're a rock musician, you're travelling all around the world, and during this, you think about other people, which means you open up. The good thing about rock music is that it lets the brain flow and that makes it open to new ideas and learning experiences. The experiences we've had over the past two years are definitely reflected in our music and lyrics. Look, we can't change the world, but we can give a little bit in our songs towards helping it. But if we were to give too much in our lyrics, like, 'You don't and you do,' then our fans would say, 'What's he trying to tell me? Fuck them!' They think we were telling them the same thing like their parents do. So we have to approach our lyrics like making a meal—you take the ingredients and mix them just right, and add just enough spice for the flavour."

"Everywhere people are the same," added Francis. "When I was a small boy in Germany, I thought that the Russians were evil, and I was afraid of them. But then we went there and discovered that they were very nice people."

"It was a luxury for us to do," continued Rudolf, on the making of the current album. "We chose the studio, and we co-produced it with the producer of our choice, Keith Olsen. Everything possible was finally in our hands. That's important to us. When we went to record the album, we wanted to do it as live off the floor as possible, and Keith had the same idea in mind. It was done very similar to what we had done years ago. We found that we were in competition with the computer in the studio before. In some situations, they're perfect, but in others they're cold. What we feel rock music needs more of in this computer world is more life, more soul. One of the reasons that we didn't use computers in the beginning was that we are from the computer music capital of the world. We feel our music is more American, more English, and that since we play what we feel, we should record it with feel too."

"We spent too much time polishing up the production on Savage Amusement," concedes Schenker, "and it came out just too produced. That's why we wanted to get back to a live-sounding album. Still, we like the Savage Amusement album for the songs, but after a couple of years, you can realise in which direction you went, and we felt we lost the feeling of the songs to the production. We never want to spend one year in the studio again. This one took us only three months to record, and three weeks to mix. Everybody has to find their own way, and we now know ours."

As for his iconic whistling in *Wind of Change*, Klaus says, "When I composed that song, I just whistled, I guess, because there was no guitar to play a cool little part that I could play. I composed that song on a piano, on a keyboard. I was just playing around with it and the whistle was not that I had such a smart idea and I thought I needed to do this cool whistle. I just did it because there were no other instruments that I could play, or fill in for a little melody. If I was a guitar player I am sure I would have tried something on my guitar like Matthias did later. He tried to do that, but they just couldn't replace that damn whistle. I remember that an A&R guy from Mercury Records in New York called me before that song was released in America and he said, 'Klaus, I like that song a lot, but we have to take out that whistle. It won't work in America.' I said, 'No, the whistle stays right there as it is an important part of the song. It's like a hook.' When *Wind Of Change* became a top five hit in America and we met the next time, he was like in Spinal Tap when the manager bends over. He bent over and said, 'Klaus, you may kick my ass.'"

Strength to strength, after the undeniable *Wind Of Change*, we're into

Restless Nights, which hits exactly the same sweet spot as *To Be With You In Heaven*, not to mention a return of an intriguing Accept vibe for a second time. It's just a really cool track, attaining an aristocratic level of melodic gravitas that could only come from a continental European band.

Lust Or Love... we're back to the band's meaty hair band rock, anchored by tradition, anchored by a sophisticated sense of melody borne of experience. The credits are crazy all over this album, this song being no different: musically it goes to Meine, with the lyrics attributed to Meine, Rarebell and aforementioned song doctor Jim Vallance.

"First of all, I've never liked the 'song doctor' moniker," says Vallance, giving us a bit of a glimpse into his world. "It implies that I parachute in and fix songs that were already written. The fact is, nine times out of ten I start from scratch, with an empty page. I occasionally take a beating for the song doctor thing, but I think I had one of the best jobs in the world. Alice, Ozzy, Steven... these are remarkable people, let alone remarkable musicians. Spending time with them was a privilege, a rare treat."

"Every project I've ever worked on, from the Scorpions to Ozzy Osbourne, is custom tailoring," continues Vallance. "In most cases you're already familiar with the artist's catalogue, either as a fan, or simply as a result of what you've heard on the radio. You have to start with respect, even reverence, for what the artist has done in the past. Then you sit down and have a conversation with them, about where they envision going, musically. The conversation gets you half-way there, then you roll up your sleeves, strap on your guitar, and spend the next day or two writing the song. Often, that original conversation becomes the song, sort of like an architect sketching a house on a napkin. The first draft and the finished product share a lot of DNA. In terms of method, you start by doing what's obvious, something that 'sounds' like the Scorpions or Ozzy. Then you try to bring something new to the equation, a bit of a twist, but without straying too far from the artist's historical style."

"Record companies like to sell records. No surprise there. I'd often get brought into a project that was 90% complete in terms of writing and recording, but the record company 'didn't hear a single.' I wish I knew what a 'hit single' was, because I'd write one every day! In my experience there are no proven, repeatable formulas. However, there are ways to push a song in that general direction. A strong, memorable melody and lyrics, for example, especially in the chorus. A good guitar riff. Dynamics in the arrangement and production, where perhaps the verse is played down, and you get swept up into the chorus, that sort of thing."

As for Jim's approach with hard rockers like the Scorpions... "When you're writing heavy songs, things tend to get dirge-like. You don't play actual chords on the guitar; it's more like open fifths, and you can easily gravitate towards minor keys. The next thing you know, your melody is dark and forgettable. I lean more towards major thirds, which produces positive, memorable melodies. As long as you don't go too far into the pop realm, your song can retain its heaviness but still sound like it belongs on the radio. And believe me, everyone wants to get their song on the radio."

"On a few occasions, artists were sent to me kicking and screaming, and I had to deal with borderline hostility," says Vallance, on the whole controversy around bands hiring on the likes of himself and Desmond Child. "They'd never written outside the band, and they weren't keen to try it, regardless what the record company said. Bands are tight-knit families, and I understand how hard it is for them to let someone in. For me, getting through the first was hell. Sometimes it was more about psychology than music. Typically, on the second day, results would start to happen. Suddenly the situation would become positive and productive, and songs would emerge from the haze. By the end of the week they'd be asking their record company if they could come back and work with me again. I got a lot of repeat business."

"I'm of two minds about 'where songs come from,'" reflects Vallance, in conclusion. "Remember, I may be a songwriter, but first and foremost I'm a *fan*. I love music. I live for the Beatles, the Stones, Zeppelin, AC/DC, Joni Mitchell, the Beach Boys, Bob Dylan, Hank Williams, Buddy Holly. They all wrote their own songs. Brilliant. But I'm also a fan of Joe Cocker, Elvis, Herman's Hermits, the Monkees, the Animals, all those '60s artists that made such listenable, enduring rock records. I continue to revere the musicians who actually wrote and played their own music, but more than that, I just simply love 'records,' the finished product, coming out of a 4" mono speaker, summer of '65. Like *Mrs. Brown, You've Got A Lovely Daughter*. Great song; it still makes me feel like I'm 12 again when I hear it. Back then I didn't care where the record came from, how it got made, who wrote it, who produced it, who played on it. It was pure magic, and that's all that mattered."

As for writing from within on Crazy World, bass man Francis Buchholz even gets in on the act for feisty rocker *Kicks After Six*, sharing music credit with Vallance, lyric credit going to the usual trio of characters. Frankly, despite the acceptable verse, this one's chorus marks a new glam rock low for the Scorpions and is best shuffled past without too much reflection.

"He's credited on eight songs," indicates Rarebell, with respect to Vancouverite Vallance. "When we started writing with him on the Crazy World album, it was because we thought then that Bruce would be our producer. You see, Bruce cancelled on us. But the songs were ready with Jimmy. Bruce said, 'Fine, yeah, do this now. I have to do Van Halen. I have to do AC/DC. I can do you guys in one year. Do you wanna wait?' I said, fuck this, we're not going to wait one year. What are we going to do for one year, twist our thumbs? So that's how Keith Olsen got in, and Keith, of course, produced the biggest hit with *Wind Of Change*. But we had lots of really good song material. We played it to him, and he really went for the Crazy World recordings, which I love, by the way, very much. There is one of my favourite drums tracks on there, *To Be With You In Heaven*, plus *Money And Fame*, for example, very heavy drumming. So we made this album in a relatively short time in LA, shorter than I actually thought for Scorpions, only three months, which is fast, unbelievable really (laughs). Compared to Savage Amusement, of course, there was great fire again and enthusiasm—Crazy World was a great album. So the album was done and it became the biggest selling one because of *Wind Of Change*."

But we're not done with Crazy World, which has fully four more tracks to go, given that, don't forget, this was the band's first album of the CD age, and thus could safely fit much more material than one could on an LP. And so the fairly gnarly rock continues, with *Hit Between The Eyes*, Mötley Crüe party rock for the verse, but a surprising melancholic and European twist for the chorus. Next is the aforementioned *Money And Fame*, a killer chunk of rock down a *China White* way, sophisticated riffing penned by Matthias, who proves right here he should be doing more of this.

Incredibly, this late in the sequence, it's time for the album's anthemic, hard-rocking title track, the band building up a wall of guitars that collapses to the tune of a highly memorable descending chord pattern come chorus time. Back-up vocals on this one are executed by the staff at Wisseloord Studios in Holland.

I suppose it was inevitable that the record would close with a power ballad, *Send Me An Angel* fulfilling that rote role. "A power ballad is really good because it's a way of having a rock 'n' roll band be accessible," muses Keith. "Because radio was not going to play anything other than the ballad. So gee, okay, what do we have to do to get exposure, to get people to actually want to go out and buy it? Because remember, the media is the message." As trivia, a keyboardist named Koen Van Baal guests on *Wind Of Change* while Jim Vallance plays that role on *Send Me An Angel*.

What did the media think of the record? Well, important arbiter of taste Kerrang! was perhaps all too knowledgeable about heavy rock and the advancements made in the genre of recent years, to be bowled right the hell over. Frankly, it was a suitable response, if a tad too harsh—this was quite a good Scorpions album.

"No, I don't hate the Scorpions' 14th album, but I don't love it either," wrote Steffan Chirazi, intelligent rock journo that he is. "Welcome to the land of passive feeling, a place where nothing really strikes hard enough to produce a supportive yell. Aah, it's a nasty old bastard, mediocrity. To be honest, it frightens the shit outta me, because I want to be challenged and turned on by what I hear, whether it means love or hate. Crazy World merely represents a job well done, and for that reason I must meet a 'job' with a 'job'-like attitude. I listened to it. Then I listened to it again. Then I came back to it after a day or two and listened to it again. Here I am, listening to it again. Nothing shocking, nothing inspiring from a band I've come to expect it from. But shopping mall sub-teenage heaven (i.e. Warrant) really seems to be the pie our Scorps are bulleting for. Who's to say it won't work? Their camp has always achieved their goal, and certainly some of the riffs are extremely catchy. *Hit Between The Eyes* grooves a fatty, *Tease Me Please Me* (smirk) has a good old footstomp to it, and there's also those soft-city night moments in the balladic hankie-soakers *Restless Nights* and *Send Me An Angel*. Quality musicians have tremendous difficulty writing totally crap music, and true to that form, the Scorpions still have the music somewhat together. It is different; more basic than before, more pounding, more, well, generic hard rock, I suppose. But thankfully, Meine, Schenker and Jabs can still elevate it ever so slightly. Crazy World is just… all right. For those middle-Americans who preserve careers, make bands millions and look simply for something to drive the car to, this album will probably constitute greatness. Meanwhile, I should just face the facts: the Scorpions packed innovation into a sealed white case around the time of Animal Magnetism. Business is business."

"As they got older, they wanted to get that one big commercial success and that's what we did," reflects Olsen, in closing. "I think we did eight-and-a-half million units of that record. Six million in America or something? Or was it eight in America, and then a bunch... four million outside?" Crazy.

"Oh," counters Keith, breaking out his perfect Klaus, "in fact it's a crazy world (laughs)."

Face The Heat/Live Bite

"Which radio station plays that?"

Touring for Crazy World saw the band work solid from November of '90 through to May 1991, support coming from Winger, then Trixter, with Great White and Mr. Big contributing as well. The record had gone gold immediately, but unlike its predecessor, kept selling, achieving platinum on July 24th '91 and then double platinum on August 7th of 1995, where it currently sits. Chart-wise, it vaulted to No.21 on Billboard, with *Wind Of Change* achieving No.4 and *Send Me An Angel* No.44. Curiously, *Wind Of Change* represents the band's only certification in the UK as a single, going silver, and same for the full album: Crazy World garnered the band its only UK award, again at silver, for sales of 60,000 units.

But dissension was in the ranks. "In the '80s, before *Wind Of Change*, we were five equal people, in the band," laments Herman. "It was very democratic. Anybody could bring anything. Then *Wind Of Change* came, and then Klaus, of course, turned around and said, 'I wrote the biggest hit for you guys. So from now on I will write the songs.' He told me, I don't need you anymore. I will write the songs from now on, because I have a big publishing offer, and I don't want to share that money. I will put that money in my pocket alone. So then I knew from that moment I was out, and it was just a question of time. After that I had no more creativity. I had nothing to do in that band anymore."

Nor did Francis Buchholz, who had been replaced by Ralph Rieckermann, a consummate musician who had done session work for Kingdom Come, as well as coming close to a deal with his progressive rock act Beyond The Blind.

"I think mostly, it was through a connection," says Ralph on joining the band. "I was already living in LA, and a friend of mine that I used to hang out with called me up and said, the bass player Francis got fired, and they need someone. I look a little bit like Francis. Like similar eyes, similar whatever. I was born in Hamburg, born and raised in the area which is like 40 miles away from Hannover, which is where they're from. I lived in the states, and I was extremely good. I was an extremely good bass player back in those days. I mean I just practiced eight hours a day. That's all I did. I came to the states with that American dream to play in one of those really big famous bands, and I liked to practice all day long. It's like shredding; I can pretty much play everything. When I met the guys, I think, not only did we have an immediate chemistry because we came from the same background, where we were born, but I lived in the states, so already had a little bit of a worldly feel to my personality, I guess. But also, Francis wasn't really a musician. He was more like a financial guy. He was an okay bass player, but you know, he wasn't like a real musician's musician, you know what I'm saying? I was 100% musician. When I came in, I don't think they ever really heard someone play bass the way I played, because I was doing all this super-fast, like slapping and fretless, and played all this classical music. I think that triggered something in all of them. Plus, like I said, we had a pretty good chemistry right from the get-go. Yeah, a little bit of luck probably paved the way a bit too."

Plus there was the LA connection. "Yes, Herman lived in LA, like I think maybe eight to ten years before I joined the band, for a while. I actually moved back to Germany after I joined. Well, first I lived in hotels for about two years, because we were travelling so much, and then I moved back to Germany for about two-and-a-half years, and I didn't like it very much. I wanted to buy a house, so I bought a house in the Hollywood Hills, and I told the guys, I said, 'What do you think if I moved back to LA?' They said, 'Well, it doesn't matter where you live, because we are constantly all over the world anyway.' I said, 'I agree,' so I moved back."

Face The Heat, issued September 21st, 1993, was recorded where Crazy World was supposed to happen, namely Little Mountain Studios in Vancouver, and upon release, it was interesting to see Herman out doing press for the album, putting on a brave face despite his growing dissatisfaction with his place in the band.

"Just being heavy is exactly what we wanted to do because we decided not to retire into ballad land," said Herman, speaking with Canadian rock media legend Drew Masters. "There's no point doing *Wind Of Change* part two—that makes no sense. *Wind Of Change* was a good thing because it was a big hit, but after that, you want to go on. We came into the studio with Bruce, and he said, 'What do you guys want to do? Do you want to do it like always, or do you want to take some risks?' We said, 'We want to go back to the roots, where we come from, another Blackout album, or another Love At First Sting. Kick ass rock 'n' roll. We want to show the kids out there that we are still there. We started to ask, 'What are we going to do here? We gonna play this the safe way and write eight ballads and make sure that we get into the commercial radio stations?' We said, 'Fuck this! Let's make ourselves happy.' We were very, very selfish this time with this music. This is what we love—it's our heart and soul. If it fucks us up, good—and if it doesn't, fucking good too! We are happy with the music, and that's the most important thing."

"It means nothing else than face the problem," continues Herman, asked for any deep meaning behind the title of the album. "There's no point in putting your head into the sand and pretending that nothing out there happens. The album is full of attitude. We have a lot of heavy things going on in the world, and I think we're at the age now where we have to write about this and tell people out there. There's no point in writing a song about a girl who's 16 years old that, at midnight, you hold her hand and give her a kiss, you know? Kids don't want to hear that shit anymore. This time we really emphasized our point of view."

"About two years ago we were not happy with our business situation," says Herman, happy to go in to what happened around the split with Francis. "Our accountant made some really wrong suggestions for a tax write-offs, so we fired the guy. Francis was always the man in our band who made the business, while the four of us made the creative part. So when we said, 'Look, we're gonna fire the accountant,' he spoke to the accountant and not the band! Until this day, I don't know why. That's all I can tell you—it smells very strong. There's still a lot of money missing, and the courts in Germany are looking into it, so it will be a couple of years before the whole fucking mess is clear. But I think with Ralph Rieckermann, we found a very fine replacement. It's sad that we had to lose our bass player after 18 years, but the saddest thing for me was to trust him completely for all these years and then find out that maybe, business-wise, some things don't always work out the way they should."

The debacle wound up getting the band in major tax trouble back in Germany. "The press was so strong against us, that it forced us to come out," explained Rudolf. "Every day it was in the news so we had to fight back. Our former business manager, who we had to fire, was building up his case in the press, and to our surprise, Francis sided with him and gave up his career. It was very important for us to stay strong."

Speaking years later, Herman insists that the problem surrounding Francis and the band's finances was the first time there had ever been any real strife in the Scorpions.

"Yes, well, I'd say, tension only occurred really in 1992, in the summer. We suddenly realised that a lot of money was missing. Francis was our CEO, in the company together with our accountant, and we put all our money at that time in a trust account in Lichtenstein, so it stayed in Europe. This money is missing to this day. We've been going to court for now for 15 years, and the case is still not solved. Francis says he never took anything, the accountant either."

"But Francis was a friend. At least we thought this. He was our CEO.

None of us wanted to do the daily paperwork, the daily business. He was in the office every day five, six hours, doing all this together with the accountant. So we were glad that he did it, you know. So we said okay, for that, we can take a person in the band who's not as musically strong as the other four. It worked good. As you can hear, nobody ever complained about the bass. But the bass player, otherwise, he made his job, he made it solid, nothing too fancy, it was okay. In my opinion anyway, it's not how good you are. The chemistry in a band has to be spot-on. Imagine the Rolling Stones without Charlie Watts. Charlie is not the greatest drummer in the world, but I cannot imagine this without Charlie. As you can see, from the moment the band restructured, the chemistry, the band usually is finished. That happened to AC/DC, that happened to Aerosmith, it happened to the Scorpions. Why do you think, on the last tour, 1000 people came? I can tell you why that is. First of all, the last three albums were terrible, they were shitty, real shitty, and then nobody comes anymore (note: this conversation took place in 2006). They ruined everything in three albums. It becomes very hard to convince people, hey, now you're going to get a good album. People don't even listen to it anymore. That is the problem."

The missing money issue aside, I asked Herman if the band managed to make good investments for themselves, along the way. "Well, yes, course. Actually, I did wise investments. For example, for me, in 1985, the accountant says, 'You're going to have to invest your money into East Germany, because we can buy there, houses are very cheap, and you can rent the house, with each house with ten apartments inside, yeah?' Then when the wall came down in '89, I bought six apartments in Leipzig. Each apartment cost about $200,000. In the year 1992, I had to sell these apartments for $50,000 each, just to give you the idea of the great investment of my accountant. That was one investment he did. It was my investment he did. Then the next investment was an investment in Internet companies. I must've spent $2 million there, because the biggest business in the world, anybody tripled and ten-folded his money in a short period of time. Unfortunately, my money, from everything my accountant invested, all those companies went bankrupt. If I would've not written all those songs for the Scorpions, and if we wouldn't have a good back catalogue, I would be in serious problems now. I mean, the back catalogue still does, every year, between $50,000 and $100,000, and the same with writing, you know. I wrote about 35 songs, and I can see *Rock You Like A Hurricane* is still played worldwide all the time. So that is a good thing."

And the rest of the guys? "Klaus is a very, very rich man. He made millions of dollars with *Wind Of Change*, and he's the sole writer there. Also in those years, he made lots of money with Ford, for car advertisements, where they used the song at the time. Then the song was

No.1 in 20 countries worldwide. Plus the record sold at the time, eight million copies, and Klaus is not a guy who spends any money. So he's worth millions. Rudolf must be the same. Matthias, he never wrote anything, but he still has a very good income from the road, and the other two are just paid salaries."

"The decision was half mine, half the band's," begins Buchholz on his break with the band, in an interview with the author years after the fact. "We could not go on like that anymore. Why did I leave? Four years before I left Scorpions, we booked into a fantastic stadium tour in the USA. Van Halen was headlining and we played directly before them at about eight o'clock in the evening, which was a very good spot to have. Metallica played before us. We had about 30 shows with an average attendance of about 30,000 fans per show. That was absolutely great."

"But directly after the beginning of this tour, it was decided that we would fire our New York-based management, CCC. While everybody was having a great time at the hotel pools during times off, I spent my time on the phone talking to Dick Asher, who was president of PolyGram Records—which is Universal Records today—in New York. Our album Savage Amusement had just been released and thousands of promotional activities had to be coordinated between the New York record company and us. I realised that we were in desperate need of a professional American management again. Asher suggested that Doc McGhee—being the Bon Jovi manager at that time—would help out with the management of the Scorpions. Asher gave me a phone number and I talked to Doc explaining the situation. I invited him to fly in from his golf training in Canada. The other guys in the band liked him, we all shook hands and everything worked out smoothly in the following time."

"For the next album, Crazy World, we did not continue our ten to 15-year-long relationship with our producer Dieter Dierks. Because my relationship with Dierks was not absolutely great, that split was okay with me. But just after the Crazy World tour, the rest of the band suddenly decided to fire our lawyers and tax advisers, even though nobody—except me—had really cared about all these day-to-day business affairs. In other words, nobody really seemed to understand how important a working business structure is for an international touring band. I was not willing to change everything around again. I was not willing to have chaos in the middle of an examination done by our German tax authorities, which took place at that time. I rather wanted to spend my time being musically creative and I needed time for my family. It did not make sense to me to fire people who had done their best. But new people were brought in: an additional manager to McGhee, a new lawyer and a new tax consulting company."

"You must know, I am a team player and I like to stick with people who are delivering high quality work," continues Francis. "Consequently I was confronted with the question either to accept these new, and in the music industry, yet quite inexperienced people, whom the band wanted, or to leave. On top of it, I felt that some of these new people were definitely not on my wavelength. They did not seem to fit my ambitious expectations. The decision was not easy. But, being a father to a little boy already, I became the father of twin girls at that time. A life out of a suitcase is not really compatible with my understanding of a healthy family life. Sometimes you've got to follow your heart."

"By then, a lot of internal problems had developed in the Scorpions," recalls David Krebs, who says the problems with Francis originated much earlier. "There was a very divisive element. There was a German accountant who was their business manager, who definitely saw himself as being the one who should be calling the shots, when he knew nothing. There was a tremendous amount of divisiveness. In the end, what really happened is, the bass player and the accountant partnered, and were thrown out. There are still lawsuits going on about it. From what, you know, once... it's like Aerosmith was cut off by heroin, Nugent was cut off by his divorce, and the Scorpions were cut off by this business manager. AC/DC, I mean, I'm a big Bon Scott fan. I like Brian Johnson, but I think it's just not the same. So there's another life that was cut one way or the other. So there are all sorts of things that happen that certainly have an effect upon your writing ability. It shows up in your lyrics. There were some great songs on Savage Amusement, *Rhythm Of Love* and a couple of other ones, but I don't think it was as strong as Love At First Sting, which was my favourite, along with our first one together, Lovedrive."

In fact, says Krebs, the root of the split with Francis might go all the way back to the Jimmy Bain incident circa Love At First Sting. "I was there, or I went there," recalls Krebs, speaking of Sweden. "I'm the manager, I'm supposed to know everything, right? So first thing, I get a call, saying (laughs)—and Bobby Rondinelli was a friend of mine from before—but there's a call saying, well, you know, we're in Sweden, and we're recording with Jimmy Bain and Bobby Rondinelli.' Now, as the manager, I'm now finding out these guys have replaced two of their five players and I have no idea?! I'm not sure if it was real or a warning. It was certainly a warning. To those guys. I always thought it was great that they were all German, but that's not true anymore, in terms of who they tour with now—there's a Polish guy and there's an American guy. But at least at that point I decided to bring this guy, Olaf Schroter in as my co-manager. I said, if I'm in New York and they're in Germany, and they're making moves, and I'm finding out after, there's no way we can deal with this. I don't remember much more about that. In many ways—and I've said this many times over the years—I think the Scorpions, in handling Francis Buchholz that way and embarrassing him, *to the world*, turned him against them. At the end, that's why, I think, he screwed them with the business manager."

As for the increasing amount of time (and times) Scorpions seemed to be dropping off the map, Herman explains that, "We were on tour for 18 months, and after that tour nobody wanted to see each other for about two or three months—we all wanted to go back to the families, relax and take it easy. But that was not possible because then the whole shit started with Francis, and we were heavily involved with the tax people, tax fraud. It kept us busy for about six months and then after that, we all finally settled down a little bit and started to write songs. Six months later we played our songs to each other, and then we went into pre-production at Rudolf's house. We must have had about 30 songs we sent to Bruce Fairbairn, and he picked 14 songs which he liked. Then we said, 'Okay, we'll come and record those 14 songs in your studio in Vancouver.' So in February 1993, we went over to Vancouver and laid the tracks in one week—there were some overdubs on the vocals and some neat guitar stuff, but it was basically the first or second take. We wanted to have it rough and tough—to have the live energy on tape. People always come to us and say, 'You guys play live so great, with so much energy, but why isn't it on the record?' So Bruce said, 'Look, play the songs three times— if you don't have it after three times, then it's not happening anymore.' So we played it rough, kept the energy, and it sounds good. It was like in the old days when the five of us would be in one room standing in a circle and then it was, 'One, two, three, four,' and here goes the song. To me, that's the only way to do records."

"In the '80s, the Mutt Lange sound was very big, and many producers tried hard to get the ultimate clean production," Rudolf told Rip's Robyn Doreian, on the press trail for Face The Heat. "After a while, the music is perfect, but nothing comes across. From hearing bands like Pearl Jam and listening to early Guns N' Roses, we decided it was time to go back and play from the heart. I've tried to play a lot looser and not worry so much about perfection. Out of the 30 songs we had written, Bruce picked those with a harder edge, and we have tried to make things a little rougher by not using overdubs."

"We are the rock, and they are the waves!" continues Schenker, asked where Scorpions fit in a world gone grunge. "Only a few of these new sounds will stand the test of time. It's important that we keep our sound and message the same as we always have. During the Gulf War, we were doing an American tour, and the whole business was in bad shape. Acts like David Lee Roth and Cinderella had great difficulty, but because of our reputation as a strong live band, we had no problems. We proved with the last album we have a worldwide appeal and message. These bands keep it interesting, as the music scene changes year-to-year. It has changed so much since we first started. Heavy rock then was more about, 'Let's have fun, get some girls and drive fast cars.' The songs had a good riff and a good melody. These days, bands like Pearl Jam have more of a message to say to the world. They are reflecting what is going on. After this album, we feel there will be a lot of young fan surprised by what we have done. A lot of people will assume that we are going to go the safe way with a commercial, big ballad kind of thing. We said, 'Shit, no!' We are a rock band, and they're going to get it right in their face!'"

"We rehearsed in the studio, all five of us in the same room," said Matthias, to Jon Sutherland. "We would do three or four takes and keep the best one. As a musician, you need to feel like you're performing and have people around. I know I like it better."

"After Crazy World, Bruce Fairbairn, of course, was overwhelmed by the success and now wanted to definitely to produce us," explains Rarebell, here with about 15 years of hindsight. "As you can imagine. So we all, Klaus and myself, flew out to Vancouver, and there we started to write. So we know Vancouver, we know Canada, and we were very glad to be back there with Bruce, and a characteristic on this album is that Bruce actually asked us, before, 'What do you guys want to do? Do you want to do a full album of *Wind Of Change*, go the safe way, make another commercial ballad, or do you want to make a rock album?' Of course, we decided to make a rock album, which became a flop, with only 1.8 million sales, where before it was eight million. Nowadays, this would be a success. Everybody would love to have these numbers. Then, you know, our first single was *Alien Nation*, which was definitely nothing for radio. It was heavy as shit, as you know, a really heavy song. Imagine, *Alien Nation* after *Wind Of Change*. Now, which radio station plays that? Zero, none. I said, we can't do this; let's give them *Under The Same Sun*, so they could play us at least. But *Alien Nation*... exactly what happens with radio, you listen to the song for five beats, and, 'No way, we can't play this; this is much too heavy for us.'

Alien Nation is indeed a total rocker, slow, doomy, malevolently Germanic even. "Well, *Alien Nation* was a pretty heavy song, and again, it had a very good groove to it," reflects Rieckermann. "That was actually a song that I refused to play on (laughs). Being my first record, because the drums didn't sound right. Because there was something wrong in the way Herman was playing it. But I literally came into the studio saying, 'Sorry, guys, I'm not going to play on this song, because it's just not right.' I was like, fuck, man, and I just got hired, and now I'm going to get fired again because I got too big of a mouth here. And Bruce Fairbairn called me aside and said, 'You know what? You're right. We're actually going to do this with electronic drums.' So he completely re-recorded the drums electronically; he had a programmer come in. So *Alien Nation* is completely 100% programmed drums, no live playing on it. Then I came in and played the bass on it, and that was pretty much the most successful song that record had."

"Bruce Fairbairn was trying with Face The Heat also to create a new sound," continues Ralph. "He said, 'Listen guys, you guys have been doing the same stuff for years and years and years, and it worked, but you know, really big bands like U2, Madonna, Michael Jackson... you take anybody who is really big and really famous, trendsetters, every time they have something new out, not only do they reinvent themselves with a passion, they have different clothing, different stages, they have completely different sound.' Just look at U2 when they came out with that album Achtung Baby. It was the most successful, but it was completely different from anything that they had done before. A lot of people in heavy rock, like in the rock world, they don't really do that. They keep sticking to the same clothes, the same style, the same poses, and it's just like, to me, it's a little bit pathetic, to be honest."

Already at track one, the seeds were being sown for Herman Rarebell to be the next member of the classic Scorpions line-up to exit stage left, although Herman indicates that it has more to do with his being frozen out of the songwriting.

"It actually started with *Alien Nation*," explains Ralph, "because honestly, he wasn't able to play it (sings that heavy military part), and it wasn't right, and like I said, I refused to play on it, and the rest of band was really frustrated. Everybody was really frustrated with it. So he started noticing that he was just not... not so much into drumming as he used to be, back in the day. He had some other interests. But yeah, in interviews, he says a lot, he wanted to be a record executive or whatever. But I think more like the real truth is that he kind of lost the interest. I actually set him up with one of the best drum teachers in Germany, that he took drum lessons from. But he didn't really do much, because he wasn't really getting into it. So he lost interest, and like I said, not only in composing, but also in playing. You had to constantly reinvent yourself. You have to practice so you can keep up-to-date; you have to be good on your instrument. Otherwise you start lagging. You fall behind. But I know he took a few drum lessons. It worked out a little bit, but for some reason, he just lost interest, and there was too much arguing about how Herman played drums. So I think he decided that he was going to go another route. And he started his company in Monaco there."

Herman also was somewhat the cause of the band having to mix Face The Heat way off in Amsterdam. "We had to make a decision to mix there or in Los Angeles," says Rudolf. "Herman refused to go to America, as there was supposed to be an enormous earthquake on May 8th. Michael (Schenker) went so far as to move down to Arizona because of the danger.

His reasoning was that after it happened, the beach would be in Phoenix. May 8th has come and gone without incident. The earthquake never happened. Herman turned to me the other day and said, 'Let me give you some advice. Don't believe what anyone tells you anymore.'"

Second track on the record, *No Pain No Gain* continues in the ill-advised lead-off single's thumping vein, Bruce adding some interesting production touches behind the verse. In fact, the production is powerful, bright, welling up from the drums, corporate to be sure, but not stripped of life like Savage Amusement. *Someone To Touch* is pure meat and potatoes party rock, and then it's into *Under The Same Sun*, a blatant attempt at a reprise of *Wind Of Change*'s worldwide embrace. It's the third of four tracks on the album to include a writing credit for Mark Hudson, song doctor.

"Mark Hudson, who wrote *Under The Same Sun*, he's an old friend of the Aerosmith guys," says Herman. "He wrote a lot of stuff also with Jimmy and Bryan Adams. Klaus and myself, we flew out to LA, we went to Mark's house and we wrote the song in one night (laughs), and then next day we flew back again, or the day after, and we said, 'Yeah, now we have song number one. This is a Mark Hudson song.' And everybody is sitting there with a long face saying, 'Yeah, that's all?! You come back after three or four days. This is not a smash.' But the producer, Bruce, liked the song, so in the end it came on the album."

Still, despite the presence of Mark Hudson on some of the record, the theme here, says Herman, is that the band was writing the songs themselves. "Yes, well, already, by Face The Heat, Klaus didn't want to write anymore with Jimmy Vallance, who was a great writer, so he went to Bruce Fairbairn with everything we had, and we did those songs. I think, you know, Bruce was biting his nails by then. But when we came to Jimmy the second time, the songs were already written, and we just said to Jimmy, 'Do you find everything okay?' 'Yeah, I find it okay.' So Bruce didn't have anything to complain about, so we could go in the direction of recording."

"The guy was one of the best producers I've ever worked with," says Ralph, with regards to Bruce Fairbairn. "Other than David Foster, who I think is a really talented guy. You know, we only did one song with him, *When You Came Into My Life*. But Bruce Fairbairn was a fantastic guy, because he really saw the art in music. Like I said, he was more like a trendsetter, wanted change. But another problem with the band was that they constantly were chasing producers that already had success, that were big time. Like Bruce Fairbairn. Like David Foster, and they had David Foster because they thought, oh, we need another *Wind Of Change*. Who can produce another *Wind Of Change*, like, who is out there that can create us another huge hit song? So they thought, we found the biggest hip producer in the world, which is David Foster, clearly. But I think that's the wrong way to go. I think you should deal more with young, hungry guys who haven't really done that much, but who are hungry to do something new that nobody has done before. You know what I'm saying? That was my vision, my perspective. That's what I would've liked to do, but they were always like, oh, no, no, we have to work together with people who are really, really successful, who had this big credit line. Some of these guys are like a little bit washed-up. To them, they don't really care. They already have the success; they already have $100 million in their account. They don't give a shit."

Fully the next five songs in a row were written by Rudolf and Klaus. *Unholy Alliance* is a frustratingly unsatisfying funky rock. *Woman*, it would be condescending to call it a power ballad, because it isn't. This was like a lumbering bluesy hard rock the sort of which Scorpions rarely addressed. The track featured a number of interesting guitar textures as well as keyboards designed to sound like a string section.

"The blues is a music that gets you emotionally, almost immediately," notes Matthias, really, the prime bringer of the blues to Scorpions, not that there's much of it. "To me it's like this: if you have a melody for a singer, it might not be a bluesy melody, but the end, the phrasing, the way he ends the melody gives it a blues touch. Like for example, I've seen Paul Rodgers sing with Queen, the stuff from Freddie Mercury. Freddie Mercury is not blues, but Paul Rodgers is very much, and he sings the same melody, but the way he gives it the blending and colouring, he makes it bluesy, and to me that's much nicer because I just like it. I think it happens subconsciously or automatically. I'm really not planning on anything blues, especially the standard… the blues as you know it. It's just something different. It's in a different dimension and it goes into whatever it is. Rock music is blues-based, I think, most of it. There's a classical influence for certain people, but they have to force that in more or less. Blues is always there, a little bit. Any Hendrix tune is blues—any. That's what he said, always. I'm just playing blues different, and therefore it's an immediate way to get emotions across. That's why I like it."

Hate To Be Nice was a cloying type of glam experiment with a conversational vocal from Klaus and a bad hair metal chorus. *Taxman Woman* was simply a different variety of hair metal, as was *Ship Of Fools*, although this one had some bite, as well, benefitting from the big beat of Herman in conjunction with Fairbairn's shiny yet muscular production job. Of note, Fairbairn would be dead six years later, May 17th, 1999, cause of death unknown. His body was discovered by Yes singer Jon Anderson who had just finished up Fairbairn-led sessions on the band's next album, The Ladder.

Nightmare Avenue is the album's hidden gem, this Matthias Jabs track hitting that *Radar Love/Kickstart My Heart* zone thanks to a verse that hangs on military snare. After this, it's onto the second power ballad on the album, *Lonely Nights* being your typical mournful slog, typical Klaus lyric, typically Schenker frame.

"Klaus is a very nice guy, but the real machine in the band is Rudolf," figures Rieckermann, concerning his two bosses. "Rudolf is the real rocker. I mean, he's the one that has always driven everything. He's like an unstoppable workaholic, amazing personality, like a real true musician, kind of like... he just doesn't stop. Also, his lifestyle, Rudolf is a very interesting, colourful and I would say almost modern lifestyle; he's very open to everything. Klaus, Klaus is a great person, but has a little bit different of an approach. He's a little more family-orientated? There's nothing wrong with that, but all the years I've ever been in the band, I've never seen Klaus wasted, I've never seen him do any drugs, I've never seen him with another woman, I've never seen him go left field, which almost every singer you know of in the rock world... I mean, if you look at Steven Tyler or any other big rock singer, they are like out-of-control, right? Some of these guys are just crazy. They're like, they do drugs, they fuck around, they live rock 'n' roll. They write about it, just like the best example: Jim Morrison. I mean, every single word that ever came out of Jim Morrison's mouth was something that he actually really lived. Like serious. People like Oliver Stone decide to make a movie about him, because he was true art, he was living art."

As for whether they had big egos, especially concerning muscling in on writing credits, Ralph says, "Of course! Every musician has egos about writing music. Especially when you've written something like *Wind Of Change*. You know, you want to do it again. But the question is, can you? Do you have, not only the skills... maybe you have the skills, but do you have a story to tell that is as deep and as important as *Wind Of Change* was? Rudolf, I mean, how many songs has he written? He's done like hundreds and hundreds of songs for years. Like 40 years, he's written one great song after another, but how long can you keep doing this? How long can you keep it up? You know, with the same technique. Because he always writes the same way."

"Mostly those visions came from the producers that we worked with," answers Ralph, asked if the band ever expressed an overall strategy for a record they were about to make. "The band was always kind of like...well, there were different opinions in the band. Rudolf always wanted to go straight rock. Klaus was always leaning more towards pop and ballads, and Matthias was somewhere in the middle. My vision, I already told you about it. But my vision wasn't really... Nobody would really listen to me very much. I was always like, 'Oh yeah, the new guy, what do you know?' Kind of like that."

"Matthias, you know, Matthias is a very talented guitar player, but he's not really a songwriter," says Rieckermann, asked about how much Jabs was listened to. "He wrote some interesting stuff, but I think that kind of bothered Matthias as well. Because he had some really good stuff as well, but I think because Klaus and Rudolf were the main songwriters in the band, that's kind of what they wanted. They wanted to be the ones that come up with the ideas, they are the engines of the band. They never said it. That was never really said in words, but you could see it. You know what I'm saying? There's nothing wrong with that. It's just like John Lennon and McCartney and the Beatles. I mean, it was a band, you know. Nobody had egos in the Beatles—Lennon and McCartney: they had the chemistry, they were the ones writing the music. They were the ones that kind of made the Beatles what the Beatles were. Do any of the other Scorpions guys say anything similar to what I do? Because, you know, in all my years, another thing, every time they do an interview, they are always pretty much saying the same thing. That's another thing that bothered me. I mean I was like, 'Guys, come on, be honest. Say what you really want to say. Don't always say the same blah blah blah.' All the interviews I've heard it's always the same stuff that comes out of their mouths."

There were still a few tricks up the collective sleeve concerning Face The Heat. First, the US edition of the album housed a hidden track, a cover of Del Shannon's *(Marie's The Name) His Latest Flame*, an amusing old rock 'n' roll cover, a rare gesture in this direction for the band, but quite nice. The Japanese version of the album included a dark acoustic ballad about child abuse called *Daddy's Girl*, plus *Kami O Shin Juru*, a similarly unplugged ballad featuring fretless bass. The European edition contains the same two tracks, although *Kami O Shin Juru* is re-titled *Destin*, with the lyrics changed within the chorus from Japanese to French (the rest of the song is in English).

As well, the *Alien Nation* maxi-single included a non-LP b-side called *Rubber Fucker*, an interesting, somewhat flippant song wedged between punk, glam and metal. Similarly, the *Under The Sun* maxi-single includes a non-LP track called *Partners In Crime*, the only song from this extras batch that is a full band production rock song, rendered with the expensive knob job found on Face The Heat. Essentially, the song is a hard-hitting, thumping melodic rock song, hair metal in the simplified vernacular, but elevated with some nice guitar textures.

You could also get the record on vinyl. "I tell you one thing, I was very much behind it and I forced the issue on Face The Heat," says Rudolf, when I asked him about the beloved format in 1999. "After Face The Heat, we went to a different record company, and then somehow I didn't force it so much anymore. I believe in vinyl because I know the sound is much better. But there aren't many people who want to eat gourmet foods. They'd rather eat fast food. But as long as you record in digital, there is no point. We recorded Face The Heat in analogue. If you record in analogue and you master in analogue, you can fill the spaces. Once you cut the whole thing out and you start with digital, in mastering or whatever you do, then you've already lost some of the sound and there's no need to release it on vinyl. It's useless. Because vinyl is only important if you record in analogue. If you master in analogue you can press it on vinyl, then it's good. The rest is bullshit."

All told, Face The Heat was the product of a band grasping at straws, forced into the proverbial "writing songs that didn't need to be written" zone, disconcerting, given that the band wasn't exactly cranking out the albums, having now made only four in nine years. To be sure, there's a sense that the band's golden run had now been ended, in conjunction with the fudging of the classic line-up, namely Francis gone and Ralph in. Or was it, as Rarebell contends, that he personally wasn't in on the songwriting anymore? Blame might be placed on Fairbairn as well, given his deep involvement in all things corporate rock, including most pointedly his ties to outside songwriters, the kiss of death for a band's credibility, commercial success notwithstanding.

Despite floating three singles from the album in various territories, namely *Alien Nation, Woman* and *Under The Same Sun*, the album didn't reach certification levels in the US, although Scorpions-loyal France sent it to gold, for sales of over 100,000 units. Touring for the album was limited as well, the band beginning in Athens on September 14th of '93 and making the rounds of continental Europe through November 10th, with Duff McKagan in tow, the Guns N' Roses bassist promoting his Believe In Me solo album. Then it was a couple of dates in Japan before alighting upon America, King's X as support, followed by Mexico and South America and then back into the US, support on the second leg coming from The Poor.

The Face The Heat tour coughed up a relatively inconsequential live album issued in April of '95 called Live Bites, which also contained two studio bonus tracks on its international release, three on the US. "I remember those songs," says Ralph, bassist on all included live tracks save for two, *Rhythm Of Love* and *Living For Tomorrow*. "I don't really remember when we did them, but I think we did them in Rudolf's studio, Scorpio, which was in Rudolf's basement, where Rudolf lives. And I mean, I don't know if it's a real studio. It's mainly like half homemade, half professional studio. It has some really professional equipment, but the rooms are not like professionally soundproofed studio rooms."

Oldest tracks on the album (track list slightly varies between the two issues) are a strange trio of *In Trance, Is There Anybody There?* and *When The Smoke Is Going Down*, with the rest being from Savage Amusement or newer. The performances hail from shows in Leningrad, San Francisco,

Mexico, Munich and Berlin, and all told, it's a better sounding record than the harsh World Wide Live. There's one composed, titled, guitar solo called *Concerto In V*, with additional wrinkles coming with the sing-along segments in *Crazy World* and *Wind Of Change*. Of the studio tracks, *Heroes Don't Cry* is a plush acoustic ballad, produced by Keith Olsen and recorded at Goodnight LA and Scorpio. *Edge Of Time* is a kind of funky hard rocker with modern rock production, produced by the band alone, and recorded at Scorpio. Finally, *White Dove* is actually a cover from Hungarian prog band Omega, although, nonetheless a conventional acoustic ballad; this one was recorded at Wisseloord, Hilversum, The Netherlands.

"Since we have 14 studio albums out, we want to take maybe two or three songs from each album," noted Herman at the time, on what to expect on the Face The Heat tour. "Obviously, we're gonna play the classics like *Rock You Like A Hurricane*, *Bad Boys Running Wild*, *Big City Nights*, *Still Loving You* and *Wind Of Change*. We wouldn't leave out those songs as people would probably kill us. But we'll be playing songs from the new album and in the middle, we would like to do an acoustic set because we have so many acoustic songs. We'll play *When The Smoke Is Going Down*, which is a very old song, and then we'll play *Always Somewhere* and then we'll introduce an acoustic version of *Under The Same Sun*. From there we go into *Holiday* and now there may be a chance that we might take Michael Schenker as a special guest on the road with us, and have him come out and play an acoustic set. Michael Schenker just made a very nice acoustic album, so maybe he can play one or two songs from his new album. That will be the first time he's been with us since 1979. We look forward very much to the tour and playing. It gets a bit boring when you sit in the studio and sit at home for so long, but it was necessary this time for us to find ourselves again. If you're on the road for 18 months, you have to have a break; otherwise you go nuts."

As esteemed journo Jon Sutherland writes, this indeed did happen as planned: "The European shows will probably be paced differently than what will appear in America. The reason? Michael Schenker. The first half-dozen songs built up steam, and the newer ones were received warmly. 'They didn't know the words yet,' Herman Rarebell would say later, 'but they knew the melodies and sang along whatever they thought were the words!' In the middle of the show, the stage was quickly sized down. Matthias Jabs sat on a stool at stage left, Rudy Schenker on the right. Side-by-side behind them were Herman Rarebell and Ralph Rieckermann. Herman was playing a small drum kit acoustically with brushes and Ralph was playing a medium-sized stand-up bass. In the centre, Klaus Meine said, 'Feels like a family reunion tonight. Would you welcome please Michael Schenker!' It was goose-bump central, and the eyes of the entire audience seemed to widen in excitement. As they sat on their stools, the Scorpions did what they do as good as anybody, played heartfelt romantic ballads. They reached into the past for *Always Somewhere* and introduced the present with *Under The Same Sun*, before Michael was given the spotlight for his brilliant instrumental *Positive Forward* off his Thank You album. When Rudolf started playing the opening chords to *Holiday*, it was absolute magic."

"A major part of it, I feel, is that we are like a family," continues Rarebell, asked what keeps him and the guys going. "There's nothing that we don't know about each other. When we were younger, we tried to change each other constantly, but now we realise that we can't change each other anymore. We're just the way we are. You know, when I go out and I go crazy, they don't even say anything anymore. They just go to the hotel and pay for the fucking damage (laughs). In the old days, everyone was screaming. Nowadays, when they hear a noise at 4:30 in the morning, Rudolf goes and starts packing, because he knows the manager from the hotel will be banging and saying, 'You guys are out of here—immediately' (laughs). There are certain things in characters and personalities of people that you cannot change anymore after all those years. We're all men over 40 now; we lived life, we still do, and we know what we want. So when we are together, we are friendly, we're very nice to each other because there's no point. We went through all the bad years, so why shouldn't we enjoyed the good years?"

"As long as people want to hear good music, and as long as we come up with good music, then we go on," asserts Herman. "If we feel we're fucking up, and we don't get any better, and people don't come to our shows anymore and don't buy our albums anymore, then it's time to stop. We are more or less kind of a legend nowadays, and our shows are now events—we find sometimes we have two generations seeing us. Age is in your head. We've never grown up. We're all kids still. We've been in this business for 20 years now. We've been all around the world 20 times, and we still play our music. That's all we care about. If people don't want to hear us or see us anymore, we'll probably just play for ourselves in the basement (laughs). If we had to play those songs every night in the rehearsal room, I'd fucking puke, you know, because I'd be dead bored after a while. But believe it or not, when you go out even after playing *Still Loving You* 500 times, and you see people crying and people's hair standing up, and people kissing each other and being happy, then I have a great feeling for the song. It's the same for *Rock You Like A Hurricane*— we see them out there going nuts, throwing their hats in the air, stomping their feet and going crazy, and then that turns us on again. Plus I think we still have the feeling musically that we haven't reached our top yet."

"You know, when I was in the band, yes, I experienced some excesses," laughs Rieckermann, offering some reflections from being on the road with the band. "But to be honest, never really with Klaus. Like I say, yeah, he was partying sometimes, but he never really got out of control. There were always boundaries for him. It reflects a little bit in his lyrics. When you listen to the lyrics that he writes, you know, there's not really much dirt in it, you know what I'm saying? Not a lot of sleaziness, not a lot of dirt, and in the end, that's what rock music is about. When people say sex, drugs and rock 'n' roll, there's a reason for that. Herman? The complete opposite. Herman was the biggest sleazeball, rock 'n' roll-like sex addict that I ever met in my life. And that's the reason why Herman actually wrote most of the lyrics back in the days, like *Rock You Like A Hurricane* and all the successful crazy-ass songs. Herman wrote the lyrics."

"The tours... I mean, Scorpions was a grand live band. The tours were always great. Every single concert rocked and it was fantastic. I had a blast being on tour; I loved being on tour. That was my favourite part. Because Scorpions is like... after I left the band, I was lucky enough to see the band a couple of times from the audience view, which I'd never done before. I didn't do that before I joined the band, because I never was a big fan of the band before I joined. I get a lot of people coming up to me going, 'Oh, Ralph Rieckermann, wow, you must've been a huge fan of the band,' blah blah blah, whatever. It's like sorry, I wasn't. Actually, I knew the band existed and I'd heard the music, but I couldn't say that I'd ever been to a concert or even bought a record."

Three early promotional photos; note the brief six-man lineup, the presence of a very young Michael Schenker and Klaus with a moustache!

free dom

PROGRESSIV ELECTRONIC ROCK

FESTIVAL LANGELSHEIM 29.30.31.5.71

Colosseum
Family
Status Quo
Brinsley Schwarz Steamhammer
Ashton,Gardner,Dyke & Co New Abraham Group
Ekseption Sam Apple Pie
Man Nektar
Can Bobbeys Children
Frumpy Clouds
Bronco Scorpions
Faces Murphy Blend
Eloy Fashion
Mythos u. v. a.

Piccadilly
presents
The Scorpions in Concert
eine der besten Bands der deutschen Rock scene,
bekannt durch ihre LP „Lonesome Crow"
Am Freitag, dem 16. 2. 1973
Beginn: 20.30 Uhr
Eintritt: 5.— DM
Piccadilly, Karlsruhe, Hebelstraße 1, Nähe Marktplatz

SCORPIONS

rock on stage

Fr. 6.2. 19⁰⁰ Uhr
1976
Glashalle
neben der Niedersachsenhalle

SPECIAL GUESTS **ARGOS**

EINTRITT 5.-

STADTSCHULRAT HANNOVER

NEW ALBUM: IN TRANCE - RCA (PPL 1-4128/26.21575 AS - STEREO)

Rudolf Schenker and Francis Buchholz, Oklahoma 1980. (*Richard Galbraith*)

Klaus Meine and a partially obscured Matthias Jabs. (*Richard Galbraith*)

Matthias Jabs conquers California on 1980's *Animal Magnetism* tour; Jabs represents within the band a presence that helped the band create a sound tailor-made for US tastes. (*Kevin Estrada*)

The band caught in full flow at the first
Monsters of Rock Festival at Castle Donington, 16th August 1980.
These shots demonstrate the physical and visual elements to the bands' performances.
(*Alan Perry*)

Although Accept gets more credit for onstage heavy rock choreography, Scorpions contributed to the game earlier, as did Judas Priest. *(Kevin Estrada)*

Matthias in 1982, sporting the trendy stripes of the day. *(Kevin Estrada)*

Klaus Meine, *Blackout* tour, 1982, California. *(Kevin Estrada)*

Three shots from the band's,
9th April 1984, Austin, Texas show,
on the Love at First Sting tour,
support courtesy of Jon Butcher Axis.
(*Richard Galbraith*)

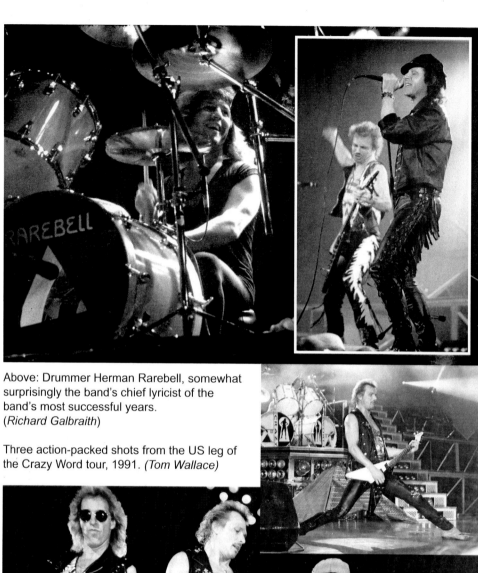

Above: Drummer Herman Rarebell, somewhat surprisingly the band's chief lyricist of the band's most successful years. (*Richard Galbraith*)

Three action-packed shots from the US leg of the Crazy Word tour, 1991. (*Tom Wallace*)

A little light music. *(Tom Wallace)*

Uli Jon Roth solo gig, 2008. Since leaving the Scorpions he has often joined them on stage over the years. *(Tom Wallace)*

Here's looking at you, kid. Rudolf Schenker, Chicago, 2010. *(Greg Olma)*

The Hollywood Rock Walk induction, 2010. *(Kevin Estrada)*

Top left: Matthias Jabs with a little extra protection at the Hollywood Rock Walk induction, 2010. *(Kevin Estrada)*

Top right: Rudolf, Matthias & Klaus with guitar. *Comeblack* tour, Molson Amphitheatre, Toronto, Canada, 2012. *(Bill Baran)*

Left: Klaus Meine, Los Angeles, California, 2010. *(Kevin Estrada)*

Below: Left to right: Pawel Maciwoda, Rudolf and Matthias, on the *Return to Forever* tour, 2015, Molson Amphitheatre, Toronto, Canada. *(Bill Baran)*

Pure Instinct

"50 or 60 things that they needed to change"

"So then a hole came."

Those are the words of thumping rock 'n' roll heart of the band, Herman Rarebell, who at this point, leaves the story, off to cavort with Prince Albert of Monaco and start up Monaco Records, a venture never to be heard of again.

Yes, it's true, says Rudolf... "Herman lives in Monte Carlo and he got into a situation to be a partner with Prince Albert to open a record company. He's the president of a record company now called Monaco Records, who put out different kinds of stuff. He sends it all to me but I haven't listened to it yet because I have no time. But he is working there and he is fine. He had a chance and he always had this in mind to do something new, so why not?"

As well, management is no longer courtesy of the esteemed Doc McGhee, who had superseded Leber Krebs in 1988. Now it was "Stewart Young and Steve Barnett for Part Rock Management and Hard To Handle Management." It marks the start of a downsizing for Scorpions, along with a downsizing for traditional rock in general, due to the rise of grunge and its successors in the realm of loud music, industrial and hard alternative. As it turns out, as defiant as they were with Face The Heat, Scorpions were now not entirely against trying to compose within the framework of modern rock.

"Klaus played me the songs for Pure Instinct," explains soon to be ex-Scorpion Herman Rarebell, "and I said, 'Klaus, no, please, this has nothing anything more to do with rock. Remember the albums we did with Blackout and Love At First Sting? They were killer albums. This is shit. You cannot give this to the fans.' He said, 'You're just jealous because you don't write anymore.' I said, 'Look, whatever I tell you now, you will pay the price. I'm not playing on there.' I said, 'If you want somebody to play the drums on there, get a studio drummer.' So he called up Curt Cress, who I know, and he played on that album. I left, because for me there was nothing to do anymore, Martin. I didn't write any more lyrics. I didn't write any more music. Creatively, I was dead. He wanted to be the new leader, musically speaking, and look where he led the band so far. That was the best proof that I was right. We have a saying here in Germany, 'You must stop when it is at the nicest point.' You know, that's what I did."

"By Face The Heat, you could feel the air was out," continues Rarebell. "Then, as I said, Pure Instinct, for me, I didn't understand. I said leave now, because I didn't want to see the downfall. Plus the argument about the writing and the creativity; that was the reason I had to make the decision I want to go. Rudolf, in particular he wanted me to stay and said, 'Oh, don't do this.' I said, 'Rudolf, look, if I don't write anymore, music or lyrics, I like to be creative, and I like to do something. If you take that away from me, you're taking half my life away, you might as well continue without me.'"

"Yeah, total dud," says Keith Olsen, on Face The Heat, after which he would be brought back to be involved elliptically with what would become Scorpions' unlucky 13th studio album, Pure Instinct. "In fact, Pure Instinct was turned down by the record company, EastWest, so they redid it. They asked me to come in, because remember, the worst thing that could possibly happen to an act is to have one of these worldwide hits. Because they go around the world, and everyone... you know, I called it the Bic syndrome. They didn't have mobile phones that they wave, they had Bic lighters, and they wave their arms back and forth at the end of the concert screaming, 'You are the greatest!' When you play, you know, for 60 weeks, five on, two off, concerts, in front of 18,000 people a night, how could all those people be wrong? You know, I must be the greatest (laughs). So yeah, what happens is, they thought they could do no wrong. And they were the greatest. They wrote these really terrible, lame songs, cut it themselves, with no production assistance at all. They had Erwin Musper, who has never produced anything in his life, act as their producer, because the record company demanded it."

"Face The Heat was such a piece of crap," continues Olsen. "There was a live album, but that didn't count, right? That was a contractual commitment album. But that was just terrible. But then they decided to do another one, Pure Instinct. As I say, they brought me in after the fact, halfway done, after it got turned down once. So they said... I gave them a list of about 50 or 60 things that they needed to change, and we went in the studio, and I was there for about five weeks, in Düsseldorf Studios, doing these changes—50 changes. They wanted to bring in Erwin Musper, who produced this one that got turned down. They didn't want me to mix it. I said, well, you know, this is kind of a mistake. But they said, 'No, we're going to do it this way, because he speaks the language' (laughs). He speaks German. Okay. So he took the 50 things I said over six weeks, and he said, 'No, you don't want to do that,' and he kept two or three of the parts in a couple of songs. It didn't make any sense. He mixed it and the mixes don't make any sense and the arrangements just don't make any sense. Therefore, the songs and the arrangements didn't make any sense, and therefore the sales didn't make any sense. It was awful."

Back in 1996, speaking with Metal Edge's Adrianne Stone, Rudolf says that the end result of the record came very much from the circumstance of its recording.

"We did it at home," begins Schenker. "Remember when you started to play music, you went to the rehearsal studio and you played fresh, without thinking. That's the same situation: we went back to where we were most rehearsing, put the microphones there, the speakers, the special mic. We moved houses and the whole house was empty. The living room was kind of the arrangement room where drums were set up and two guitars and bass and something to sing with. The sleeping room was the acoustic guitar room. Every room had a different kind of atmosphere. When you're recording in Los Angeles, especially when you're doing overdubs, there's four guys sitting in a hotel room, killing their minibar and only one person is with the producer. So you're getting nervous, thinking, 'Why didn't they call me?' Then they call and say, 'Hey guys, what's happening?' You say, 'I have a great idea' and they tell you to wait. Then we are frustrated, sitting in the hotel room, going to the Rainbow, getting drunk. In this case, what's different is because we're living very close to each other, when somebody was working and recording something and he was finished, he called and said, 'Hey! Rudolf, you have time?' Or, 'Klaus, you have time? Come over.' It was very relaxed."

"A couple of years ago, we used to have a real ego about things," adds Klaus. "We liked to read on the back of the albums, 'Recorded at the Power Station in New York' because it was really cool. But today, really, who cares? It's more important that there's authentic feeling on the record. We felt that by working at home, we would get this feeling and really make it 100% a typical Scorpions album. I mean, America's changed so much, so what do we do now? How can we reflect the American feeling? We did in the '80s because we spent so much time here. But all the bands from our generation, the American bands, they even cannot reflect what's going on here in America. It's another generation and they're doing it their way. Which is very good. But this is our 13th album and we don't need to look for whatever can maybe make this a strong album. We just said, 'We need to look at ourselves, inside of us. That's where maybe we'll find that inspiration that makes us special.' Because we are different. We are a European band."

"I hope the fans in America will find this out," continues Klaus. "What I'm afraid of is just that in America, program directors will say, 'You know, the '80s have passed. Scorpions, yeah, normally I would like to play them, but I'm afraid I'd lose my job. My boss will kick my ass because I played some '80s stuff here.' This is not the '80s. The Scorpions are the '90s. The Scorpions are the Scorpions. We're not competing with alternative music. We're just doing what we're doing."

"We just let the surroundings be there," reiterated Klaus. "That was one of the reasons why we recorded most of this record at home this time. I know that American bands from our generation haven't been able to pick up this vibe in America. Those bands started in the '80s and even earlier. They do what they do. The greatest bands like Aerosmith and Van Halen are still going strong. Other bands from that era are gone, because all you remember is an image. They were too busy being stuck in this heavy rock cliché kind of thing. For the Scorpions, I hope people remember some songs. I think that's why this band is still here. There's a lot of talent in this band and I hope we continue 'cause we still have some great music to offer. This is not about image—it's about music and songs. This time around we felt we didn't need the most famous producer in the world or the most famous studio in the world 'cause it looks good in the credits. We didn't believe in writing with an outside person to get another hit. All we should depend on is us, because of this change to alternative. In order to record an authentic Scorpions record, we had to find the strengths in the band. In order to do this, we decided to record it at home. Since we write our music at home and we've got the studios that we usually do pre-production in. But the most important thing was that we had to find Scorpions music inside ourselves. That's the only way to get out there and be successful. It would be stupid for us to try and catch up to what's going on in America. We've never done that with any trends and we've seen many trends come and go. All we had to make a really great album was to bring out Scorpions pure—pure instinct, pure magic, pure Scorpions. It's called personality. To find personality in songwriting is what it's all about. We haven't mastered it quite yet, but hopefully we are heading in the right direction. But that's all that matters—it's not the pose you strike on stage."

"Look at it this way," says Schenker. "Here's a stone, a rock in the ocean. When the waves come in, they come over it and a little bit stays on the rock for a moment and then, the next wave comes. But the rock stays there. For the moment, it's gone! But it's always been there."

"He was calling," answers Rudolf, asked about the idea of the guys working with Bruce Fairbairn again. "He wanted to do something before he went to work with the Cranberries. We were also in touch with Keith Olsen." So they ended up with Erwin Musper... "our long-time engineer, who worked with us already on Face The Heat and Crazy World. He asked us for a chance to be a producer with us together and he asked for seven days and somehow, seven days became three months. Later on, for the last songs, we worked with Keith when Erwin was working on another project." Adds Klaus, "The first idea, basically, was to work with different producers. Not wait until there are 30 or 40 songs written and then have some genius producer come in to pick some. We wanted to say, 'Here are five songs. Let's produce three with this guy and let's produce two with this guy.' Like that. But it didn't work out that way."

Pure Instinct, issued May 21, 1996, actually starts fairly strong, with a Schenker/Meine song called *Wild Child*, not an uncompromisingly heavy opener as had become tradition, but kind of a cool melodic hair metal rocker. Then there was *But The Best For You*, not a disaster but probably too poppy to show up at track two, followed by a ballad called *Does Anyone Know*, both of these written by Klaus and Klaus only, true to his articulated character as the soft side of the band. Next up is *Stone In My Shoe*, again, a new direction for the band and not horrible, Rudolf and Matthias strumming a variation of those dependable *Louie Louie* chords from the '60s, but toughened, not without sophistication, come chorus time. Notes Klaus, "*Stone In My Shoe* is a rocker kind of song, and I wrote some of the lyrics here in America. But the hook was missing. I couldn't find it. It drove me crazy. On the way back to Europe, I was sleeping on the plane and I woke up in the middle of the Atlantic Ocean because of turbulence and thought, 'Well, it's so close to heaven, maybe I'll have some inspiration.' So I started working and when I landed in Frankfurt, the chorus was there and the song was finished."

An even lighter song comes next, *Soul Behind The Face* being a serious song with uncharacteristically smart and empathetic lyrics, essentially a mournful ballad with a beat. Again, no outside writing here, this being one of eight tracks on the album with music by Rudolf and lyrics by Klaus. *Oh Girl (I Wanna Be With You)* certainly evokes the arrangement oddness of which Keith speaks, this one being a rocker with some nicely eccentric touches—at least the band is exploring some new terrain. "It gives it colour," answered Rudolf, asked about this one's doo-wop intro. "There was a problem in the late '80s. Everybody was building out of one formula, always the same thing. Now to mix different kinds of things together... it's like a painting. We use different colours to make it interesting."

"We were looking for an intro," adds Klaus. "Normally this song would have been the opening track on the album. Then we worked around with this and then we came up with *Wild Child* as the opening track. But we thought, 'This is fun,' so we put it on anyway."

Man, *When You Came Into My Life*... for a Scorpions ballad on an album with supposedly waning batteries, this is not hard on the ears, especially given its passion-filled chorus and delectable Eastern influences.

"Yes, that's because when the album was almost completed, we went to Bali to write with Indonesian musicians," explains Klaus. "It was a songwriter workshop kind of thing. It was not to write for Scorpions, not at all. It was just a cultural exchange. There were more than 30 songwriters from America. We were the only European guys in this event and it was a lot of fun. We wrote some great songs, and when we came back, there was one song about which everybody said, 'You must record this for your album.' *When You Came Into My Life*, which we recorded with Keith in December of last year. When you hear *When You Came Into My Life*, you don't hear Bali. Probably say, 'That's a typical Scorpions song.' But this is the only song we wrote with outside writers on the whole album. With Indonesian people. The Indonesians wanted all of us to write with Indonesians."

Adds Rudolf, "Music has no borders and there were no language barriers because there was some people who didn't speak English, and you have to only hear the sound of the guitar. There were longer lines with us because we are so popular in Asia—Pure Instinct went triple platinum in Malaysia on its first day out—that everyone wants to write with us! (laughs). So it was in Bali that I worked on *When You Came Into My Life*, but I didn't have the time to finish it. But when I came back home, somehow, I was thinking, 'What can I put in to make it really interesting?' Then when I took it home, I came up with the idea and I wrote it then."

Next up is *Where The River Flows*, a mid-paced folk song, quite nice, mournful melody, catchy chorus. *Time Will Call Your Name* is another smart bit of craftsmanship from a softer rocking point of view. Again, if some of these soft songs were on some of the earlier records, Scorpions wouldn't be as ridiculed as unimaginative or even worse, kinda dumb. As an arrangement goes, well, sure, there's more texture and all manner of Zeppelin touches here, some tasteful percussion, an odd but refreshing break... while in the past, essentially the ballad would be full electric band and not much else just playing quieter. *You And I* just might be one ballad too many, and this one is quite saccharine down a '60s pop pathway, or at least a little too much Klaus commiserating over the April Wine.

Did I say one ballad too many? The album actually closes with yet another peaceful piece, *Are You The One?*, very soft, Beatle-esque with strings. Bonnie Tyler, same label as Scorpions, covered this one with a slight change to the title. Explains Klaus, "I wrote it when I started working on the album and it was on some of the tapes, I think, on a demo. It was the first song I completed. Rudolf did the music; I did the lyrics. Then the record company called and said, 'Guys, do you have a song for Bonnie Tyler?' We said, 'Yeah, maybe.' So I played this song over the telephone and the guy said, 'I love it.' Bonnie Tyler liked it a lot and then she went to the Bahamas and recorded it and made her version. When Erwin went through all our songs, he picked that song and said, 'I want to do this.' We said, 'No, we can't because we gave this away.' He said, 'It doesn't matter, it's your song. You should do it.' But since she did a band version of it, we did it differently. That's why we did it with a string quartet, to be completely different."

That's it, although there's a Japanese bonus track that is at least a loud rock song, *She's Knocking At My Door* again featuring an odd '60s pop progression or two, but miles smarter than yer *Kicks After Six* or *Tease Me Please Me*.

All told, Pure Instinct, just might be one of the buried gems of the Scorpions catalogue. Indeed, if one can put aside the lack of any heavy rock past one or two tracks at most, then there's some classy songwriting to be had and heard.

"Part of Scorpions is heavy rock; the other part isn't," reflects Rudolf, at this point speaking 15 years past Pure Instinct. "I think in the last years we always called ourselves a classic rock band. I think that comes close to what we really are by all these different waves. We always created the line that all the waves are coming but the big rock is always there. We feel ourselves to be a part of this big rock. Where all the small waves are coming and going but the big rock is standing. It's classic rock music. I feel better if I'm not restricted to anything. I feel better when we our music is not labelled. I know that Germans always think of a new term, a new way to describe certain music and are very creative about it. I'm fine if our music is called rock music and we are a rock band, and that's it."

"Pure Instinct to me was kind of like 'la la la,'" offers Ralph Rieckermann, nowhere to be seen in the credits. "Because we did that one... we didn't really have a producer, but Erwin Musper, who is not really a producer, he's a nice guy, but he doesn't really have an artistic vision, like a real producer, like Bruce Fairbairn or Peter Wolf. So the lyrics, I mean, if you listen to the lyrics, to me they sound like they're written by a 15-year-old. They are just 'la la la.' *Where The River Flows...* I mean, there was nothing new, no depth to it. There are a couple of songs that are nice, but that's exactly what they are. They are nice, but just there's no balls, there's nothing to it, you know what I'm saying?"

"I don't know," says Ralph, asked about his lack of credit. "I actually wrote a few other songs that people like a lot better, than some of the other songs. But because no other band members had any other writing credits, I think they didn't want to have them on the album. I don't know if that was the reason. There were some before Eye II Eye's *Mysterious*. There was a ballad, a couple of other songs, but no, the other ones were mostly written by Rudolf and Klaus."

Pure Instinct, despite its show of maturity and play for acceptance beyond the headbangers, was a disappointment in the sales department. Still, it achieved gold in Germany and France, actually a higher result in Germany than had been afforded Face The Heat. Fully five different songs were floated as singles in various territories, *You And I* achieving the best result. But nothing could budge the fan base, who didn't buy into the experiment. Pure Instinct really is a good album. It's just not, as they say in these situations, a good Scorpions album.

Three years after the fact, Rudolf looked back on the Pure Instinct experience with dismay, hard to understand around these parts, given that he had just put to bed Eye II Eye, a record that would take the band even further away from any degree of "thorniness."

"When we came up with Crazy World, I think that was the peak of '80s rock," explains Schenker, providing a survey. "1991, we had a big success, seven or eight million sold around the world. And then grunge came. Even when we were on tour in America with the album Crazy World, grunge was already there. We said, hmm, something has changed. We can't do the same thing again. When we started in the '70s, we tried to experiment and find our right style, and then in the '80s we found our style and we played our style until 1991, when the timing was perfect for that."

"Then when grunge came out, we feared that the times had changed drastically. We had in mind to come up with something new so we didn't become an oldies band. How can we make something that fits the times of today? Then we did Face The Heat, and it was dominated by Bruce Fairbairn—too bad he is not with us anymore—and that was an album that was okay. It had some good things like *Alien Nation* on it. There is the possibility that you would say that it is a little bit heavy rock, right. Because when grunge came, Bruce Fairbairn was pushing us, especially with that *Alien Nation* song... it's very hard and strong; I like the song very much."

"Then after we came back from the tour for Face The Heat, we said to ourselves, okay, we were on the road so long, what can we do? Because I have a studio in my house, and I moved houses, which means I had a new house next to my old house, and the whole house was available as a studio to record in. I said, 'Look guys, why not let's try to record something here?' with our sound engineer Erwin Musper, who has been with us since 1987, and why not try something very relaxed, without thinking. Then we did Pure Instinct, which I feel is a nice album, but not enough edge, you know? It was missing that edge a little bit. It was too straight. It was very European. It was too nice. Nice is not enough today. It's like when you have the rose without the thorns, the rose is not a rose anymore. With Pure Instinct, the thorns were missing."

The first leg of the tour for the record was a co-headlining North

American jaunt with Alice Cooper, beginning in early May '96 and winding up August 17th, mostly in sheds, amphitheatres. Japan got the band next, followed by Europe with Gotthard as support. Russia and South America got the band as well, before it was over and done in November '97. Scorpions were easing into late life cycle as a band that could still sell tickets, but with records that were meaning less and less to anybody as the years wore on. Nothing left to do but blow it up completely, and that's just what they did.

Eye II Eye

"I was never dancing to Scorpions songs"

Eye II Eye, issued March 9th, 1999, is a perplexing and perplexed record that is without a doubt the most reviled album in the Scorpions catalogue. When the author interviewed Rudolf about it he put on as positive a spin as he possibly could. "It's very important for a musician to see how far you can go and what you can do. Technology and music and everything is changing, and we're looking for a new way to bring Scorpions into the year 2000. That was the basic idea. Play music, make music, and play around in the studio and look for different ideas and try things you've never done before."

Additionally, the band seemed less like one. Only Matthias, Rudolf and Klaus were pictured on the (artsy) front cover, while Ralph Rieckermann and new drummer James Kottak anchored, not the back cover, but the back of the CD booklet. Plus a producer we've never heard of wrote half the songs.

"The way we recorded it," answers Schenker, when asked what excited him about the process most. "Normally we went into the studio with a producer and he would pick out of 30 songs the 14 he wanted to do, and then we did basic tracks and overdubs and mixing and then the album was finished. This time we met a producer, Peter Wolf. We talked together and he invited us to his studio in Austria and take a look at it. First of all we weren't that excited because Austria isn't our favourite country, to make music in anyway. But his idea was, let's make music for ten days and see what comes out. We went there and the studio, which is called Little America, is a great studio with everything you need."

"Peter Wolf worked for 24 years in America on different projects, producing Heart, Jefferson Starship, playing keyboards for Frank Zappa, and then had a studio in Los Angeles and then after the earthquake, he made the transition to move to Austria. So we played for ten days with him and three songs came out. It became clear that he was a great man and a great person to work with. He listened to our songs, our demos, and said, 'Look guys, that's great, but it's time to start writing again.' He wanted to have different teams and work with Klaus and Ralph etc. He wanted to change the format which we always worked in to try to get new ideas."

"So we started writing, writing, writing, and recording, recording, recording. Then the picture became clearer to us, and we went on a tour of Scandinavia and Russia in 1998. Then we worked again on the album and new songs came out, and we tried to play it, arrange it, and we were actually building the album up. We weren't recording playback and then adding overdubs, and all of that, no. Here we were working from song to song, and I think that was a really good thing because you are very close to the song and you try to give the song what it needs and you make the best out of it."

"You know, I think we were never a metal band," continues Rudolf, uttering the proverbial famous last words. "We've always told people that, but after awhile you shut your mouth because you can't tell people that. They aren't going to listen to you anyway. As far as we were concerned, we were always a rock band. And we are always open to put different spices in. In this case, we're living here in Europe, and here the music changes faster than in America. We somehow got this fear that we have to refresh our music. Because the '80s are gone, as you know. We, as a rock band, don't want to be known as an oldies band; we want to be known as a band of today. How to do it? That's a difficult situation. That is what we tried."

Listen to the record, and one is shocked how ruthlessly the band's big celebrated sledges of tandem rhythm guitars has been sent into exile.

"Give the song tasteful guitars, and don't overdo it as perhaps we did in the '80s," is how Rudolf describes the limited role he bestowed upon the guitar, for Eye II Eye. "Give the song a tasty guitar part, and make the guitar sound a little different; don't play the normal scales. We wanted to do it different than in the '80s where guitar was all over the place, give the song more air, give it a different vibe. There are no new techniques, except for stuff like burning it on CD. Then we would scratch the CD, and we would play the CD back and you would have this cut-up distorted noise. We tried different equipment, acoustic guitars, different kinds of electric guitars, different microphones, AKG microphones. We are always looking for a way to give the songs a special kind of thing. It was important to us for each song to be different from each other. I think if you listen to the album, you'll see that every song has a different kind of vibe."

Illustrating different strokes for different folks—as well as why Rieckermann is not the Scorpions bassist anymore!—Ralph says that Eye II Eye is "actually the one that I like the best. I mean, first of all, I'm not what you would call a big rock or heavy metal fan. I've done lots of other music in my life, and I grew up listening to all kinds of other stuff, like Pink Floyd, Yes, Genesis, more... I wouldn't say more sophisticated, but more musical, like more depth to it. I do like on the album, *Mysterious*, because I'm always a believer of being a trendsetter. So I thought we should have evolved; that was my personal opinion. To explore different horizons and create a sound that the Scorpions didn't have before, which we tried on Eye II Eye.

Opener *Mysterious* sets the shocking tone for the record, Scorpions turning in a dance track heavy on bass guitar, basically U2 in those insane mid-years, Klaus even crooning like Bono.

"*Mysterious*, which I wrote, that was the first song we'd created," explains Ralph, this being his only credit on the album. "Then all the other songs were created after the sound of *Mysterious*, which didn't really work out as well. I think personally, because either you write a song a certain way, or you can take a song that is like a rock song, written as a rock song, and try to make it modern and funky. Just because you put a few loops and create some electronic sounds underneath it, it doesn't really work. It has to be written that way. So *Mysterious*, my song, I wrote it that way, I wrote it with loops, I wrote it with a funky feel to it. It was written like that. That's why it works. I mean, the radio took it well. It was played in nightclubs; people were actually dancing to it. I remember before, I never heard Scorpions in nightclubs. I was never dancing to Scorpions songs and that was always bothering me. Because at that time, I used to go a lot to nightclubs, and you know, I heard Bon Jovi, Aerosmith, AC/DC, even in nightclubs—people danced to it. But never Scorpions, and that always bothered me. I wanted to challenge the guys, 'Listen, guys, we need something that has a groove to it, the people can dance to it, and that the DJs would put on in a nightclub'."

To every old Scorpions' fan's horror, the second track on the album, *To Be No. 1*, was pushed out as a single. In the vein of *Mysterious*, this one pushes even more buttons, including a ludicrous little keyboard blurp. One thinks of the abomination that is Def Leppard's X, or Aerosmith's Just Push Play, but even that record didn't go this far... into the dance clubs.

"Yes, well, with Eye II Eye, the record company made a mistake," continues Ralph, clearly in another world, or, one supposes, a world Klaus and Rudolf were sincere about visiting with him. "They should've released *Mysterious* as the first single worldwide, and they didn't; they released that other song, *To Be No. 1*, in Europe, as the first single. That was a big mistake, because in Europe, especially back in those days, they had drawers for music. You either had to be pop, rock or jazz or whatever. They have these drawers. They had to actually put music into a category for radio stations, to be played. But that song, it was like half rock in the chorus, and it was like soft pop music, almost electronic pop music, in the verses. So the radio stations refused to play it. That was a mistake. Whatever, it doesn't matter. There was a lot of money spent on a video that was really... whatever, it didn't really work out."

Next up was a crap ballad called *Obsession* but then a skilled and mature ballad called *10 Light Years Away*, good because it's outside the zone and not particularly saccharine, recalling the storehouse of impressive lighter experiments all over Pure Instinct.

"It was like this," says Rudolf, on collaborating with song doctor Marti Frederiksen on this track. "After Pure Instinct, we had this fear that we wanted to try and write with other people. Because when you write with the same people all the time, you end up repeating yourself. We said to our manager Stewart Young, 'Can you find some people we can write with?' We also had in mind that we wanted to go to Los Angeles to write, because our bass player has a house there, and our drummer lives there also—it was only us three that had to move to Los Angeles. Stewart found Marti and we were sitting together talking and we found out that we fit together very easily. We started writing immediately. He lives in the Los Angeles area too."

Foreigner's Mick Jones is in on the credits for this song as well, as Rudolf explains. "Mick came over to the studio in Austria with us, because we wrote one song with him, *10 Light Years Away*. We wrote it together and said, 'This is great; why don't we also record it together?' So he said, 'Sure, I'll come over.' He came over in the snow and chaos, but he made it, played acoustic guitar, we played together, and in-between we talked about things. He mentioned, 'I'll tell you what, I met your brother in the early '90s, in New York and we were the perfect team in table soccer for four days, and then after four days I never saw him again.' He said, 'How is he doing?' I said, 'He is fine; he's sometimes with UFO, sometimes with MSG.' But then I called my brother because I had to talk to him anyway, and I said, 'By the way Michael, here's somebody who wants to talk to you.' I heard him yell—he couldn't believe it!"

Brave and yet mature of architecture is *Mind Like A Tree*, a Zeppelin-esque stomper with interesting light and shade, killer production through and through by this Peter Wolf, in Austria, who also gets five writing credits on the record, including within this Queen-touched track of whack.

"It was made in Austria because Peter Wolf was living there, and had a studio in Austria at that time," explains Ralph. "Peter Wolf was a fantastic visionary and a very good composer and producer, and also happens to have the same type of music background and the same tastes in music as I do. More sophisticated, I mean, he played with Frank Zappa and lots of jazz players, lots of orchestral stuff. He has done pretty much every style of music there is on the planet."

"He's like a highly honoured musician in Austria who is like the real deal," continues Rieckermann. "Anyway, we were sitting in the studio for a very long time, just listening, almost like a week, just listening to songs that Klaus and Rudolf wrote, and some of Matthias' stuff, and finally Peter got up on his chair and said, 'You know what guys? We have a problem. We don't have anything. We need to sit down and write some music first, because there's not one single song in here that I hear that is worth being recorded.' Because he was under the impression that Scorpions needed a new sound. Also, another person that was trying to do that was the guy that did Face The Heat; what's his name? He's dead now."

"That's something we found out later, because people kept saying that," laughs Rudolf, asked about the Queen flourishes on the album. "When we did it, we never thought about it, but then people would come up to us and say this sounds a little bit like Queen. But it could be an influence, because Queen was also a band that later tried to look for new sounds. Because for a band who has been this long in the rock business, you can't do the same thing over and over again. Because when you do that, you end up in a dead end street. Like in the garden, if you want to see something new, you have to go in and put the earth upside down, so something new springs out. That's what we tried to do. We said, look, we're a rock band, we know that. But we don't want to stick in one format. We don't always want to be in the same position. That's what we tried and we will see how it works."

Next up is the album's anonymous, innocuous title track of muzak, followed by housewifely pop ballad *What U Give U Get Back* and then *Skywriter*, a slightly darker yet still poppy ballad, ambitious arrangement but not much else. "When you make a move like this, you have to all agreed on it," says Rudolf of the title Eye II Eye, changed to *Eye To Eye* for the title song. "And eye to eye, one definition of that is total agreement. Unspoken agreement."

Yellow Butterfly is impressively proggy, yet still annoying, and then *Freshly Squeezed* is another dance track, which is followed by *Priscilla*, yet another twist on disco rock, Klaus not believable as lecherous lounge lizard—club-goer's dad looking to drag his drugged daughter home, more like it.

"We've been working together so long that everything is worked out already," reflects Rudolf, on working with Klaus on these Meine/Schenker compositions. "That is why we need to change the format some times. So in this case, I compose myself, put a melody on that, give him the tapes, and he puts the lyrics on them and finds out whether they fit or not. Or he gives me his stuff and I think about it and put some guitars on that, and that's what normally happens."

"In the early days, not so much. But now he does," says Schenker, on the degree to which Klaus enjoys writing lyrics, here in 1999. As for collaboration or corroboration... "Mainly with producers. Or managers. He will go to them and say, 'Is it possible to say it this way?'"

Du Bist So Schmutzig is another braying, ear-yanking U2 joint, distinguishable in that it is the first credit on a Scorpions album for jokester drummer James Kottak—hopefully he isn't responsible for the rap bit. Yes, the lyric is primarily in German, but I'd venture to say that any given Anglo Scorpions fan would rather get their foreign language fix from good old Rammstein than a track from Eye II Eye.

Says Kottak, regarding his introduction into the Scorpions' ranks, "I was in Kingdom Come from 1987 through 1991. We had opened for the Scorpions in 1988 on the Monsters Of Rock tour. It was Kingdom Come, Metallica, Dokken, Scorpions and then Van Halen. We did 32 stadiums and it was amazing. Then we did an indoor arena tour with the Scorpions for about another 20 dates. So, of course, you get to know the guys. Keith Olsen produced the second Kingdom Come album, In Your Face, and thereafter, in 1990, he produced the Scorpions album, Crazy World. I'd see the guy hanging out at the studios down here in LA and I played on Michael Schenker's album. The rock 'n' roll community is pretty small. Then the '90s came along and I joined The Cult, played with Warrant and played on 30 different albums over the years. In 1995 I got a call from the Scorpions' manager and he said, 'The band would like to know if you'd like to come and play with them?' I said, 'What made them think of me?' They said, 'They remembered that you were a nice guy. Plus, you're a great drummer.' That said it all right there. The Scorpions are class. They've never been dirtbags. That touched me in a heavy duty way. Rudolf and Klaus came to Los Angeles and we met. We were like friends. It just clicked. I have a very powerful bond with Rudolf and, of course, Klaus. I've been so honoured and fortunate to be part of this organization."

Eye II Eye mercifully closes off soon, first with *Aleyah*, another thumping dance rock track, and then a classical piano ballad called *A Moment In A Million Years*. The sum total was a record that was almost begging to be marketed differently, if it was to have any chance at all.

"That could be a possibility," agreed Rudolf. "I know one thing, in Asia, it was marketed different and it was a very big success there. It was in the Top Ten and went No.2 in Europe; it's No.2 and No.1 and stuff. Okay, it's not doing extremely good, because in the European market you need something airplay-wise. *To Be No. 1* was played okay but not very much. What you need is a song that is played five times a day, and then you will have success. This album is good; the fans took it okay but for the right audience, it's okay. We have a new single coming out sooner or later, either *Eye To Eye* or *A Moment In A Million Years*, not the piano version on the album, but a different one. Because Europe is very ballad-oriented, and as you know, we are a rock band, and that always is our problem. We operate on two continents, and America is more rock-oriented, but Europe is more ballad-oriented. So now we have to find the right way to move. But marketing, that's a good question, I think that is now up to the people in Canada and America."

When I asked Ralph why the band, as it turned out, never experimented quite to this extent ever again, he's off on a tangent, but an interesting one... one that actually results in a pretty deep answer: write about what you know, or even more cogently, write your nature.

"I think it's because they never really reached the peak again of the success that *Wind Of Change* had. Which was also an experience, because at first the record company wanted to take the whistling out, and then everybody was like, 'No, the whistling stays in.' I think Klaus was mostly voting for it, which was a great idea, because that's part of what made the song what it is. But in a way, *Wind Of Change* was an experiment too, and *Wind Of Change* was one of the most serious songs the band ever had done, because it was a true-life experience. So that's what I've been talking about this whole time. It doesn't matter whether you use drugs or have sex with 10,000 women or whatever, or decide to live your life to the fullest the way like Jim Morrison did. But Klaus wrote *Wind Of Change* based on his experience, when they did the Moscow Music Peace Festival, which was before my time, in Russia. So he wrote true-life experiences, and that's what made the song as strong as it is, because it's true. It's not something you make up and try to write a good song. Do you know what I'm saying? I wasn't motivated anymore either at the end. I just didn't like the music, for some reason."

Given Ralph's insights and perceptions, I thought I'd ask him what he thought about the way Scorpions ran their business. "You know, they have this guy, this lawyer, who is now their manager," explains Rieckermann, referring to Peter Amend. "Who is always, you know, handling all the finances. The guys are really generous, all of them. But I can't really say too much about the business. All I know is that they had a lot of problems, before my times. That's why I came into the band, because Francis Buchholz, the former bass player, was handling the band together with this other guy, the business end. So that's why there was the split up. Then business-wise, this guy Peter Amend, who is now the manager of the band, came into the picture. I think he is a very, very good business person. The band kind of put all of the business power in his hands, like a long time ago."

"I don't really know how the sales were," says Rieckermann, asked how the records he was on did in the marketplace. "I know I have quite a few platinum and gold records hanging from my walls, like quadruple, triple, four, five times platinum, whatever. So I know they sold well. None of the albums ever sold like Crazy World, and I think that was the ultimate, that everybody was trying to achieve, you know what I'm saying? But like I said, if you're not willing to take risks and reinvent yourself, like they did when they wrote *Wind Of Change*... I think that was completely fresh wind, not only like the song talks about, but also they split away from Dieter Dierks, who was their producer for a long, long time. That was the first time they actually worked with an American producer, a different kind. They were set free from the old contracts, and all the emotions that they came back with from Russia, seeing behind the Iron Curtain for the first time, seeing the Kremlin for the first, first Western band ever in the history, and that was very strong emotions. I think in order to write a real successful piece of art or music, you have to have some kind of experience or emotions like that in your background, whether it's a book or a movie or a piece of music. It doesn't really matter. It has to be based on true life events. That's my belief. Unless you're a very good fiction writer."

As we've discussed, Eye II Eye would turn out to be an aberration. Says Ralph, "So after that, then it was like, oh shit, we need to go back to serve our old heavy rock fans, from like 20 years ago. We need to serve their needs. We need to make music that they want to hear. Scorpions fans... and I kept telling the guys, they are 20 years older now! They listen to the radio too. They're not going to... When they were 30 or 40, they're now in their 50s and 60s. Yeah, maybe some of them... But let me tell you something, if they wanted to hear how Scorpions sounded 20 years ago, when you did Blackout, they're going to put on Blackout, they're not going to buy any record that sounds like it was from 20 years ago. It just doesn't work like that. At least that's what I believe. We need to do something completely radical, new, like shock people! Completely go where people go like, 'What the fuck is this?!' Then maybe it either works or it doesn't, but it's a risk you have to take. It's music, it's an art form. You constantly have to reinvent yourself. You don't go back in time! You actually try to create something that people haven't heard before. You are a creator. You're not a follower."

Initially there was the immediate problem of playing the new material live. "The set list will be different for America," said Rudolf at the time, which is consistent with his thoughts above on the material on the album itself. "But at the moment we have five new songs on it, which is very abnormal; usually we have only three or four. We play *Loving You Sunday Morning*, *Mysterious*, *Mind Like A Tree*, sometimes *Is There Anybody There?*, sometimes *Bad Boys Running Wild*, then we go to *Coast To Coast*, then we do the German song, then we do *10 Light Years Away*, we go for *Always Somewhere*, *Holiday*, then *You And I*, to *In Trance*, to *The Zoo*, then *Tease Me Please Me* and *Blackout*. Sometimes we get to *To Be No. 1*, a different version, a rock version kind of, then we went to a short drum solo that James can play really good, because he's a very, very good drummer, and then we might end with *Big City Nights* or *Blackout*.

186

Then the next songs for the encore in Europe were *Still Loving You, Wind Of Change*, then *Rock You Like A Hurricane*, then with the three guys in front, *A Moment In A Million Years.*"

The Eye II Eye tour began in Germany, April 27th of '99 and then lumbered through continental Europe, the band sporting their new close-cropped, non-rocker look as they confused fans 'round the European union. June 29th saw the start of the North American leg, all of it with Mötley Crüe, with opener duty split between Flash Bastard and Laidlaw. By September 6th of '99, it was all over, and Scorpions would enter a period of intensifying drift, not coming back to us with a new studio album for full on five years.

Moment Of Glory/Acoustica

"Matthias and me on guitar and a little bit of shakers"

On August 29th, 2000 Scorpions followed rock 'n' roll suit and issued an album that saw them play with a bunch of classical dudes, namely the Berlin Philharmonic Orchestra. The album was called Moment Of Glory, and it was typical of these affairs, although certainly not worse than most.

Interesting wrinkles included the title track, a song written for Expo 2000 in Hannover (where the concert took place as well), plus a Diane Warren song first covered by Tiffany ten years earlier, called *Here In My Heart*. Both are quite maudlin ballads, but *Moment Of Glory* is quite ambitious of arrangement and crackles with life. *Crossfire* includes a little *Moscow Nights*, and the *Deadly Sting Suite* was a twofer that pasted up *He's A Woman - She's A Man* to *Dynamite*. Again, this was classical fused to rock that went far beyond the norm, with a ton of writing taking place in service of a huge and epic experience. Still, all told, it's really a bunch of ballads, other than the rousing *Big City Nights* (sung by brief Genesis member Ray Wilson) and *Hurricane 2000*, which incidentally wound up as the official theme song to the Sabres Hockey Network. To give credit, *Hurricane 2000* is insanely orchestrated and arranged, beginning full on classical, and then well integrated to the band, high fidelity, nice mix, a ton of orchestrated parts and not just sawing away. Verdict? If you like this sort of thing, probably no one's executed it with more gusto, aplomb, brain power and sonic clarity.

"It was hard work to keep it up there and keep it going," Klaus told Dmitry Epstein, referring to the band's career itself. "In 2000 we did the project with the Berlin Philharmonic Orchestra, which was like a whole new challenge on a very big level. I mean, this orchestra approached us and asked if we would do this project with them—and this is one of the best classical orchestras in the world! This was something you really had to put your heart and soul in, and that's what we did. Moment Of Glory was a monster challenge. To play with the Berlin Philharmonic Orchestra... they are really, really good players, and in 1995 or 1996 they said, 'We want to play with you guys. We don't want to do this album with Pink Floyd. We want to make it with The Scorpions.' We were, like, 'Wow! Here comes one of the best orchestras, the Herbert von Karajan orchestra..."

The band's pleasant experience with Moment Of Glory, as Rudolf explains, put the wheels in motion toward sister record Acoustica, issued May 14th, 2001.

"I'll tell you one thing," Schenker told me in June of that year. "First of all, the first people who asked us—I think it was 1988 or 1987—MTV asked us to do an Unplugged thing. But at that time we were in the studio doing Savage Amusement, and we couldn't do it. They asked us again in 1990 or 1991, and we were in Asia on tour, and we couldn't do it. Then somehow we thought, we don't want to be last in line doing this acoustic thing. But then we realised this whole concept, acoustic unplugged, is a concept that can go forever."

"So people have asked us, why are you not doing this? After the success with the Berlin Philharmonic thing, Moment Of Glory, where we were working with Christian Kolonovits, who arranged most of the stuff for this symphony album/crossover album, we had a very good time with him and somehow the chemistry was working very good together. So we said to him, look, when people asked us so many times to do this unplugged thing, the best time would be now. Because we are somehow in the frame of mind of doing side-projects. So he was interested and we said, okay, let's see how we fit together, him on the keyboards, Matthias and me on guitar and a little bit of shakers and stuff like that. Let's see what we get out of it, and let's see if it's any good or not. Because we want to do it only when we can do it right."

"So we sat in my studio and went through songs and we found out more and more, hey, that's great stuff. Also stuff like *Holiday*, which we played live since '79, when unplugged pretty much wasn't a concept... we already had a song called *Holiday*. When we played the song in England, I remember we did the first tour after metal was back and we came with our acoustic guitar and it was like, 'What are you doing with that?' Because we have a song in the middle where we played acoustic. 'Oh, you can't do that! You can't do that!' We did it and people liked it. So in this way, we've been doing unplugged in our concerts since '79."

"When we really started to get into the arrangements, especially *Holiday*, which I like very much, I was always unhappy that we put this *Longing For The Sun* as a tail, somehow at the end. I said, you know, it's really a great chorus, why not try and make the whole arrangement in this direction? So we did it and the song came out great. We had so much fun and we were getting more into different songs, and thought it would be a great thing, even though everybody has done unplugged. I still thought this would be a great thing for us with this kind of chemistry."

"One thing is clear, you have to arrange things into different ways, especially *Rock You Like A Hurricane*," continues Rudolf, asked about the challenges of playing acoustic. "When you have an electric guitar, you can have a sustain which goes forever. But with an acoustic guitar, after a while the tone is gone. In that case you have to get something out in a different way. You have to somehow give the songs the same drive as when you play with an electric guitar. You also have to get a special rhythm, a special feel. The whole album has different colours, but you have to somehow give it the same atmosphere."

"If we couldn't rise to that challenge and still have fun, we would have said stop it and not do it. There's also new songs. I composed two songs especially for acoustic, *When Love Kills Love* and *Life Is Too Short*. I said okay, this is a different thing, and the challenge was to make those fit with the old songs in the new arrangements. Then people said, 'Look, why don't you do cover versions fully acoustic?' So we went through all the history, Led Zeppelin, Deep Purple, and in the end we came up with these three songs that we thought Klaus could sing the best."

"In terms of a place to do it, we thought Portugal was the most interesting. Look, we tried Paris, Milano, Madrid. There was no place as good as this place in Portugal, because what we had in mind was to do a DVD, which is two hours long and has more songs on it than the CD. The atmosphere of this place was great, because it was a monastery where monks were living in the early days and it's a very special vibe. It was cool because it's not only unplugged, but it's live, not in the tradition of MTV. This had a different atmosphere because MTV unplugged is very quiet. We didn't want to stop the people from enjoying it. They made a lot of noise. It was great. One year after doing the symphonic album, we did this thing and it was very good for us and now the mind is free to go back to the roots."

"We have extra people on stage," continues Rudolf. "We have one guy from Chile who's doing the percussion (Mario Argandona), backing vocal singers from Belgium, and then we have another guitar player who is from Holland (Johan Daansen), and we have one keyboard player now, because Christian's doing something else. So we have a guy from England, and we have a cello player (Ariana Arcu), a girl, and she is from Romania. Then there is James from America, and us four from Germany, so it's a very international kind of crew."

"There was always something new and exciting," mused Klaus, asked about Acoustica. "We'd always wanted to do this, and this was about picking the right songs and maybe some covers, but it was us with a few guest musicians, so it was under our control. With the Berlin Philharmonic, Moment Of Glory, with 80 or 90 musicians, you not only record an album but you must please them with arrangements, and they said, 'Give us a challenge!' So the guy who wrote it, Christian Kolonovits— he's also on Acoustica—came up with amazing arrangements for the songs, from *Rock You Like A Hurricane* to *Wind Of Change*, and a couple of new ones like the anthem for the Expo 2000, *Moment Of Glory*. And to play a show live together... I know, Acoustica is very popular, it came off pretty good, but you can't compare it to Moment Of Glory."

As for the extra songs on the DVD version of Acoustica, these would be *Rhythm Of Love, I'm Leaving You, Is There Anybody There?, Loving You Sunday Morning, Back To You, Tease Me Please Me* and *Under The Same Sun*. Highlights of the regular CD are the opening swampy blues version of *The Zoo*, as well as the two new ballads *Life Is Too Short* and *When Love Kills Love*, which benefit from not having to be power ballads. *Catch Your Train* gets a boogie woogie vibe that works splendidly, and hearing the Scorps do Kansas' *Dust In The Wind* is pretty much the treat of the package. Along those lines as well is a cover of *Drive* by The Cars and *Love Of My Life* by Queen, the latter of which, just like those magical times, is accompanied by a huge crowd singing along.

"We had a few," says Rudolf, on songs that didn't make the cut. "A Beatles song called *Golden Slumbers*. We tried *Angie* from the Stones and *Radar Love* from Golden Earring and also from the Rolling Stones, *Paint It Black*. In terms of Scorpion songs, it was mainly the harder ones that we just couldn't make work, songs like *Can't Live Without You*. You just feel that when you miss something. In the end, you have only this much space and then you make a decision and say, look, the songs are coming so good across, and they are such good arrangements. I think we played nearly three hours at this concert in Lisbon, and we couldn't put everything on the CD or the DVD."

"We needed some kind of new kick," is the way Klaus looked at all this, talking with Mark Syrjälä, snapping his fingers for emphasis. "A new kind of inspiration. After our last studio album, the confusion was bigger than before to be honest. So this opportunity to work with the orchestra, The Berlin Philharmonic, that was not a new idea. They approached us in '95, way before Metallica did their album. So we thought about this many times. In all those years, we never had the right guy. So I think between '99, we found Christian Kolonovits a great composer and arranger from Austria. He did the right arrangements and everybody said, 'This is great!' So, the timing for us was great, to do the project and play at the Expo in 2000. It all came to us at the right moment and it gave us a way to use our very best material for a very exciting project. We learned a lot from this experience and it was very inspiring and motivating. So even though it was not a typical Scorpions rock album we worked with our best material and it became successful. It gave us a whole new world to work in. It gave us new life. So demand was on the upswing again and it created demand for an unplugged record. It basically came from Asia and we had the same team. We had Kolonovits and we built a band, an acoustic band, around the Scorpions and it gave us a lot of opportunities to work with different styles around our music. But it was quite a while since our last album. We did a lot of touring and then classic rock came back in America in a big way. So in the last 12 months we have played over 120 shows and over 80 in the States."

Surveying at this point where the band has been and where it's going, Rudolf explained that, "if you think about it, '98, Eye II Eye came out and now we have 2001, and in this short time we've put three albums out. So now you know how much we were working. The interesting thing we did is that now the Scorpions are able to play three different formats: rock, classical and unplugged. We came back from Russia, and we played in about six different countries, because they now have the new countries there, and always with the national orchestra. Our conductor went one day before. We sent all the material to the orchestras four weeks before and always one day before, our conductor went there and rehearsed with them. On the day when we arrived, around 3:00 was our rehearsal, and then in the evening we played. We played in Kiev, Moscow at the Kremlin, St. Petersburg in a new ice hockey arena to about 12,000 people. We played in the Baltic states; it was like Kiev, Tallinn, Riga, and always with a very, very good orchestra. Then from Kiev we went straight to Zurich to one of the highest possibilities where you can play, on top in the snow; I think this was up 2600 meters in the snow, open air, a rock concert. You see what I mean? We are now really doing different things and enjoying it. It's always good to do something different, not always the same thing. So we don't have much time to do solo projects. I think we start working in the studio again around September or October. I tell you one thing, it was a really hard thing for Klaus. But now he knows how to train his voice, warm his voice up, which is very important."

Interesting in the above that Rudolf provides an echo back to the band's original premise and purpose as stated as early as the mid-'60s, this idea that the Scorpions provides a ticket to ride, the passport to adventure, like stowing away on a merchant ship and working your way around the world.

However the band's bass player was looking at all this with some disdain. For example, asked about Acoustica, Ralph comments, "I just have a few words to say for that, and it's like, 20 years too late, sorry guys. It's like, you've got to be kidding me. I've seen acoustic versions on MTV going back decades. It was a little late, I think. I mean, it was a nice album and it was a nice try, and it was a great time working together with Kolonovits, great guy, very talented, who also did the Philharmonic stuff.

It had moments. We did some nice shows, but then again, it was nice, it was good, it was there, but it wasn't. I mean, same thing—like followers. Yeah, okay, acoustic versions of the hit songs, great, wow, there's something new. You're like the last band who did it. I mean, that's my reflection on it anyway. Yeah, it was nice, it worked, a lot of people liked it. But to me it wasn't really necessary. That was my opinion."

"So again, toward the end of my career with the band, I kept saying the same thing. I was like, guys, we need to reinvent ourselves. We need to come up with something new, something, you know... like look at Aerosmith. They had that *Walk This Way*, whatever, where they worked together with rappers. Whether you like it or not, they did something different, something new."

"But they never really gave me the chance to run free," continues Rieckermann, at the proposal that right now, in their bassist, they had probably one of the best musicians in the band they'd ever had. "They never really gave me the chance to... because always, for some reason, they always called me the new guy. Like the new guy, like 20 years younger than the rest of guys: 'Yeah, what do you know?' That's exactly my point. I was hungry, I wanted success. I have like hundreds and hundreds of songs that were so strong and so powerful—one of them was *Mysterious*—that never really saw the light. *Just For You*, Scorpions did that song. That would've been another *Wind Of Change*. It would've been a huge hit, but because my girlfriend wrote the lyrics, I wrote all the music, so no one in the Scorpions wrote any part of the music, I think that was the main reason it was cast out. Because when we had a listening session, we had about 25, 30 people in the studio. That was actually for Pure Instinct, the EastWest one. That was song No.6. We gave everybody a sheet with numbers on there, and we had 16 songs on it. My version on YouTube is acoustic, but Scorpions' version was more of a rock version, like a rock ballad, but it was the same song, the basic structure and everything, same lyrics. Then almost everybody in this listening party in Wisseloord Studio in Holland, everybody jumped out of their seat, 'Song No.6, song No.6, that's the best song, that's a total winner! All the other ones, we don't really like that much.' This is for Pure Instinct. I looked around at Klaus and Rudolf's faces, and their faces turned green, and their chins just dropped because that was the only song that they had absolutely nothing to do with, when it came to the writing. At that moment I knew, the song is out, because they don't want... the last thing they want is the new guy in the band writing the next big hit song."

But Ralph got to go to India. "Yes. I would say, for me, that was the farthest, strangest and most impressive: India, plus Beirut. India was amazing because when we arrived we were shocked by the poor around us. The more we stayed the more we got impressed with the attitude of the people there, so we had an amazing time. We had close to 50,000 people in the stadium, maybe even 60. The next day, in India Today, which is kind of like USA Today, the main paper, we were at the top, front page, with a big picture, so it was a big deal. We went to Beirut, first time in the Middle East, and just on the way from the airport, which was like a half hour drive, we heard four or five Scorpions songs on the radio station, and we had a really big turnout too. I think that was about 60,000 people there too. We were really surprised how famous the band was over there, which no one really knew."

"We just toured, in the states at least, last summer, with Deep Purple and we missed out on Canada," said Matthias in 2003, with the band back to playing loud and live in '02 and '03. "One of the reasons why we said, let's complete the tour, so to speak, was because we played for only three months in the summer and obviously you don't make it everywhere then. So we said, okay, a few places we haven't played and Canada especially, the eastern part especially, since we remember it was always a fantastic time. Not only Toronto, where you're from, but also Québec City, very special area, where they speak French, and if you're an English-only, you are (whistles) (laughs). I always thought it was a funny place. I speak French so it helps a bit. So we decided to go on the road again, even though we have to finish the new album this year. We're thinking, oh, does it take away time from the recording schedule? But we decided differently. We said, okay, it's great to go on the road—also with Whitesnake; it's a good opportunity—and play some of the places we haven't played in the summer. But we also converted the back lounge of our tour bus into a recording studio. So I think we get more done when we're on the road, you know, with all these long night rides. After the show, everybody's wound up anyways. All five are together and it's music from morning until late at night. So it should be the right inspiration and the right environment to write songs. Better than sitting at home."

"Yeah! We're good friends," says former Dio drummer Simon Wright, recalling days on the road with the Scorps at this juncture, in mid-2002. "We toured with them with Deep Purple. I forget what year but, I know James, Rudy, Klaus and Matthias real well. I think their contribution has been awesome. They've done some fantastic arena songs. They're just a brilliant band and to watch them too. They really know how to put on a show on and how to handle a crowd. They're just great performers, all of 'em. James is amazing on drums. He's like a really incredible performer. But we were always hangin' out and you know, big waves and saying hello. We had a couple of parties on the road. There was a Scorps party, there was Deep Purple party and there was a Dio party. Obviously the German one was like a beer-fest with lederhosen and stuff, and boy did we get hammered! Purple's was kind of like the tropics, with a lot of Hawaiian shirts goin' on (laughs) So we all had to go out and find Hawaiian shirts. I forget what ours was. I think it was just beer night, ya know. But they're just really friendly people; a great band and a great bunch of guys."

The following year it was another journeyman drummer, Dokken's "Wild" Mick Brown who got to sing the praises of the mighty Teutons. "I mean, what a band! That band still is just amazing. We have a long history with them, being sort of thrown into the studio together back in the old days, the '80s. So there's a lot of camaraderie there and they're really super nice guys. I go back with James Kottak pretty closely, and I tell you, the whole damn thing was just a bunch of fucking fun. I think we all enjoy each other and there's a lot of respect. God, these drummers I was playing with are just incredible. I'm like, oh, I hope I can hold my own. He gave me the thumbs up, so I thought, my God, it's great to be part of the club. It was just really nice, a really great moment and a lot of great music. Some wonderful music, man. Scorpions were just big, man. They were gigantic; I loved it."

But as Matthias alluded to, even while the band was doing all this live work to re-fill the coffers, thoughts were turning to a record that would somehow right the train after the ill reception afforded Eye II Eye.

"If I would know now, I would promise you something," laughs Matthias, asked at the time what he though the next studio spread would sound like. "But I can only hope that we are sticking to what we've been talking about all the time. We want to, basically with the style, go back to what we think is the real Scorpions style, meaning the Blackout/Love At First Sting days. But obviously, it's 20 years later and therefore, song-wise, we can do what we are able to do these days. We hope it's going to be much better. So something sounding like 2003/2004 but as far as songwriting and the edge, I would say, think about Blackout."

Jabs figured the band wouldn't be trotting out anything new live. "I don't think we're ready for that now. I don't think it makes that much sense because people don't know it and 'whoops!,' it goes by and usually the majority of the audience wants to hear the songs they know, especially if the band hasn't played in town for a long time. So I don't think it makes sense. You have to think about, well, somebody is recording it, and are they putting it on the Internet and dah dah dah dah. In the old days you could do these kinds of experiments but today, you've got to be so careful."

"He's in excellent shape," said Jabs with respect to Klaus's voice, more of a positive spin than the one out of Rudolf at the time. "I think we played seven months altogether last year and we just did six weeks in Siberia and it was cold and miserable and he didn't have a problem. That's all good. So he's in great form and he never had the problem again. Every singer has to watch over his voice, but at the time he didn't know. Nobody had told him and he didn't have any training so he went onstage and started screaming. These days, he warms up well and he has a little device that massages the vocal cords, like from the outside, with magnetic power. We also structure the songs in a way that he has a break here and there and we don't really start with a song that is much too high to sing, like we did in the old days. You have to pay attention to this. It's always good for three shows in a row, but not for 53. You have to balance it out."

Commented Rudolf on the direction of the next record, "I'll tell you what, we did some shows unplugged, but we don't want to go too much into it and I'll tell you why. We want to do a real rock album again. We need time to write new stuff. The last two projects were very good for us to go back to our old material and see what Scorpions is all about. We did a few big shows here. We did a big concert in Germany with 40,000 people and then we came back yesterday from France where we played in front of 80,000 people, this concert, and also in the south of Germany. We go down to Asia because the Asian people were the crazy ones. They really want the unplugged concert. So we're going to all the Asian markets, and then I think we'll go back to writing and try to make a great rock album."

"The last three albums, you can look at them as three of a kind. Especially the last one, Eye II Eye; we said why not play around with new technology, try some new things? Then the Philharmonic thing was a new thing, and now this unplugged thing. The next one... when we went to our old material to create new arrangements, we saw that the basic sound of the Scorpions was that we were a really great riff-oriented band with good melodies. What we have in mind is to make an album in the direction of Blackout again, perhaps mixed with Love At First Sting. That will come out maybe at the end of 2002, the beginning of 2003."

"We have written a couple of songs," noted Klaus. "There is some new material… tons of new material actually. There are not so many songs fully worked out. We are in a session with an American songwriter called Eric. We wrote a couple of tracks a couple of weeks ago before we started to go back into the touring thing. But we said that after all the touring we did, last summer flip-flopping headlining with Deep Purple, we did three months in the States…then we went on a *big* tour of Russia in the fall and played shows, everything east of Moscow, between Novosibirsk and Vladivostok—we did it all!"

In the spirit of those five kids from Hannover garage bands playing rock 'n' roll to see the world, Klaus looks at the far-flung Russia trip as another notch on the belt.

"Throughout the '90s we played some shows in Russia but we always played Moscow and St. Petersburg. After we played two shows at the Russian palace, the Kremlin, a guy we know who owns an internet company, we were in his office and there was this big map of Russia. He said, 'Do you know how *big* Russia is?' We all said, 'Yes of course.' He said,

'You have no idea. Look at this, you have played Moscow and St. Petersburg. You should go all the way!' We said, 'All the way?' (laughs)."

So, as Klaus's interviewer Marko Syrjälä brings up, the band did it, and did live broadcasts from the extreme road just to prove it. "Yeah, on the Internet, from Germany from Samara and Omsk and cities you have never heard of before… that *we* had never heard of before (laughs). Some of them were bigger than Helsinki! (laughs). There are millions of people; we played Samara, Ufa, many cities all over Siberia… Novosibirsk, Celabinsk... We played *every* show. We had a big jet; otherwise we couldn't make it. You know there was 3000 miles between Krasnoyarsk and Vladivostok, maybe more, I don't know. When you are in Valdivostok, you are an hour from Tokyo! (laughs). So we went all the way; it was exciting and it was a big adventure. We felt like pioneers again *and* the great thing was we played all summer in America. We played *everywhere* in the States for three months and then we went to Russia and we played *everywhere* in Russia. It was like the '80s, except for playing everywhere in Russia. Back then it was the Soviet Union and it was a different thing, but what I want to say is both poles, America and Russia, are very much a part of our lives."

"With the side-projects and adventures…we did it," said Klaus, realising that with all of this extracurricular activity, the eye was off the ball when it came to the sculpting of new Scorpions anthems. "Very successfully and we enjoyed it, but what we got out of it was that there are many fans around the world, not only in Finland but in places like... Scotland! They appreciate us, they like what we are doing and they say, 'Thanks for the shows,' and they know that we are playing with the best orchestras in the world… 'Acoustica, the DVD is very nice; we like it a lot.' Even in America. But they say, 'The best thing for us is if you come out with a new rock record.' So after all these project we did, it takes you right back where you come from. What are the strengths of the band? The strengths are *Rock You Like A Hurricane.* But, the strengths are also *Wind Of Change* or *Still Loving You*, so you know, it's like Bryan Adams said way back, years and years ago. He said, 'You guys could have a very successful record if you had *Rock You Like A Hurricane* and *Wind Of Change* on one record. It would be smash.' (laughs) He's right."

With that bassist Ralph Rieckermann was gone, replaced by Pawel Maciwoda, who is still with the band today. "I do film music," says Rieckermann, successful in Hollywood. "I've done 45 movies now, it's all on my website. But yeah, I do film scores; I have a scoring stage here in LA. But most of the music I do is all orchestral stuff. I also write songs, anything from rock to death metal. I mean, I've done everything like hip-hop, techno, house, pop music, soundtracks, everything."

On May 28th, 2002, Hip-O Records issued a fairly high profile

Scorpions compilation called Bad For Good: The Very Best Of, spanning the length and breadth of the Matthias Jabs era. Along with some singles versions of songs, plus Who cover *I Can't Explain*, there were two new songs produced by key man from the past, Dieter Dierks.

"We recorded a couple of songs at Dierks Studios," explained Klaus. "All the fights of the past… it's all gone, and everything is cleared up after so many years. So, we said, let's go to Cologne for a couple of days and work with Dieter and just have some fun. We recorded a song called *Cause I Love You* and *Bad For Good* which basically came out in America on the Bad For Good compilation last year. It was good and it was weird at the same time (laughs), like a time-travel kind of thing. We worked with Dieter for so many years and it worked. So we said, 'When we are going to do a new album, we might come back.' Right now, we will definitely do something with Dieter. I don't know if we will do the whole album but we'll definitely do something."

Bad For Good finds the band locating for themselves both a gallop and a melody out of the NWOBHM, but then tempering it with their newer laid-back vibe, an odd accessibility. Still, despite the evocation of hair metal, and even glam circa Sweet, there's something appealingly Germanic about it. *Cause I Love You* is heavy as well, heavier even, with a bunch of cool talkbox and a verse that is classic magical molten Scorpions rock recalling the epic mid-paced tracks from Blackout through Face The Heat.

It all bode well for the record that Rudolf, Matthias and Klaus had started promising for us through 2002 and 2003. Whether they could deliver, having gone so far afield for well on eight years now, was another matter.

Unbreakable

"The rock is still standing"

O n June 22nd, 2004, Scorpions made a game attempt at putting
"heritage act" status behind them, issuing a new, more
conventional Scorpions record, shiny and embossed of cover,
called Unbreakable. The acoustic album, the classical album, touring just
because it's there... the band was moving on, giving notice that they
wanted to remain participants in the game.

Surveying the years from this vantage point, Klaus remarked at the
time, "We just didn't even think about it; we take life as it comes and try
to work our way in the business, in the world of music. In the first ten
years it was more about finding your own style and the right people to
work with. Like Dieter Dierks: we did our first album with him, In Trance,
in 1975. That was very important to us, to grow up as a band, to write
strong songs and to have the right camaraderie in the band, just the right
mix of people. So for us, the fact of friendship was always very, very
important. I think the reason it worked with Uli is because of the
chemistry: with all the differences we have in personalities, in the big
picture, when we're going to sing together in the studio, there is
something very, very strong. The philosophy of friendship has definitely
paid off, because after all the highs and lows, we're still sticking together
and we haven't lost the passion for what we're doing. In the '70s, there
were a few changes, then we had this line-up with Herman and Francis
for almost 20 years. 18 years is a long time! A couple of years ago Francis
left and Herman retired, so James Kottak came aboard, and since the last
year we have a new bass player, from Krakow in Poland, Pavel Maciwoda,
a very nice guy and a great musician, so the line-up now is very strong. I
also have a wonderful family; my son is almost 20 now and he just went
through his exams, so I'm a very proud father. But I'm a Gemini, so one
side of my heart is my family back home and the other side is the Family
Of Spiders, The Scorpions! (laughs). Our fan club, they call themselves
the Family Of Spiders, because when you look in the books, a scorpion—
the animal—is a part of the family of spiders."

Unbreakable, the band's 15th studio album, would prove that there was no longer any such thing as a conventional Scorpions record. Fairly heavy and guitar-laden as it is, the writing of old was gone, or had changed, or matured. In any event, the resultant complete record wouldn't exactly match the aggressive rhetoric, and that's what upset the fan base more than anything.

"Let's say this way," Rudolf told me, asked for the reason Unbreakable is the way it is. "We know that the '90s weren't so good for heavy rock. I mean, classic rock in the '80s was big, and then with *Wind Of Change*, we had a good bridge into the '90s, when grunge and alternative and stuff like this came. But somehow, especially when you live in Germany, you feel that new wave of alternative and grunge. So we were in a position, after the big hit, the fan base of the rock freaks weren't so happy about the success of *Wind Of Change*. Also a lot of the '80s bands were splitting up because there was no work anymore and everybody was sick about this kind of music. We were looking, what can we do? We were looking for a new way, through the '90s. We knew that rock would come back, no question about this. Because if the rock is in the ocean, with all the new waves coming and going, the rock is still standing, no question about this."

"But we didn't know when it will be. So, we were very lucky that we had the Berlin Philharmonic Orchestra knocking on our door and asking to work with us. We were very surprised. We didn't know whether we would do it. But somehow we thought it would be great, when we could do it. We were looking for a conductor and an arranger. We tried to convince Michael Kamen to do a song with him together, but he couldn't get somehow the right conditions, the right situation with the record company. So he went to Metallica and did the whole thing. But then we found somebody from Austria, and he actually made the great job and we used them for the Berlin Philharmonic Orchestra project, which gave us a really good way of working on our music in a different way, and learning about music and ourselves. Also with Chris Kolonovits, who was our arranger, we had a good time working together, because the Asian market asked for an acoustic album for over ten years. We said, okay, we are good team now, let's do the acoustic album, which we also did."

"So, in this case, we did these two tours of America, with Deep Purple co-headlining and also as a headliner in 2003 with Whitesnake. We felt very strongly, now classic rock is back. So that gave us inspiration to really, besides the side-projects, which also includes Eye II Eye, we said time is over, now we go back to what we can do best, Scorpions, great guitar riffs, great songs, good hooks and great vocals. That was the inspiration. The last two tours in America gave us a lot of inspiration and also writing... we had about 50, 60, 70 songs that we could pick from—with Erwin Musper. We had a producer review already and we told him we wanted to do a rock album in a traditional Blackout style, but with the sound of today. We also tried to work with Dieter Dierks, but he is very much involved with his company now, DVD Plus, and in this case, he couldn't come up with the right timing. We did everything with Erwin Musper, and we were around three months in the studio, and it was really fun to come up with the rock album again. Because after all the side-projects, we were really full of power to show people that we still kick ass."

Unbreakable would, in fact, deliver something that almost defiantly didn't kick ass, but more so rocked with an element of grunge, or the morose and slow, somewhere between moody pop and heavy rock. That's a fairly accurate description of opener *New Generation*, which... with a title like that, you are setting yourself up for some degree of ridicule, and indeed, the song over-reaches on the youth angle.

Second track *Love 'Em Or Leave 'Em* emphatically delivers on the proposed Blackout formula, Rudolf expressing his favour for the track foremost on the album (and certainly his favourite guitar solo), calling it, "a straight rocker which really has the Scorpions kind of signature sound; a great song, a lot of drive, basic rock, good riff—everything is inside that makes a good Scorpions song." True to that, it's got a circular rock riff that stands alone without the lyric, a verse of Germanics, and then a chorus that is pure catchy hair metal.

"I also like *Deep And Dark* which is a great song," says Rudolf of track No.3, one very much in the poppy yet moody hard rock zone, sort of a fit to Face The Heat. "Matthias composed this one, actually the first time he composed a song all by himself, the whole song, which I like very much."

Borderline combines straight, simple riffing with a psychedelic chorus melody, the Beatles by way of Aerosmith... or Dokken circa Shadowlife. *Blood Too Hot* is one of the album's more successful rockers, brisk, strong of Euro rock melody for the verse, also regularly strafed by a circular riff, pure party hard rock for the chorus. Essentially, it's like a sped-up version of *Love 'Em Or Leave 'Em*, the band taking the unremarkable and adding their pan-world attitude and experience, sending it into the successful zone. Noted journeyman bassist Barry Sparks plays bass on this one, plus *Borderline*, in place of Ralph Rieckermann's official replacement in the band, Pawel Maciwoda.

Maybe I Maybe You finds Klaus in his comfortable classical ballad zone, writing with Iranian pianist Anoushiravan Rohani, Rudolf and Matthias adding some harmony guitars to reinforce the Queen-ness of it all, circa that band's Made In Heaven or Freddie solo. Added flair comes with the engaging and epic "classical rock" piece late in the sequence that turns this one power ballad but without the clichés, Rudolf, in fact, stating that this one has his favourite lyrics of the whole album.

"I remember that song was included at the last minute," says Rudolf of this ballad, a track that could have slotted right in on Moment Of Glory or Acoustica. "Klaus had composed the song for a charity situation two years ago and he played it to us, and it was very much only piano and his voice. It was very clean and somehow the whole live feel didn't come across. Then I remember when we were working on Unbreakable that Klaus had to get the vocals from the playback. He needed the vocals by themselves. I heard it only with the vocals and I said to Klaus, 'Hey, what's that?!' I said, 'Hey, this song with a great arrangement would be unbelievable.' Erwin Musper came with his friend who was also involved with keyboards on Unbreakable, they came up with this arrangement and we said, 'Hey, that's great. We have to put this song on the album.' Because it's really outstanding and has something special that nobody else can do, except Scorpions or maybe Queen. Because Queen doesn't exist anymore, it's a great way to do something. Because everything is allowed for The Scorpions, except to be too normal."

Someday Is Now is one of those oddly sour melodic hard rockers that could have been a heavy track applied to Pure Instinct or Eye II Eye, an experiment. *My City My Town*, completely written by Klaus, is a catchy and simple hard rocker with a bit of a bluesy yet somewhat Euro-tinged turn for the verse, even more Euro for the pre-chorus, but then a poppy hard rock chorus that somewhat undermines the gravitas of the rest of it.

Asked about the simplicity of the new songs, Rudolf, somewhat circuitously offers, "I'll tell you one thing, when we started writing songs, and when we started to work with a producer, in pre-production in my studio here, we really... because we were working with side-projects with the old material, because we polished this one and put it into a different arrangement with the Berlin Philharmonic Orchestra, we really noticed with a strong situation what Scorpions music is. Out of this, going in and writing new songs, you actually find out what it really means to have a great Scorpions song. When we play now—we've done a few festivals already, Sweden Rock and we did a big festival in Holland—we play around seven songs from the new album. Never, never have we done so many songs from the new album. Why we can do that is because the songs have no problem being played with the others; they're not falling apart. They're really strong enough. I think that's the secret of the Scorpions. When you have to do a great album, you have to have songs you can play on the big stage. They have to be powerful and they have to have the right frame."

Through My Eyes, another Schenker/Meine proposal, is another one that fits into this Blackout framework, in a *No One Like You* mode, again, simple, passion-filled at the melody end. "Yes, I think it's close to Blackout and Love At First Sting," affirms Rudolf, of the wider album's vibe (or maybe more so his hopes for it). "Maybe you can even count in there

Lovedrive, those three. Crazy World is already a little bit different, so I think we're quite close to those three albums, but with the sound of today."

As for what "sound of today" means, Schenker says, "We tuned our guitars down, some of them two steps or four steps down. Which we already did years ago, because our songs for Klaus were already too high. You know, we always pushed him to sing very high. When you're on tour for a year-and-a-half, you have to be careful that you don't make it so he can't finish the tour. So in this case, when we went on tour, we always tuned the guitar, first of all, half a step down and then one step down. We noticed how powerful the guitars came in. They had much more punch. Also, when we started writing, Klaus couldn't sing the songs how they were composed, in general, in E. Klaus knew it was to high, and we didn't change the chords then. We said, okay, let's go down and see what's happening. We found out when we tuned down the guitar that the song becomes more powerful."

"So on this album, the riffs sound stronger, and with a new bass player, we were trying out different bass players, we noticed that Pawel was a guy who really played the bass somehow that allowed the guitars more space to punch through. Also how he plays the bass, it was exactly the way we were thinking how the bass had to be on the Scorpions songs. So in this way, we have freshness in the sound, we have the right bass, we have the right technology. Of course the recording of the new stuff with ProTools... before we always work with 24 track analogue with digital Sony 48. But this time we did it with ProTools because now ProTools is somehow good enough where you can use the new technology and not lose too much. So this is the way we recorded the whole thing. It sounds like the Scorpions, but with the sound of today."

No question that at least production-wise, the album is powerful and punchy, plus very bright, which is very much a characteristic of Love At First Sting but even more so Blackout.

"Erwin did a very, very good job with guitar sounds," says Rudolf, of Musper, as we've discussed in past chapters, first an engineer and now a producer. "I think the guitar sounds excellent. I think the whole album is good. I can't say this one is a better guitar sound than that one. I think with the technology of today, it's easier to get great guitar sounds than 20 years ago. I remember 20 years ago, we'd try different ways with different speakers. We did it also this time, but we know how to do it to get the best out of the speaker cabinet. This time we tried different speaker cabinets, Marshall, Yamaha, some others. But with ProTools, you really can make the A-B process much easier, to find out which you get the better result with. Also the equalizers today are much better, more sensitive. You have many very good possibilities, and as I said before, the ProTools, the converters, are much better now. They're coming now very close to analogue, not as good, but quite close."

As the album weirdly, frustratingly ambles to a close, we've got another slightly psychedelic hard rocker called *Can You Feel It*, followed by *This Time*, a thick, funky, noisy rocker which again, helps paint the portrait of a band grasping for grind but then often ill-fittingly tempering it with melodic parts that don't quite fit. Then there's a fairly maudlin (and again Beatle-esque) ballad called *She Said*, the album closing with *Remember The Good Times*, which can be described as a pop punk, glam, bubblegum rock, undermined further by a lyric that is pretty much a syrupy sentimental mini-history of the band. "It has this kind of retro sound," agrees Klaus. "The version we used was from one of the first studio sessions, when that song was still in a demo mode, so to speak. Later on, we had a proper studio-recorded version but we went back and took the demo as an extra track, a bonus track: it sounds rougher and we like the feel of it. It also has this retro feel in the lyrics."

Additionally, there were two Japanese bonus tracks, *Dreamers* being a solid, ambitious ballad, and *Too Far*, being an even better mellow track, sort of a southern rock acoustic song, a bit of slide included. Still, reach back a few records and it was becoming expected that the bonus songs were usually going to be some form of softer rock, granted, usually well-produced and arranged somewhat expensively.

"After I left came Pure Instinct," says now long-time ex-Scorpion Herman Rarebell, offering a point-blank take on the band at this juncture, a matter-of-fact summation that lines up closely with that of the fans, now long-suffering and still quite dissatisfied, "Pure Instinct had only one song on there which was commercially enough to go on the radio, *You And I*. And Eye II Eye, I don't even want to talk about. That is a complete disaster. The last album is in the right direction, Unbreakable. But it needs... there's no song on there. *Rock You Like A Hurricane*, this isn't. But it's in the right direction."

Unsurprisingly, the band's lead singer saw the future for him and his band in rosier terms... "In-between all these records and projects we're still touring all over the world: last year, with this latest album, Unbreakable, we went back to Japan and played in Scandinavia again. Before we come to Tel Aviv, we play in Paris, at Olympia, we go back to Russia, we play Kazan, the only show this year with an orchestra. So there's a lot of things. I think that keeps us going. The fact that after all these years we have a chance to come and play in Israel is very, very exciting and emotional, and it also feels like a new chapter."

Humanity Hour 1

"People want to take you seriously"

Okay, so it wasn't too left-field that Dio and Rush would finally craft and crank out concept albums, but Scorpions? Apparently so, even if the concept was a bit hazy and crazy, and yes, completely unexpected, especially since a very different mandate had been stated back at Unbreakable, this idea that they were going to try and recreate the glory years.

"I mean, this was a very, let's say, unusual situation," begins Rudolf, laying down the whys and wherefores. "Which is always good, something new, working as a team. After a long career, you really end up doing albums to let the fans know you are still alive, but then nothing else comes out special. In this case it was a different situation. First of all, after Unbreakable, and after all the side-projects we did with Eye II Eye and Moment Of Glory and Acoustica, just to survive the '90s, instead of doing solo projects, we did side-projects, and learned about ourselves, and worked with one of the greatest orchestras in the world. Plus we pleased our Asian fans by doing Acoustica; they had been asking for this kind of stuff for years."

'In this case, Unbreakable was the start after many fans asking us again and again on the Internet, 'You do great stuff, but can you do an album like Blackout again?' We said we can do a traditional album, but for the year 2004. That's what we did with Unbreakable. For Unbreakable we were happy, but we knew there were some points where we could do better, composing and sounding, and so in this case, we had it in our mind to do an album ourselves in 2006 in my studio. But then we said, you know, to do that, it's maybe not a good idea, because it's much better to have somebody from the outside, to really lift up the band, a great producer who can really do it strong enough, to give it new spark."

"So we had some big names, and Klaus and me went over to Los Angeles in 2006, February, and met with these people, and the one who came the closest to our vision was Desmond Child. We asked the guy, 'It would be great if we could do something with a concept album, something like this.' Because it was a message. He said that you guys really gave a great message with *Wind Of Change*, the soundtrack of the most people for a revolution of the century, and you guys can make an album where people will believe it, coming from you,' and stuff like this. We said, 'okay, let's do something together.' He said, 'okay, you have to wait until October because I'm still working with Meat Loaf.' We said, 'No problem, we will wait for you.' We had lots of stuff to do with playing live around the world."

"So when we arrived in October, to start with the album, beginning of October, we had a lot of songs with us, but then Desmond was surprising us by presenting us his idea of Humanity Hour 1, including already... he brought a guy in called Liam Carr; he's an artist to do covers and working on the Internet, the artist who really came up with a great cover, with a great booklet and everything. He said, this is the way of doing this idea, Humanity Hour 1. Then we talked about it, liked the idea, and Desmond said, 'Guys, I have a lot of good writers around who can help to make this album a great album,' including Eric Bazilian, who we knew already from working on Unbreakable, and Marti Frederiksen, who we knew already from working on Eye II Eye, and Jason Paige, John 5 and stuff. So in this case it was great teamwork."

"Also Desmond mentioned that, 'I want to do the overview. I'm going to do the vocals. But for the guitars, I have a new upcoming guy named James Michael, and he is the guy who will work with bass, drums and guitars.' So in this case it was a good idea to work in two studios, and really watching each other that nobody went too far. We had around 18 songs. First of all we had 14 or 15, and then we noticed that this album was becoming too dark, and it was important for us that this album has the dark side of humanity, but also the hopeful side of humanity. We had to write three or four more songs to make the balance right."

"Also for us this album was not to go too far with our sound, a bridge between the older style of Scorpions and the up-to-date style of Scorpions. So the way we were working on it, everything came naturally, and really arranging, working on it, some talk about it, and then things were building up, until the end of February. Then the time for mixing the album was a little bit difficult. We already had an invitation from Putin to play the Kremlin Palace in March. Which means we had to leave, and we had to do the mixing online. We were on tour then, in Moscow, in the Baltic states, in Kiev, in Kazakhstan."

Asked to what extent he had any indication that Putin actually knew much about the band, Schenker says, "I think one thing, he wanted to meet us, a few times when we played in Russia. But somehow, because of different schedules it didn't happen. We met his right hand once. He came to us and said hello from Mr. Putin and stuff like this. So I don't know if he's really a fan or not. Maybe he knows about the Gorbachev thing, *Wind Of Change*. By doing this Russian version of *Wind Of Change* and being invited to the Kremlin in 1991 in December, when Gorbachev was still in power. I think this was a message that went all around the whole world— we were the only band. Even Gorbachev we met later. He said, 'You know, you're still the only band who has been in the Kremlin, and even jamming there.' So in this case, of course, we have a different position. The other position is that Putin is doing very well together with the Germans. In this case, of course, it could be a possibility."

Returning to the odd assemblage of Humanity Hour 1, Rudolf explains, "So on this trip, we got the mixes then online, and we had to make our notes and everything, send it over to the guys, and James and Desmond said they like this more, so it was a very interesting procedure. A different production. In this case, everything was not planned. It was teamwork, being inspired, by, let's say, lifting up the consciousness, the global collective consciousness, of people, like Linkin Park or Bono is doing it, to let people know and to be more aware of the planet here. That we can't fool around with nature too much because we will hurt ourselves. Everything is connected. When something is happening in Brazil, in the rain forest, the lungs of the world, it gets killed, then we will get hit terribly. So that was a good thing about Humanity Hour 1. When we started our American tour, we started in South America in Manaus, in the jungle. The promoter. Paulo Baron, who did the South American leg, he came to us to Spain when we played in Spain for the Humanity Hour 1 tour, and explained to us, 'You know guys, there's this rain forest, Manaus. Many people living there, two-and-a-half or three million people, and it would be a fantastic idea, connected to Humanity Hour 1, where you can play to Manaus, it in the rain forest, supported by Greenpeace, and let the people know that you have to be careful with the rain forest.' So we played there in front of 30,000 people, and we recorded everything with 13 cameras, and we will release this for a charity album for saving the rain forest. So we did Brazil first, and then we'll see what we do next."

"In this case it's a good way... you're not coming from a position where you are repeating too much," says Rudolf, summing up. "I mean, you are repeating because of the way you write and everything, but that's also why we were happy to work with other writers together. Because it's good sometimes to really get fresh blood in your own way of working, to see how other people are working. Create with different tunings, different sides. That's very important. We wanted to continue to be ready to give another spark to another album. You have to be ready. You have to work your way through it."

Humanity Hour 1 (issued May 14th '07 in Europe and August 28th in North America), included this tiny note that really is the key to cracking the whole confusing thing open: "Humanity – Hour 1, based on an original concept by Sir Desmond Child and futurist Liam Carr predicts a world torn apart by a civil war between humans and robots. This apocalyptic nightmare serves as a warning shot to all mankind... our only hope of survival is to reclaim our humanity."

Musically, anyways, the album bears a similarity to the dark melodies and simplicity of Unbreakable. *Hour 1* is pure tribal, down-tuned grunge rock. *The Game Of Life* is an example of the band's new curiously morose pop rock. *We Were Born To Fly* is a mix of both those ideas, but quite catchy and nicely European of melody. *The Future Never Dies* is a big, ridiculous Desmond Child ballad, with equal additives from Queen and Diane Warren that become disconnected and maudlin come chorus time.

Incidentally, the credits are dominated by Child and Bazilian at the lyric end, with Klaus, Rudolf and Matthias essentially splitting the music credits. As alluded to by Rudolf, the production credit is shared by Desmond and James Michael, with Desmond additionally getting the executive producer credit. None of this matters outside of the splitting of the money, because Humanity Hour 1 fits uninspiringly right in the middle of the tight sonic range established and mapped by every Scorpions album since and including Love At First Sting.

Moving forward through the track list, *You're Loving Me To Death* is acceptable grunge rock and so is *321*. Then it's into another ballad, *Love Will Keep Us Alive*, more epic, down-tuned grunge rock in *We Will Rise Again*, which is half ballad, and then an odd uptempo ballad called *Your Last Song*, which includes shades of Porcupine Tree in the verse and pre-chorus. *Love Is War* is yet another ballad, this one acoustic and bluesy, again, a bit of Porcupine Tree to it. With *The Cross*, we are back to circular Soundgarden riffing, followed by *Humanity* to close this downer of a baffling record, the ersatz title track beginning as a typical Klaus ballad set to a soft military beat, and then turning into a progressive rock-type song of pretty cool movements, sorta Pink Floyd-like in tone, vibe, melody, and daft concept. There were a couple of radio edits for Japanese bonus tracks, but also a new song called *Cold*, which was a thumping rocker fully within the dour and direct spirit of the album at large.

As for Klaus's view on the strange Humanity Hour 1 exercise, he figures that the band, "wanted to follow, definitely, like what we did with Unbreakable, and hopefully top it. We wanted to make a rock album with lots of energy. We'd left the stage of experimenting and side-projects behind us. Since Unbreakable, we tried to really follow that way again. A lot of rock fans all over the world, and especially when we played the Wacken Festival last year, they really appreciated it. Because especially in the heavy rock community, they thought the Scorpions had mellowed out and became a ballad band. I mean, we love the ballads and we are proud of them, but we're not a ballad band, we're a rock band. And we wanted to prove that this band is still rocking, and still got the sting, and haven't lost anything."

Indeed Scorpions headlined the main stage early at Wacken 2006, playing the Thursday, August 6th, with a few intriguing twists to the tale planned and executed...

Explains Klaus, "We did a show called A Night To Remember. We invited Uli Jon Roth, Michael Schenker and Herman Rarebell to join us on stage. We put 50 songs on the Internet and we asked the fans to tell us what they wanted us to play. It was a hardcore audience. Again, we wanted to prove that this band is not a ballad band and that we like to rock. It was also a challenge that we threw ourselves into. There were 60,000 rock fans there and they freaked. We filmed it and we will hopefully be putting it out soon. We enjoyed playing songs with Michael and Uli. A couple of weeks back we played some shows in Europe and we had Uli Jon Roth with us. We played songs from way back like *Dark Lady, Speedy's Coming* and *Fly To The Rainbow*. Uli is an amazing and legendary guitar player. Uli had a lot of fun playing on stage with the Scorpions. We played *In Trance*. It was fun for us as we would play *Humanity* and then we would introduce Uli and we would play *Pictured Life*. It is so cool to do that and the fans really loved it. It would be great at some point to do this in the States as well. It shows that it was an important part in the Scorpions history and it still works to go from the present to the past. It also shows that we are not just riding on the glorious old days. We have something new to present but it really is like going full circle. Michael Schenker is going through difficult times right now and we hope he gets back on track soon. But that is the story of Michael's life. He was back at the Wacken show and a couple of weeks ago, MSG opened the show for us in London and Manchester. The fans just freaked. It was difficult for Michael though. We hope for the best and that he is alright soon. Uli is a very organised person and he is a great artist. When we play a show in Paris then you know he is going to be there. With Michael you never know."

"I think it's definitely a more mature kind of record," continues Klaus, back to Humanity Hour 1. "And working with Desmond Child, and some of the best artists, writers, in rock 'n' roll: James Michael, who also produced the record, Jim Peterik, Marti Fredericksen. So in a way, we're back with old friends and family. But it was different because it was a collaboration with all these writers, and when Desmond introduced to us to the idea, the concept of Humanity Hour 1... so we have a redline all throughout the recording sessions. It was a huge pool of creativity, working with all these people, and still trying to come out with hopefully another milestone record. Hopefully another album that rocks, with a lot of attitude, great lyrics, and not so much boys chasing girls, but like a deeper meaning, and carrying the message of humanity, where all the songs are connected with this kind of concept."

"But at the same time, of course, it's another rock record, and we want to entertain the audience, but we want to fill it with some meaning. If you see the artwork, this cyborg standing in front of a crater—in a way, it's all of us facing the future. So where do we go from here? The big question mark. It's time to turn around and get back on the road of humanity, get back to respect for each other on this planet. So that's how we started. It was a whole different set-up, but going for a record that has the signature Scorpions sound, the Scorpions DNA, what makes the Scorpions so special. We have our own brand of music, but at the same time, moving ahead as artists. Not trying to become a Spinal Tap act but come up with another classic album. We wanted to make an album that sounds 2007, and there were a lot of things that were completely different."

I wanted to check with Klaus, Rudolf's curious comment about adding some light to Liam's and Desmond's concept, and if, as the lyricist in the band, Klaus had any part in that process. "Yes, I'm definitely the kind of guy who would come up with *Love Will Keep Us Alive* rather than *Love Is War*. We had a big argument with Desmond about it (laughs), because we tried to find a balance between those darker songs on the record and songs of hope. I'm certainly more the guy, more romantic, more... I never would come up with a hook line, 'love is war.' Well, you know, for a Scorpions song, that doesn't come together. But Desmond really convinced me in the end and said, 'Klaus, come on, we can't have an album where we have 12 songs and they're all about we're happy campers.' So it's got to be more down and more dark—if dark is the right word—and more dangerous—to find a good balance. Singing, 'Humanity goodbye,' you know, of course is one thing, but we mean, 'Humanity, it's time'."

"This is also an issue where we said, it's got to... we've finished the record with that song—the message has to be, 'Humanity, it's time,' in the very end. So this child saying, 'It's time.' This New Orleans kind of orchestra or band is breaking down, and it looks like the Titanic is going down, so you hear this child, and the message is, 'It's time.' We know we cannot change the world with music, but as grown-ups, adults, artists, with a long-time career, 35 years plus, you don't just want to concentrate on songs with, 'Hey baby, let's rock.' There's more to it. When Desmond came up, he said, 'You guys, take this to the next level. Lyrically, it's very important for you. You've been out there for a long time as artists, and people want to take you seriously. Not a comedy act, like a Spinal Tap act, hair metal from the '80s'."

"It's very different," says Klaus, asked to contrast Desmond with Dieter. "With Dieter, the way the band worked at the time, it was this dirty rock 'n' roll animal, working this dirty attitude. So many, many songs, from *Lovedrive* to *Another Piece Of Meat*, so many, (laughs)... and of course, being the romantic guy (laughs), I always had my share of putting those songs and lyrics like *Still Loving You* and so many, many others in there. With Desmond, so many years later, he was so aware of where the band is now, and after this long, long career, really wanted to come up with something that should be amazing. If the lyrics are in the centre of attention, of course, the music too, but he wanted the whole thing to be very meaningful. So therefore, it was really great to have a chance to work with all these great people together."

"But don't forget, we're an international band, but we are Germans. German is my mother language. So to have all these people working together, that was just fantastic. For example, there was a song *The Game Of Life*. Actually I wrote that with two Swedish guys, and Desmond liked that song a lot, and he wanted it to be part of the whole set. He did like the lyrics though, so we were starting all over again, and it was exciting, you know, to work with Desmond, and how he works and how he comes up with ideas. He's throwing, kicking out these hook lines, it's just amazing. It was never a big deal, you know, 'Hey, we need another pre-chorus; the words are missing.' It was a constant flow of ideas because so many people were working on this project. So it was fascinating and I enjoyed it a lot."

"With Desmond, I must say, he's a legendary songwriter, producer—his list of success is so impressive," continues Klaus. "He knows totally what he is doing, and he lives also for his vision, and what he wants to do. When you are with him in the studio, in a way it was very similar to Dieter, because he worked me very hard as well. It was like a challenge, after all these years. 'Okay, come on, let's get something out of this.' You know, even if it's really tough, you know that it's the only way to get something out that is really top class. When you work with a top class producer like Desmond Child, you know up front that this is going to be a challenge. After all these years, I know we want to make something that is hopefully great and outstanding. You have to go through this kind of process, and have somebody who works you really hard."

"In the end, it shows in the performance. With Desmond, you go at some point, 'okay, Desmond, you're sitting there in the control room, the studio, I'm singing my ass off, and now I'll show you what I can do.' (laughs). At the end you come to something, and if you listen to it, I think you can hear it, it's very powerful. So I'm very thankful if I have somebody who works me that hard, and still after all these years, you learn a few things. It was a very exciting trip. When you turn him on, then he's the kind of guy who really shows it. He's really inspiring to me, 'Oh, Klaus, that was really fantastic! That was amazing! Give me that exact thing again!' He was very exciting. At the end of the day, everybody walks out there, and he's never giving up before he has a first-class performance."

Then there was the whole other skunkworks of the organization, namely what was going on with the guitars. Bizarre when you think about it. I mean, it's almost like Desmond hijacked the band, to the point where this could have been billed as one of these rock opera projects and not something under the Scorpions brand. "Well, Rudolf, I mean, he's very creative guy," explains Meine. "He comes up with the typical Scorpions riffs. I mean it is so Scorpions-like, what he brings to the table. Same with Matthias. This time, they worked, both, with James Michael. So also, I think what makes this album so special is the combination between Desmond Child and James Michael. Because James Michael worked with Rudolf and Matthias, and Desmond was focused very much on the vocals. So between the two, you know, they could always figure out who should do what, and I think there was a lot of stuff that completely worked out amazing on this record. I think it came out very powerful and supporting every song really well."

Back to vocals, as the years wear on, quite surprisingly, it seems that Klaus's scare back at Blackout was a one-time event. "Fortunately no problems," says Meine. "I mean, this was heavy, in the early '80s. I'm very thankful that I have my voice back, and I get a second chance as a singer, artist. No, I take much better care of myself these days. I know it's an ugly word, together with rock 'n' roll; it's called discipline, but that's what it takes. To go through all that crazy touring and those heavy recordings to those sessions, where you sing for months and months or for weeks and weeks. You've got to have a strong voice. With Desmond, he set me up with a vocal coach. He wanted my voice to really be strong during all those months. Well, again, I learned a lot of new things. With this guy, when I was in his house for a vocal session, another client was coming in, and it was one of those famous Hollywood actors. I was introduced, and he kind of went, 'Klaus, you don't need a vocal coach after all these years!' I went, okay, man, check it out, that's very cool, you will enjoy it. I think it supported a lot of our recording process. Well, whatever it takes. There's no point going on tour or making a record when your instrument is not in shape. I try to take care of it, and since I had that experience in the early '80s, I don't ever want to go through something like this again. I think I learned my lesson."

"I know that people think that maybe we are running out of ideas," said Klaus, to Jeb Wright, who played devil's advocate, saying that the perception is that when a band goes this deep into outside songwriters, it's because they've lost the plot. "It is not so much that. The whole world of music has changed. We made this album in an old-fashioned way, in that sense. We worked in Los Angeles, in the studio, for four months, working every day. We could have gone into our basement and made a cheap record and put it out on the Internet and hopefully we would have a hit. We made it the old-fashioned way to convince the fans, and the new generation of fans who may be listening to our music for the first time, that this is very powerful music. We put everything into this.

We wrote a few hits and we know what we are doing. Of course we can do it all ourselves. We know what to do and we are definitely not running out of ideas. We are touring all over the world and that is still the biggest source of inspiration. But to make something that is outstanding and amazing you have to have a good team around you and you have to open up. Desmond has worked with artists that we really respect, like Aerosmith, and he really knows what he is doing. He lives for his passion and his music. Desmond is a guy that you can trust if you want to go somewhere else and you are ready to learn another lesson in the new chapter of this band."

Asked by Jeb to compare it with the last time the band stepped out this extensively, namely Eye II Eye, Klaus says, "The difference is that this album still incorporates the Scorpions trademark sound and ingredients—even with all these people involved. Desmond really put his stamp onto this as well but you still recognize that it is the Scorpions. With Eye II Eye it was a different kind of sound. We were experimenting. Peter Wolf produced it. He played keyboards with Frank Zappa. He was very talented but it was not a very professionally produced record. For some reason the Scorpions' sting was not shining through. The fans couldn't identify with it. The album had no Scorpions DNA. People did not like the album because they could not connect with it. With Humanity, we were not experimenting. I think we all learned our lesson—I know I learned my lesson. This album is truly a Scorpions record but it has a more current sound. It sounds very much 2007. A lot of rock magazines back in Europe said that a lot of rock bands that are just starting to make rock albums should listen to Humanity Hour 1 because it is very cool."

If you cop to calling this a single tour, and further cop to calling it a tour for Humanity Hour 1, Scorpions executed their most extensive world trek ever, playing everywhere for near on three years, from March of 2007 through December of 2009. Indeed five different tracks from the album were played at various times, with three from Unbreakable living on past that album's ill reception.

Still, one would have to admit that the only scattered applause for the recent studio albums, plus all the compilation and quasi-compilation material, had worked to turn the band into little more than a fairly thriving live experience, trotting out classics whose origins faded further and further back every year. What were the guys thinking? Well, one would have to say that they were sincere about changing things up, like

Rudolf says, injecting some new blood into the process. It also seems that the guys found appealing the possibility of recapturing some of the political capital they had with *Wind Of Change*, this idea of being associated with a story that had some intellectual heft to it, although ultimately, Desmond's attempt went the way of Pete Townshend's Lifehouse. And perhaps it would have worked, if the music had had more pep, i.e. less ballads and a bit more uptempo and riffy at the rock end. Fortunately for the band, they would finally heed the messages being sent by their suffering fan base and soon return with their best firecracker of a record since certainly Face The Heat, if not Crazy World.

Sting In The Tail

"There was no big wave lately"

Amid rumblings that they would be retiring after the long goodbye tour following the new album, on March 14th, 2010, Scorpions issued, Sting In The Tail. Traditionally awkward as that title is, it sounded like a message that the guys were going to out injecting a bit of venom, the mighty album cover reinforcing the crude communication.

"The way we recorded this CD was a little different," explained Matthias Jabs, in conversation with RockMusicStar, who had just congratulated him on the album's robust chart positioning across Europe, particularly the eastern side of it. "We started in May of last year; we got together with the producer team of Mikael Nord Andersson and Martin Hansen in Sweden. We had some songs from recent albums that we didn't use and we re-arranged them and wrote a few new ones. Then we went on tour in the summer and came back in August and really started working on the songs, and then we played a few shows again and then went back into the studio, sometimes in Sweden, sometimes in our place. Because of this, it always felt fresh. We would work for a week or ten days then take two weeks off from recording and play a few shows. When we finished with all the songs, we invited people from management and from our record company to listen to the rough mixes. After, we heard the whole thing, we went wow! The management said that we should consider calling this our last album, because it's really a great one. This followed by a world tour, that usually will last two-and-a-half years because we play everywhere. They said this will be a great way to end your career on a high note. So we thought about it, but not for too long. We decided that it was a good idea and made the announcement in January that this would be the last CD and tour for the Scorpions."

Whoever they are, Andersson and Hansen no doubt got one of the punchiest, most explosive sounds for the band in years, the brightness and vibrancy of the production reaching back to Blackout. Says Jabs, "The producers of this CD have been fans of the band since the early '80s, and if you ask them or any of our fans what their favourite Scorpions album is, 95-99% will say Blackout or Love At First Sting. I think during the early '80s the band finally found its sound and style. Love At First Sting was the essence of the band's sound. I think that the new CD comes closest to Love At First Sting. It wasn't intentionally done this way, but looking back, Sting In The Tail could have been the follow-up album to Love At First Sting during the '80s."

Amongst all the preposterous statements we could cherry-pick out of our interviews for Unbreakable and Humanity Hour 1, mainly from either Rudolf or Klaus, there's one from Matthias that rings perfectly true like a bell. Sting In The Tail sounds vacuum-packed in the Scorpions sound of 1984, churlish lyrics included, for better or worse, but mostly for better.

"We had recorded probably 16 songs for Sting In The Tail and nobody was happy with the way it was coming along, amazingly enough," says James Kottak, asked about the production on the record. "Then Mikael Andersson and Martin Hansen took the songs and turned things upside-down. All of a sudden we're like 'whoa' and that's the job of a producer. They have to take a diamond in the rough and turn it into something polished. They gave us new perspective and we went back and re-recorded everything. The album was done, but we went back and re-did it. They were able to get to the root of what the Scorpions are all about and I think it's one of the best albums we've ever done—well, since I've been in the band. There's four songs with the work 'rock' in it, so that's perfect (laughs)."

"I keep it simple," says Matthias, asked about his molten tone all over the record and on stages worldwide. "I don't put any effects between my guitar and amp. My guitar goes into a cable that goes into the amp and there is a microphone in front of the amp. The tone comes from my fingers. Our producers asked the same question. Whatever guitar I play, I still get the same sound. If you use foot petals and all that other crap, it gets lost. Your true technique will never shine through. But, I keep it simple and that's my well-known secret. Thank you very much for the compliment. I also play a lot too! I played most of all the lead guitars on the Scorpions albums. Sting In The Tail, I even put down the rhythm tracks and then I worked on the overdubs and guitar arrangements. I did the leads last. By the time I play the leads, the song already has its sound. In case you are interested, I developed my own amp over the years. I road-tested it the last two years on tour. So it's reliable. I use it now in the studio as well. It's called Mastertone. It's my own brand, my own amp and does exactly what I like."

"Desmond is known as being a hit-producing producer," continues Jabs, asked why the band didn't work with Desmond this time. "We went with him three years ago in LA. But he made us follow his concept too much. He put his producer stamp on the Scorpions too much. But I like the album; I liked what he had done. But the Swedish guys, Mikael Nord Andersson and Martin Hansen, were who we were originally going to record the last CD with, but decided to go with Desmond. But it was their turn now. They wanted to do what we wanted to do and not bend it out of shape. It was more like a unit, a band with seven people rather than a producer and a band."

Asked if it was uncomfortable working with Desmond, who indeed did impose his will upon Humanity over and above production, namely lyrically, Matthias says, "No, not for me. I think it was more uncomfortable for our singer Klaus because Desmond is so particular about his lyrics. He liked me and my guitar playing and we didn't have any problems. I mostly recorded with James Michael anyways, our co-producer. But it was hard working with Desmond because lyrics are his main thing and the Scorpions are a guitar band. You have to pay attention to that and the results will be a lot better."

Embedded in that, ahem, jab, is a truth about Humanity Hour 1. Not only did Desmond bring to the band something he wasn't in the least bit famous for, a concept album, but the end result did go against the band's nature, putting the guitars in a subservient support role, support to the whole ill-advised futuro-tale, which again, ain't exactly adjacent to the nature of the Scorpions... or Desmond Child. Sure, maybe this Liam Carr, but not Desmond Child or Scorpions.

Efficiently putting all that in the past, Sting In The Tail opens in fine Love At First Sting fashion with *Raised On Rock*, a song too stupid to be on Blackout, but firmly as good as *Bad Boys Running Wild* or *Big City Nights*. It's a simple chord progression, but there's an anthemic chorus, not to mention talkbox, as well as some tasty leads colouring the positive experience.

The album's heavy, rocking title track is next, featuring additional guitar textures, this time wah-wah and an oddly clean guitar solo, plus a weird guttural Klaus vocal as a sort of b-chorus. "That was Klaus's idea," says Matthias. "He came up with it when we were doing some recording in our studio, which is very close to where Rudolf lives. Klaus and I live on one street within crawling distance of one another. So we took a car every day to our studio and it's a 20-minute ride. When you're in the car, you try to use the time to come up with ideas or get inspired. He had the idea while driving, but it was just noises and not words. It then turned into, 'Bang, bang, rock will again.' He had the sound in his ears and that's what came out. It's like a sound effect, but it's just voices. We open the show with that song, at least so far. We have played a few shows already to test everything out for the tour."

Next up is *Slave Me*, which in fine Scorpions tradition, holds back on the creativity for the verse to explode with Teutonic glory come chorus-time. Already, true to Matthais' words, Scorpions have built a punchy record as stadium-loud 'n' proud as Love At First Sting, no speedy, smart, technical rock feat to be sure, but a decibel-drenched party all the same.

"Not only Love At First Sting, but also Blackout, and I would include Lovedrive in there," enthused Rudolf, framing the album in conversation with Andrew Bansal, but really giving Sting too much credit! "The good thing about the whole album is, we are getting back to where we've come from, and by accident, the time is right again for classic rock. There was no big wave lately. The latest waves were grunge and alternative. Now, because the grunge and alternative guys can play their instruments, they are becoming like classic rock bands. You have Nickelback, 3 Doors Down, Green Day and even the punk bands—they are playing classic rock now! We are getting the essence. If you take the best songs from the '80s, from all the albums on one album, you have Sting In The Tail. That's the reason why we noticed and mentioned that this is going to be the last album and tour. We can't beat this again. That would be hard and even if we do it a bit better than this album, the people would not respond as strongly as right now, because the time is perfect. It's like a big wave. We are surfing on it and enjoying it!"

Things settle down for *The Good Die Young*, a ballad, but, in the spirit of success established by the album so far, this is a top-flight and largely epic ballad, with a powerful chorus that features a guest vocal courtesy of ex-Nightwish legend Tarja Turunen.

"We met her at the Live And Loud Festival in Sao Paulo," explains Matthias, "at a few shows actually, but that was the most popular one. The idea always comes with every recording. It usually comes from the record company. They go, 'We would like to have a duet.' Mostly it doesn't work out. But this time it worked out (laughs). We met her doing a German TV show together. She's a nice lady, she looks good on TV and she sings well. I think it really adds to the atmosphere of the song. It gives it a mystical touch. It really pays off and for the harmonies with Klaus in the chorus, the voices fit well together."

But taking Tarja on the road to do the song isn't really an option. "See, that's the problem," says Matthias. "She has her own career. While doing duets we are always careful, because then we have to depend on somebody. She's not too loud on the song but if we do a duet where the guest really plays a major role in the song and you can't take them on the road... if it's going to be a hit, maybe people will be like, 'So, where's the person?'"

"We have an idea to bring her in by video during the shows," adds Rudolf. "That would be good. We even formed a new version of the song, which will come out as a single in Europe where she even sings one verse and also louder in the chorus. When we have that one, we will include it with the video."

One of the band's crunchiest rockers in years comes next, *No Limit* fitting well into the simple driving hard rock of the record, but definitely striking more of a heavy rock pose over and above the opening three tracks. *Rock Zone* is a refreshing bit of Mötley Crüe party rock, housing a riff with a bit of AC/DC to it as well. *Lorelei* opens like the more famous *Lorelei*, and then becomes yet another high quality Scorpions ballad, high rent due to its Mediterranean vibe.

Up next is *Turn You On*, another tight, taut rocker, elegantly drenched in distorted guitars, simple, to the point, infectious, old school of chord progression, and then again, as so many times before, gilded in a bit of Euro rock. After what is the album's weakest ballad, *SLY*, then it's back into the punchy material, *Spirit Of Rock* being a bit poppy, but saved by a Boston-like twin lead and other guitar embellishments, typical Scorpions moves including short bursts that are nonetheless built of thick, rhythm guitars, filling the spaces usually saved for piercing lead licks.

The album closes with another ballad called *The Best Is Yet To Come*. "We didn't do it on purpose," laughs Matthias, with regard to the title's sense of irony, given the retirement announcements. "The song is actually six years old. It came in at the last minute for Unbreakable but we didn't record it. In 2003 it was already there. But this time it was right. For the previous album Humanity Hour 1, any other song wouldn't have fit in—it all had to do with that special concept. That's why, even though it's a very good song, we couldn't use it for that album. Now the time was right and it's pure coincidence. It makes some people think and wonder. You never know. It's a nice way to finish the record."

"You can look at it in different ways," adds Rudolf. "Ironically on one hand as he said, and on the other hand you have to always see the next step forward as a better one to make your life more interesting. That's very important. It's also a very true thing. You work in the studio, you try to make the best for the fans. Then you have the result and go on tour. The tour is actually the best! So you can see it in different ways."

Of note, the European version of the album carried an extra track over and above the American version, a fairly aggressive yet slow and grinding heavy rocker called *Let's Rock!* which is clichéd part of the time but richly Teutonic in the breaks and chorus, featuring some tasty drumming from Kottak as well. There's also a Japanese bonus track called *Thunder And Lightning*, which is a powerful yet melodic Euro rocker fully supporting the idea that this was Scorpions on a songwriting roll. Arguably, these were Scorpions' best two bonus tracks ever, all too many in the past falling into the paint-by-numbers ballad zone. The crescendo of Scorpions tones and tails... the way *Thunder And Lightning* builds to epic conclusion should be the way the career ends, a heavy rock flourish for the ages, moody and mystical of melody, loud and proud.

Two weeks after the issue of the album, Scorpions were made part of Hollywood's RockWalk, outside of the Guitar Centre on Sunset Boulevard. Remarked Rudolf, "Among all the awards we've got so far, this is the most outstanding one because the other ones are made by jury or by people because you had some hits or whatever. This one is a musical thing. We are the only German band ever to get this. To get it alongside Jimmy Page and all the other people, it's unbelievable! When I think back, I spoke to Conny Plank, the producer of the first album. I remember speaking to him because he also wanted to have us in his company. We said, 'No, it's too small. We want to focus worldwide and want to play in America.' He was laughing like crazy (laughs)! He said, 'Do you know what kind of musicians they have there?' We didn't care. We wanted to play in America. So, we knew that we were already included in the rock family of musicians. But now, we know that we really are. So that's the point and that's the reason why it is very special."

Despite the tease, the plan really was that Sting In the Tail would be the band's last album. "The reason we said we were going to do a farewell tour was Sting In The Tail," affirms Rudolf. "Because when we finished the album, shortly before mixing, our manager said, 'Hey guys, that's a fantastic album, how do you want to beat that? It's unbeatable.' He said, 'Hey guys, I would think this would be a great album to make a farewell tour.' First of all, we were shocked, but then oversleeping the whole thing, we said, maybe it's right. Klaus and me, we were 63, the time is right, we have the '80s big sound with a twist, we have an album which is fantastic, and it now has the DNA of the Scorpions completely in it. That would be fantastic, and that was the reason, because this album became very successful, and it put us in the Top 20 in the Billboard charts, in 2010. And we have a tour now around the world, since March 2010, a sold-out tour with lots and lots of people. We came lately from the French tour, and Portugal, sold-out places like Lisbon, 20,000, and France, 19,000, the other places full, sold-out. That's fantastic. I think that's how you have to finish a career of over 40 years. On a high note. Not fading away. On a high note, have a great time with your fans, and enjoy it, and so in the collective mind of the people around the world, hey, the Scorpions were a great band. I think that's a good thing, instead of fading away, or maybe crawling in front of your fans; that's not the way the Scorpions are. As an animal, it's a very strong animal. But in the moment, the animal, the scorpion is not as healthy and strong as the scorpion wants to be, then this dangerous animal becomes a weak animal, and we don't want to become weak."

Comeblack

"A holler-out to the bands that inspired us"

Comeblack is, unfortunately, one of those goofy incidental releases that one would have hoped would not serve as the last Scorpions album ever (and as fate would have it, it wasn't). If it was supposed to end according to plan, best to remember the robust Sting In The Tail than this hodge-podge of half re-recordings of hits, half ill-advised covers. But you know what? Given yet another studio album we would see in 2015, Comeblack would not be the last spot of product from this band.

"There is no mission!" begins Rudolf, running down the state of affairs as Scorpions, ostensibly, wind down their affairs in 2011. "Only an inspiration, finding out that we have in our concerts now, on the farewell tour since 2010, many, many, many young fans. We were wondering, couldn't believe it, couldn't see it, but then we found out that we have over one million users on Facebook, and that 80% of this one million is people between 14 and 28! So in this case, we saw the people singing the songs with us, *Blackout, Rock You Like A Hurricane*, and seeing how the record companies are falling apart, and all the backup has gone away, gone, we said, 'Yeah, let's do it. Why not do the best songs from Scorpions, the classics, and put them on an album, using ProTools, use technology, use the sound, more punch?' I mean, I love analogue, of course, but that is more for heart and soul. But the digital has a good part also, because you can put lots of energy in, and put it in for the young kids, and of course for the old fans also, too, where you have something for the modern way of listening."

"So in this case we started working with our Swedish guys, after 2010, beginning of 2011, after having, being in the Top 20 of the most successful tours around the world... only four rock bands were in front of us—it was U2, Metallica, Bon Jovi and AC/DC. So we said, hey guys, let's go for it, and so we worked on it. Then somebody's idea, why not put in also half-and-half, bands who inspired us? Make some songs, cover versions of Kinks, Stones, Beatles, Pretty Things or whatever, and let's see how this sounds. Then we started working on that, and also found out what Klaus could sing, and we were working with around 20 to 25 songs, cover versions, and out of the 25 are the songs which you hear, now made it on the album. In this case, we give a holler-out to the bands that inspired us to make music, and also give our 'best of' from the band on this album, and give it as a project, as an extra, to our fans."

There's definitely more crunch to some of these re-recordings. "It's the reason why we did *Rhythm Of Love*," says Rudolf of the opener, which sounds like a tank rolling through the desert compared to the original. "*Rhythm Of Love* is a great song, and now on the Comeblack album, many people told me already that it's so much better. Also *Blackout* I like very much, because it's so powerful. I get so many fans writing that, 'Oh, I can't believe this song, *Blackout*, it's amazing.' It's young kids! 'It's got amazing... you sound like a young band, and you guys are already 63' (laughs)." Not unarguably better, this version of *Blackout* is thicker, more garagey from a drum point of view, and then it seems like everybody reacts in Kottak kind.

"It was a privilege and honour to re-record such incredibly wonderful songs from the Scorpions and I was thrilled to do it," says James, speaking with Montreal's Mitch Lafon a couple months after the album's November 4th, 2011 release date, vinyl included. "We've actually re-recorded *Wind Of Change*, *Still Loving You* and *Rock You Like A Hurricane* for TV shows over the years, but this was a little more official and I had complete freedom. They recorded these songs in Portland, Oregon. Then they sent the tracks over to me with click track and I had the freedom to add the drums on my own. I had years and years of preparation because we'd played those songs hundreds of times. It was a real thrill. I was so pleased and proud of how they came out. When I joined the band—and I still feel this way—I need to honour these songs. I need to honour the way they were written, the vibe, the certain drum fills and the feeling, but I've been in the band 16 years and I think we've evolved. I feel I'm as big a part of the band as Herman was and I feel I was able to make them my own."

Elsewhere, *The Zoo* holds back and then grooves, banged up real nice by Kottak for the chorus, the production explosive, Klaus creating cool new melodies because of the necessity of ducking a few notes here and there. Similarly, James is a huge part of driving *Rock You Like A Hurricane* to new headbanged heights and it's huge grinding guitars that make *No One Like You* more potent than the original.

Asked about picking the covers, James remarks that, "It shows how deep the history of this band is. Rudolf's favourite band is The Kinks. He was so influenced by The Kinks. Klaus loved The Stones and he loved The Beatles which is why we did *Across The Universe*. These are songs that Rudolf and Klaus grew up on back in the '60s. That's the honest to God real roots of where the Scorpions started. That's going back to when they were young teenagers and they were sitting in their room listening to the radio. It was such a thrill to be part of that. But these songs were a challenge and very difficult for me to record. My roots are very different from theirs because I grew up in the '70s. I was a Led Zeppelin and Grand Funk Railroad kind of guy. Grand Funk were my heroes. It was just The Kinks, because it was a little before my time. I mean I know these songs, but not the names of them and it was a challenge because I'm supposed to put my drumming to these classic, classic mega songs. You want to do them honour, but you also want to make them 'my own' and not just some generic cover. There are too many bad covers out there and I don't want to do that."

"Honestly, I did not know that," continues James, after Lafon tells him that supposed odd-man out on the album, *Tainted Love*, is in fact a 1965 composition, despite everybody knowing the Soft Cell version. "I thought it was Soft Cell, but what a great classic song. We ripped it. We killed it!" Ergo, it's a fit, Gloria Jones having first recorded it back in the mid to late '60s, which is more or less where the rest of the six total covers originate.

"We announced the album Sting In The Tail in conjunction with this tour that will take us all over the world," summarizes Klaus, also letting on that Comeblack was somewhat of an olive branch to the label. "It became such a huge success that Sony said, 'okay, we want to support this with some product.' What can you do? We just announced our last album and then things are so huge that they want us to get back in the studio. We decided that if we were going to do that then we would just go in and have some fun. We decided to re-record some of our classics like *The Zoo* and *Rock You Like A Hurricane*. The idea was for us to blow off the dust from those vinyl records and to present them to a whole new audience in the sound of the 21st century. It was a lot of fun because you can do so much more today in the studio. At the same time, we thought that this can't be enough as we didn't want to put out a new album without some new songs on it. We thought about recording some covers and paying tribute to some of the legendary bands who inspired us in the '60s. We had a lot of fun trying things out and seeing what worked and what didn't work. We really were enjoying playing music from all of our heroes like the Beatles and the Stones. We did songs like *Tainted Love*, which is a song that many people might not expect to hear us do, but the riff worked well. We gave it a try and it worked. We did *Children Of The Revolution* by T. Rex, which was outside of us in a lot of ways. They are all great bands."

"Those are all legendary compositions," continues Meine. "You have to find your own adaptation of that music. You better do it good; it doesn't make sense to record any of those songs unless it is going to be great. At this point, we had to be convinced that it was not only a great song but we had to put our own Scorpions DNA onto those songs. It was a very difficult issue to even choose the songs. You can't go in and choose *Hey Jude* or *Strawberry Fields*, no way. When I did *Across The Universe*, it worked well with my voice and everyone said, 'Let's do it.' Then Matthias said we should do a Rolling Stones song. It is impossible for me, with my voice, to sing a soul song. We found *Ruby Tuesday* and it came out not too bad. Then we went to Led Zeppelin and we figured out, no way could we do that. We love Led Zeppelin and they are one of our favourite bands of all time, but at the end of the day it was impossible to pick any of those songs. I think we were talking about *Good Times Bad Times* but it didn't work. At the end of the day, we took a deep bow to Jimmy Page as we couldn't do justice to any of their songs. Doing this album was so much fun that if someone had not told us it was time to stop, then we would probably be in the studio still recording. We didn't need to write songs and we didn't need to write lyrics. We just had a great time."

Some songs, like *Across The Universe*, are kept aptly mellow, but *Tin Soldier* and *Ruby Tuesday* turned into a Scorpions pop, while *Children Of The Revolution*, *Tainted Love* and to some extent *All Day And All Of The Night*, are given the full metal jacket racket treatment.

Bonus tracks include the Yardbirds' *Shapes Of Things*, a new version of *Big City Nights* and *Still Loving You (Je T'aime encore)*, with Amandine Bourgeois. Makes sense, says James, because, "it was the No.1 song for like two years in France. For some reason we have a huge renaissance in France and it's such a wonderful country to tour and play. So, the song makes total sense to me. It flows. It's wonderful and I think there's a version in Spanish with Klaus, or maybe that's *Wind Of Change*."

"I have to say that I, personally, am not that crazy about the title," muses James about calling the thing Comeblack. "It was meant to be a new word like Lovedrive or Blackout. It goes in the tradition of the Scorpions coming up with new words. It's so close to 'comeback' that people are going to say, 'But didn't you just say farewell?' They might take that the wrong way. It is what it is."

At this juncture, Rudolf was still sticking to his guns concerning the band's retirement, at least from record-making. "I mean, we told the fans, when we started to play the world tour, and we told the media, that this will be the last tour and the last studio album, and we stick to it. Comeblack is a side-project. It's something that we did, but there are no new songs on it. It's not an album with new songs. We having our library, and in our warehouse, we have tons of bonus material. You know, remember from the final days, there were only nine songs possibility of bringing on an album, and we always recorded around 14, to find out of the 14 or 15, which songs we want to put on the album later. So in this case we have a lot of songs, and what we want to do, especially after we finished, we want to give the fans a box or something, with maybe bonus tracks from the Scorpions, and maybe another film, a DVD, or blu-ray, with a live concert of the Scorpions, which will be happening the end of 2012, the beginning of 2013. We have to think about what else we can do. But no, we also have 900 hours of film material in our warehouse, in the library, playing in front of the pyramids in Cairo, playing in Manaus in the jungle, playing in Red Square and other very outstanding places. So there is a lot of stuff for where we want to go then. But we need lots of time to put things like this together, to make it really great. So that will be the next thing we are doing in 2013, '14."

"I've been asked this question many times," laughs James, asked about the tail end of the Scorpions. "When the Scorpions announced their farewell tour, it meant it's the farewell tour. It is time to say goodbye and call it a day. You don't want to go out on a sour note. This band is going to go out on top. Our normal tour lasts two-and-a-half years, so this one will last three-and-a-half. It really is our farewell tour and I don't think there will be another studio album. I'm sure there will be plenty of live albums. We have our Live In 3D album and DVD coming out (note: also known as Live 2011 or its subtitle Get Your Sting & Blackout). There will be all kinds of archival things. We're working on a documentary. That'll satisfy the fans' needs as well as our needs. We're in the home stretch here, but the planet is big and to satisfy everyone is going to take a long time. We'll really be done by 2013."

"Knowing how restless Rudolf and Klaus are, I would think there will always be some kind of 'special' thing here and there, but that's just my thought," continues James. "At the same time though, it's only fair to say to the fans that this is it, we're done. Rudolf and Klaus want to go out on top. There are injuries... I'm a drummer and have been doing this since 1978, my first tour. I've got some injuries and I'm in great shape. Rudolf Schenker is in better shape than most 25-year-olds. The guy is a machine and Klaus Meine is the same thing. He's phenomenal. The whole band is, but you can't turn a blind eye to age. It eventually catches up to you and the very important point to make is that the Scorpions never stopped. Bands like Mötley Crüe and the Rolling Stones have big gaps in their career. Mötley Crüe weren't together for five or six years and they didn't do anything. The same thing for the Rolling Stones and many bands. The Scorpions never stopped. There has never been a gap. Motörhead is one of the only bands that I can think of that has consistently put out album after album and toured and toured."

"This was a good situation," reflects Rudolf. "We noticed already in 1984 that when time is on your side, everything goes automatically. You do something and in the end you notice that the puzzle finished without knowing that you are part of the puzzle. So in this case it was the same situation. During Love At First Sting we put all the pieces of the puzzle together and even when we started that tour, it was terrible with the worst stage sets. But the people didn't care. They loved the album so much that even when we played it only with amplifiers they loved it. Later on the stage set came in. It's the same here. We did Sting In The Tail, we enjoyed it very much and the management gave us the idea. We said, okay, our age is not 24 and we don't want to die in front of our audience (laughs). In my time, I went to many parties. Mostly I took the wrong decision by not leaving at one o'clock—I left at maybe six in the morning. So like Joe Walsh says in the song *Life's Been Good*, I couldn't find the door. That's the situation when you make the wrong decision at one o'clock. Instead of leaving when the party is over, you think that maybe there's a little more. So we don't want that now with the Scorpions! The first album we put out was in 1972, Lonesome Crow, and when we'll finish in 2012, we'll exactly have 40 years. That is perfect."

"It is a weird thing to think about after 40 years with this band," wonders Klaus, perhaps dreaming of the day he could give his vocal chords a proper retirement party. "We are family. On the other side, we are a band that after 40 years has survived punk and grunge. Classic rock music seems to be very popular with the new generation. Right now, we can put all of our energy into our concerts. We are really happening right now and we feel the energy. Our fans around the world will keep this energy going until the very end. They will keep it going until our rocking hurricane is downgraded to a tropical storm."

But... of course, as we know, Scorpions would pull one of the biggest retirement reversals in rock since The Who's multiple out-bows.

MTV Unplugged

"If this is retiring, then I like it because it's pretty crazy"

Provoking the band and their love for ballads, the folks at MTV talked the heroes of our story into postponing their retirement plans further by recording an elaborate and involved unplugged record. Captured with much splendour at the Lycabettus Theatre in Athens, Greece, September 11th and 12th, 2013, the band configured into various arrangements and with various guests to lighten up on many of the hits but also *Where The River Flows*, *Hit Between The Eyes* and *Rock 'n' Roll Band*, among myriad others in the complicated release history confronting these old-timers in the digital age.

"The answer must be the songs," muses Klaus, speaking with Classic Rock Revisited's Jeb Wright on why the band's material translates to well to the unplugged format. "It is the quality of songwriting and the quality of the songs; that might be the difference. You're right, we do all of these different formats and now we are releasing this Unplugged concert in Athens with many different instruments, from mandolins, to accordions, to harmonica, to strings. We just came back from a stretch of concerts we did between Russia and the Ukraine and Finland...some of them we played with symphonic orchestras. We shared the stage with 65 to 70 musicians from these State orchestras. I think those arrangements, if you would have had a chance to listen to them, it is much different than what we just did in Athens, but they are so strong, as well.

It is the music and it is in the songs. You take your own rock song, the way we play it live on stage in every regular rock show, and you take it and add a whole new dimension to the music. That is the reason why not everybody can do it. If you're only a band that has screamer material or whatever, there is not so much you can do other than to scream it out loud. The music has many dimensions and that is why we have a chance to do this sort of thing and that is why we reach a huge audience."

"It is not just the hard and heavy fans," qualifies Meine, "although we can play at Wacken, like we did in August, which is the biggest heavy rock festival in the world. We can, however, do many different things like

Unplugged as well. This is the sort of thing that keeps us going, keeps us awake and keeps us inspired. There is nothing more boring than when you do the same thing over and over again for years and years and years. We have a chance to do different things and they are also a challenge because those sets are not easy to play. When you do just a few a year, or maybe just one a year for a huge event, then you have to get back into it. With MTV, we had six months of perpetration."

"We had the offer right at the end of the tour and we were surprised," explains Klaus, offering some specifics on the situation. "We were talking about MTV Unplugged back in the glory '80s, I am sure, but it never worked out. With this offer, we wanted to come out with a whole new show, playing and performing songs that we've never played live on stage before. We wanted to play new songs as well as the classics. It turned out to be a very long set of songs. For the diehard Scorpions fans around the world this is the real deal, this is the bread and butter and the meat and potatoes and they will love it. There are a lot of songs that they know, but there are a lot of songs that are out of the mainstream. *The Best Is Yet To Come*, since Sting In The Tail came out in 2010, has been in our set list as it is a great live song. *Born To Touch Your Feelings* is from 1977 and we never played it live, never. It was one of those ballads that we never touched for a live show. For this show, with the accordion, it was just perfect. We had a Greek actress for the speaking part of the song. I don't know if you've seen it yet, but this lady was so emotional she started crying. It was emotional for everyone. You will have to check it out. I mean, if this is retiring, then I like it because it's pretty crazy. We have a new album coming out and a DVD of MTV Unplugged and the whole world seems to be excited about. If this is retirement then this is cool."

"This was the very first MTV Unplugged under the open sky," notes Klaus. "It was not recorded in a studio where they usually have a few hundred fans gathered around the stage, very relaxed and listening to the music. This is not a big rock show. They wanted the artists to sit down on the stage and perform the songs in a whole different way, which is cool. The focus is totally on the music. It was impossible to nail the Greek audience down on their seats, as they were going crazy. It was an amazing set-up. The theatre holds eight thousand people, but we cut it down to four and a half, or three and a half, or something like that, which, for an MTV production, is a lot of people. We played two shows and we recorded them for MTV and then we had another show crammed with 8,000 fans in there and played the whole show for our fans. We had two shows we filmed and recorded and we pretty much took everything from the second day. When you see the DVD, it is really cool and it is very different. Historically, it is the first MTV Unplugged under the sky. The temperature—this was in September—it was perfect, it was 27 degrees. I am not sure what that is in Fahrenheit. It was really nice. You don't need a rooftop on your stage. It was really under the stars."

"We decided to do a lot of songs that we had not done before and we decided to do more up-tempo songs," adds Matthias. "For example, we rearranged *Blackout* and *Hit Between The Eyes* which are not so obvious when you think of acoustic guitars. I think it came out great. The visual is also quite interesting as it was filmed in an outdoor theatre. The Greeks have these great outdoor theatres. This one was not an ancient one. We tried to play at one in the Acropolis, but it was a bit too small and there were too many regulations and limitations from the government side. It is old and no one can drink anything in there. There are also sound limitations because otherwise it would fall apart. It looks pretty fallen apart already; maybe they should renovate it."

"It was like we were doing a new set," continues Jab, asked about all the deep album tracks retooled. "We didn't even want to do *Rock You Like A Hurricane* on Unplugged. We wanted to do completely new music that we had not done. We had done the other songs with different shapes and forms and with orchestras and we have done them electric and we have live versions that are different. We didn't want to do this, but the fans love them and the record company wants them and then MTV said, 'No, you must do them.' The new arrangements make the songs have new sounds to them. Of course we've done them enough times but, overall, it feels like a new project and it is the most complicated one that we've ever done. It was more complimented that the classical things we have done. That was easy compared to this."

Asked by Jeb about his life outside Scorpions, Matthias says, "I have a guitar store in Munich. It is nice and I like guitars and it is a good place. It is a wonderful store. I have vintage guitars, but I also have new ones. In the States, you have more stores like this. In Europe, you either have tiny stores that have nothing interesting, or you have stores that are like Walmart. They are superstores. They have no atmosphere. You go in my store and it is almost cozy, very special. It has turned out to be a meeting point for Scorpions fans. I will do events once in a while, and I will play a few songs with a band on a small stage and people love it. It is worth keeping it. I don't do this for business. It is just a hobby and it actually costs me something, but I love it. Sometimes, I will have an exhibition. I am going to go down and bring my pre-CBS Fender candy apple red guitar collection and make a Christmas display. I will add a few evergreens and a few decorations and I will have a nice Christmas card for next year. I show people guitars that they can never get close too. I show them some Scorpions touring guitars and then I take them away again. I will bring out the guitar that I played on *Wind Of Change* and I will let them see that. People can talk to me and they don't have to stand in line backstage trying to get an autograph. I am a regular guy and I just talk to the people. I love it and it is fun to have the store. I will tell you a story. One woman who is a fan, was probably about age 60, showed up with her son and they flew over from San Diego just in order to come over and meet me and buy a guitar. They spent two days there and then they visited castles and made a trip out of it. It was really great. If you ever come over here then you need to come see me at the guitar store."

As for solo plans... "People ask me so, so many times, 'When is your solo album coming out?' If we are not so busy anymore then maybe, but I am the busiest now because I did all of the arrangements and I am getting ready, believe it or not to record *Temple Of The King* from Rainbow because they are releasing a tribute album for Ronnie James Dio. We are taking two days out of our tough schedule and recording that song. You're the first to know. I have the '57 Strat ready. I have the '59 Les Paul and we use that in the studio as well. I have one that is so clean and so mint it is unbelievable. I will play these fantastic guitars on it. I checked the song yesterday and it is easy to do, so we will do that. I would love to do a solo album one day, but I would need to be able to focus on it. The Scorpions has always been—and will always be—my priority. As long as we are so busy, then I wouldn't find the peace of mind that is worth releasing. My goal would be that it has to be at least as good as the band's album where I have a lot of impact. Otherwise there is no point. Lots of musicians' solo albums are not even half as good as the band effort. I am not stupid. I would not release anything that is not as convincing."

And Rudolf's take on the Unplugged situation?

"It came at the right moment. I know that in the late '80s we had few options to do MTV Unplugged. We had already booked the Savage Amusement world tour when they came to us and we told them that we couldn't do it because of that. I think it is good that we didn't do it then. Now, we have much more experience to do it in the right way. When we started to do MTV Unplugged we decided that we didn't want to do things the same way we do it with electric guitars. We wanted to change the arrangements upside down. I think now, when you listen to the songs, you will have a completely different feeling. I think we use acoustic guitars to make an acoustic guitar orchestra, and that gives the songs new energy. I think *Hit Between The Eyes* is a good example of this, as well as *Blackout*."

"We are very happy to have done this concert under the open sky," continues Rudolf. "The theatre is a fantastic place. It was built into a rock back in 1965, which happens to be the year that Scorpions were born. It was a great thing to do it in front of the Greek people. MTV Unplugged is already released in 78 countries and now you guys in the USA have it. I think it is going to be something like 80 countries by the time it is all done. This makes this a monumental success."

Addressing the bank of rarities on the record, Rudolf explains that, "When we did Acoustica in Lisbon, Portugal, in a monastery, we played the hits on that one. For MTV Unplugged we really thought about not playing the hits like *Wind Of Change, Still Loving You* and *Rock You Like A Hurricane* but MTV said, 'No, these are very important songs and you have to put them on the album.' Our producers, Mikael Nord Anderson and Martin Hansen for NordHansen Productions, did a fantastic job by arranging this stuff. It is very, very good. Matthias went to Stockholm very often to work with these guys that we call The Swedish Rock Mafia. The producers did it the right way and in the Scorpions way. I said in the beginning that I didn't want to stop the other guys from getting crazy with the arrangements because I was so involved with the songs when I composed them. I was very close to them in the beginning. In this case it was a good mixture of songs and also the idea of what became the heart of this MTV Unplugged where everybody, Matthias, Klaus and me, performed a song each without the other two guys. It was very interesting and we got a lot of applause. Klaus played guitar. We worked very hard to give the people something special. We wanted to make this the icing on the cake."

"But I immediately mentioned this to the producer: 'You can pick whatever you want from the catalogue. If you were to ask me then I would tell you that I would love to do *Born To Touch Your Feelings* because I know this song has so much soul and so much heart that it has to be on MTV Unplugged.' I think the version we did is very good. It gave me goose bumps. I tell you one thing, it was unbelievable when the video producer was showing us this performance and our background singer cried. Then we cried too. When the girl performed the song she was so touched, and the song was *Born To Touch Your Feelings*. It really touched her in the right way. And *Speedy's Coming* was great. Klaus was not so sure. I always mention *Speedy's Coming* because it is an interesting song. I remember when Alice Cooper was supporting us in America in 1999, we told him about the song *Speedy's Coming* because his name appears in the song. It is a naïve kind of lyric. Klaus changed it a little bit and it came out great. We did a great version of *Pictured Life* and also of *In Trance*. The guest singer with Klaus, a German female singer named Cäthe on *In Trance* was great. She really has a great voice and a great personality."

"The other German guy, Johannes Strate from Revolverheld, was great," continues Rudolf, clearly enthused about the extended cast. "Many people ask how this came about. It was very easy; we played in Russia one half year ago and we got a phone call from his management that said he was in town and that he would love to come to our concert. We had passes and tickets for him and we met him backstage. I think he was very touched when we performed the concert. When MTV was looking for guests he was the first one to say that he wanted to sing with Scorpions. MTV was very much into getting some new guys into the game. We thought about maybe Steven Tyler, Jon Bon Jovi or David Coverdale of Whitesnake but MTV said, 'No, no, no, we want to have young kids.' We said, 'Okay, let's see what we have.' We ended up with the guests that are on the album."

"We had three days on this high mountain making the album," continues Rudolf in closing. "My father was a philosopher. He was also an architect. He was always talking about Socrates and the other great philosophers. When we were in Greece for the first time in 1982, and from then on, we always went through the city from the Acropolis and to all of these magic places. We went to the tree where Socrates was talking to the people and things like that. We went to these magic places and we had many magic moments. It is interesting that the essence of democracy was born in Greece. We had around nine different nationalities on stage from American to Polish to Russian to Greek to Norwegian to Swedish to Finnish and beyond. We were showing people that when politicians have problems with different countries and different systems that music does not have those problems. We were a great family and we had a great time. We were literally crying when we had to leave in different directions and go back to where everybody came from."

Return to Forever

"You have to train even after you are not competing anymore"

S o as discussed and snickered over, as we crossed into 2014 and 2015, Scorpions flamboyantly reneged on their promise to retire. "It is wonderful," waxed Klaus, refusing to wane.

"When you take a look at Scorpions' Facebook site and you see that we have four-and-a-half million fans with the average age between 17 and 27, that is pretty crazy for a band that has been around for 40 years. It shows in every show we are playing, wherever we go, we have a whole new young audience in front of the stage. They make a perfect mix with all the fans who have been followers of the band for many decades."

"I think we are getting to where we have this Rolling Stones-like audience. There are a lot of young kids and they are singing along with songs that were written way before they were even born. If just feels great and it gives you so much energy. We have toured all over the world the last few years and we did over 200 shows in something like 30 countries and we have sold out shows from Moscow to Paris to Los Angeles. It is really wonderful to see that we reach so many people around the world with our music. When you're a boxer and they knock you down then it is important to stand up again. That is what we did, always. Who would have thought, a year ago, that we would be doing MTV Unplugged? This came in a time in our lives where you really don't expect it. This might be a whole new page in the book of Scorpions—we will see."

"The most exciting thing," continues Klaus, "after all of these years, is that we never lost the excitement for what we are doing and the passion for music. With all of those classics you look back and you see all the excitement and you reach out to a whole new generation of Scorpions fans and it is really wonderful to get that feedback, especially when you're out there for such a long time. We feel very privileged that we have this worldwide stage and that there is such a strong demand. At the same time, you say goodbye, but at the same time it is almost impossible to say goodbye because of this demand from all over the world. It is wonderful, but at the same time, it keeps us going, but at the same time, we know, at some point, you need to step down a bit and recharge your batteries. Right now, it is as crazy as it's ever been. If this is retirement, then I think we will just keep going."

Rudolf was sending out pretty much the same signals, that Scorpions would in fact live on.

"It's like a sportsman. If you are doing sports in the highest league then every doctor will tell you that you should not stop immediately. You have to train even after you are not competing anymore. You have to train because it is important for the whole body.

It is the same in music. You can't take the car and go 300 to zero immediately. It means we are going away slowly but surely from the scene, but we are always open for new challenges. When somebody comes up like MTV, we will do it. We have a cinema for next year that is 50 years of the Scorpions. This film will be presented in Berlin on the history of the Scorpions. In this case there are a lot of things happening. We also want to give the fans a bonus track album. In the '70s and the '80s, when we recorded on vinyl, there was only the possibility of nine or ten songs on the album. We always recorded 14 or 15 songs. In this case, we have a lot of songs from this time that are still in our library, but never found their way on the record."

"Two of them are on MTV Unplugged," continues Rudolf. "Before we did MTV Unplugged we were supposed to do this bonus track album. They came along and we put the album behind and we did the Unplugged first. There are two songs which we took from the bonus track project and performed on MTV Unplugged. One is called *Rock 'n' Roll Band* and the other one is *Dancing In The Moonlight*. Most people think a bonus track is the last shit a band has and that they are trying to make money with. No, no, not this time. These are good quality songs and I will tell you one thing, that when we do this bonus track album, which should come out at the end of this year, or early next year when we do the 50 year anniversary, then people will think it is unbelievable. They will say, 'They are not going to stop. They have to stay.' When people come to us like they do on Facebook and say, 'Please don't leave! Don't leave and don't go away,' that really kicks your ass. We announced the Farewell Tour because we didn't want to end up in two years announcing another tour and a new album that isn't good. We don't want to end up in a situation where we can't deliver to the audience how we like to deliver. If you do that then the audience goes, 'Oh shit, the Scorpions used to be so good. Why are they doing this?' We want to say, 'Yes, we want to leave' or 'Yes, we want to go on stage.' At the moment we have everything in our hand. Klaus says to us, 'I have to sing so high in range. I can play maybe three or four concerts a year.' We would do that. At this moment, however, everyone is fit and we are having a great time."

"I don't want to go until the Rolling Stones leave," avows Schenker. "I saw them one year ago when they toured in London. It was fantastic. I tell you one thing, Jagger was running like crazy and he was singing fantastic and the whole band was playing fantastic. Keith is playing his rhythm and it is always fantastic. When I saw the Eagles, Joe Walsh was just fantastic. This generation, and this music, will go away when these people go away. You will have the CD you can put in your CD player, but to see them live, people like Joe Walsh and the Rolling Stones, is something special."

"We learned from the first day on that you have to prove yourself onstage playing live. If you can win the people over there, then people will go to the record store and buy the record. When you do that, then you know you're good. We went from France to Belgium and then to England. We went to England, as a German band, and it was something like the biggest risk. People told us that we were crazy to go to England, as they would kick us in the butts like crazy. They said we would be back in Germany faster than you think. These magazines came and saw us and said things like Scorpions are the Blitzkrieg, as they have a special kind of humour. It was fantastic. We proved it to ourselves. I think that brings up an important point. You have to prove it to the people when you're onstage and that is why we have so many young fans. When we put out Sting In The Tail the young people went to YouTube and saw videos and they wanted to see us live so they came to the concert. That is the new way of getting new fans. You always have to prove yourself. If you are good onstage, then you can make it."

And so Scorpions was back, yes, vigorous live, but willing to pony up to the studio album bar as well, with an ersatz, complicated "bonus tracks album," which wasn't really, but rather greatly reworked shelved songs plus a pile of new ones. In a somewhat endearing, the rationalisation on the subject of return had evolved by 2015, but with many of the original kernels intact, Rudolf telling me, "Because this record was planned to be a bonus track album, after the last tour... well, not after, but in our situation doing this album and this tour, we promised the fans a bonus track album from the leftovers. Because we went to the leftovers, and we saw that we have a lot of fantastic material which didn't make it to the album. Especially in the late '70s and the '80s, when vinyl was still happening. So in this case, we promised in interviews, yeah, get the fans some bonus stuff and very good stuff, and we had started working on it, already in 2012."

"But somehow in the summer, and in-between shows and concerts and tours, we found out that we had very good material. But then actually Unplugged came in-between. We thought that maybe we could have some time off in 2013, but no, MTV called us and asked for an MTV Unplugged. Of course, we always wanted to do it, but we had no time. In this case we said yes, we're doing it. It was a very big success, so we start working. Then, in 2014, we started working again on this bonus tracks stuff."

"But by looking for one tape in my office which I couldn't find, because I thought there was very good stuff on it for the bonus track album, I found a book my mother did. And the situation was my father, when I started the Scorpions, gave me money to buy equipment. But my mother said, you know, you have to pay the money back because you have to know what it is, what it's all about, to really get so much money and then to appreciate maybe, the reason much better. So in this case, she was doing a book, by getting the income into the book, and splitting it half to the guys in the band, and then for the half to pay my father back, and then also for cables and stuff, some preparation and stuff."

"Then I found out, this book was started in September in 1965! So I took it downstairs in the studio, and said, 'Look, guys, here, next year is 50 years of the Scorpions.' Our manager immediately said, 'Of course, hey guys, that's fantastic, I will call the promoters around the world and tell them. Because you have to bring that forward, in that case.' We said hey, but we can't come out with a bonus track album. We started over-thinking the whole thing, and said, okay, there is parts of the old stuff, which really has the DNA of the '80s and late '70s, and we also started writing new stuff. So we have a complete, fantastic kind of bridge between the late '80s and the new time—classic rock with a twist into today."

"But in the end, you know, you maybe even can't tell what comes from the '80s and what comes from today. When you go and look at it. So in this case, it was a great kind of inspiration, first of all, to start celebrating 50 years, which we have now. The time is right, like crazy, and on the other hand, you have the later stuff. Of course, we changed the choruses a little bit on the older stuff, because I saw my songs then and thought, oh, this chorus is not strong enough; I have to rewrite the chorus. By this working on it, which is very important, you always get new inspiration for material. If you go into a new album after nearly 50 years, this album can be made good if the right inspiration comes. Some times it comes from tragedy or something. But when you are in a routine, you never get something very special out of it."

Why the title, Return To Forever?

"That came from the record company, from telling them every second day a new title. The record company, said, 'Look guys, people are always... you did the farewell tour, but what's happening?' In this case, Return To Forever doesn't mean that we will be there forever, but that our music will be there forever. That's a great situation. That's a good story. It also created in our band a certain new kind of energy, which gave us the possibility to really make a strong, new album."

Once again producing was the team of two Swedes, who take an increasingly active role by writing the new songs as well. Already we have a compromised record, an album by committee, but then again, when haven't the Scorpions relied on strong personalities to push the process.

Return To Forever, issued February 20, 2015, kicks off with two new autobiographical compositions, indicative of the band's hard rock with rounded edges all over the three most recent albums. *Going Out With A Bang* instantly puts on the display the organic high fidelity achieved by the producers, while *We Built This House*, a paean to panorama of the band's career, is essentially a poppy yet uptempo stadium ballad. Proud of the lyrics, the band put them up on the screen as they performed it on subsequent tour dates.

Rock My Car is an old song that has kicked around the Internet in live form, and is here buffed to the band's tidy standard, complete with hair metal gang vocals and phase-shifter. But there's also considerable heft from the guitars and from James Kottak's booming drums.

In fact, once the band hits the stage these days, James is featured very much as one of the stars of the band, with Rudolf particularly proud of his place in the band...

"See, I saw in him the first time... when Kingdom Come was supporting us on the Monsters Of Rock and later on, on the American tour in '88, I was very hypnotized by his kind of playing and his personality. Then when Herman left, he even recommended that, 'You know, the only guy who can replace me is James Kottak.' We said, 'Yes, great' (laughs). We thought the same. So in this case, he came into the band. But you know, the important point is, is it's the same situation again! You know, everybody in the Scorpions, when he gets into one role, he can do what he wants to do, and we enjoy watching him and everything. He puts more and more into the show and we say yes. But of course, when he sometimes did over-drumming, a little bit... you know, James it's great, but sometimes we have to cut a little bit of this down, because it's maybe not sympathetic anymore. You know, there's a fine line between playing a superstar and then overdoing it. The good thing is, he likes that, and he enjoys every day, playing on stage, and playing good for the band—and also for himself. That's the power and energy which we need, especially these days, where everything is done already, from this band and from that band. We want to enjoy playing and we want to give people a great show."

Back to the record, *House Of Cards* is a bluesy ballad with some sweet David Gilmour-like playing from Matthias, while *All For One* is another new number, featuring those iconic stacked chords from Rudolf, and classy, intriguing Germanic melodies deftly placed against stadium rock tropes. *Rock 'n' Roll Band*, surprisingly a sole Klaus Meine credit, is one of the record's fastest and heaviest tracks, lifted by a riffy chorus punk-rock slammed by James.

Next up is *Catch Your Luck And Play*. Awkward title aside, this one's got an Animal Magnetism vibe, once more the band mixing somewhat offensive hair metal melodies against sophisticated Teutonic colours. Again, the listener is immersed in huge, warm production values, testimony to the skills of Mikael and Marten.

"They're fantastic," explains Rudolf. "And Mikael is a very good guitar player as well. He was growing up in the north of Sweden, and one of his first albums was In Trance, and he became a Scorpions fan. Somehow he became better and better. He started producing soundtracks and stuff like this, and we found him by... I was listening to an M and M song on the radio, which I liked very much, from The Rasmus. I was looking at the credits to this and I said to my manager, 'Look, can you find out where we can find these guys and set up a meeting?' Then we met them, and we found out that we have the same kind of vision—what the future Scorpions songs are, and what Scorpions are all about—because he was, of course, following our career, and he saw that we were jumping a little bit to the left side."

"He said, 'Look, guys, I know, because I've seen you guys over the last 20 years, and I think that I know what to do.' It's a producer team, two guys, and that's very good. One is very good on guitar and the other one is very good in recording vocals. So in this case, by starting with them working in 2009, on the album, Sting In The Tail, we loved them very much, because they really understand the DNA of the Scorpions. Same like with the Stones and Don Was. Don Was did the same thing. He said to the Stones, 'Hey, we love your direction.' So in this case, they were asking what is happening in the career and why, because, of course, you want to be better as a group. You want to be better as a composer. You want to be better as musicians. Then you are jumping into different directions, and maybe your fans can't follow you. So I think that these guys did very well, especially also on the last album, in getting us on the right track with new material. They were even part of composing the new material, which was very good because they have the DNA. Their material fits perfectly into our role, and that's fantastic."

Back to the record, *Rollin' Home* is a piece of puerile pop, slap rhythms which hearken back to Mack's '80s production but also to today's kiddie pop. *Hard Rockin' The Place* offers bold correction, housing the most heavy rock riffing on the record, along with texture and chatter between the guitarists. Once more, there's a Germanic quality to some of the chord changes, but this time, there's no tempering with hair metal melodies from the American left coast.

Eye Of The Storm demonstrates some growth in the acoustic ballad department for the band in terms of arranging, ideas that had been explored on MTV Unplugged, which, as facile as much of it was, did indeed show the band striving hard to dress up the tracks and champion ambition. *The Scratch* is an experimental, almost swinging hard rocker that recalls, perhaps, the party rock aspects of Savage Amusement and Crazy World, and closing the record (the short form version, anyway), we get something called *Gypsy Life*, yet another ponderous, bluesy power ballad from a band always searching for the next *Still Loving You.*

As for the bonus material, suffice to say it's a mix of the above mix, namely ballads against rockers, a bit of pop, some experimentation, any of which could have been inserted into the album proper, given the stamp of these completely not eccentric players and producers, the sum total of such surety being an eccentricity in itself, or at least an identity cultivated now continuously since 1983 outside of the odd side trip in the '90s. Of particular note among the bonus tracks is *When The Truth Is A Lie*, which suggests an interesting and intelligent synthesis between light and shade that the band rarely achieved without some degree of awkwardness.

Given the lack of sales prospects for new records—and especially new records from heritage acts—perhaps even bigger than Return To Forever is the magnitude of the live presentation executed on the record's tour. Stage-blanketing video screens painted colours, told stories, and in the case of one part of James Kottak's drum solo, splashed across huge continuous screens all of the album covers from the band's catalogue back to 1972, revealed one drum whack at a time.

"Look, we always, from the beginning of our career until now, were trying to use new technology in a new way," explains a proud Schenker brother. "First of all, having great amplifiers, then having a great stage look, and then later on, more and more, technology came into the whole thing. Also because we went through the video times, you know how very important the whole look is. It's the same situation with the whole band foundation we talked about. If you're only looking for one thing, you know, 'I'm a great guitar player—look how I can play,' you are losing momentum in what you can give the people."

"The music and the look fits together, and we really work very hard on it," concludes Rudolf. "We have production meetings, we found the right people, and we spend time comparing who does this, who does that. We couldn't even put the whole show in Toronto. We have lots of more stuff we use in Russia and in Europe. But the problem is sometimes the outdoor amphitheatres or sometimes even inside, they don't have the possibilities because the production is so big. But on the other hand, we also have to play in smaller places sometimes and we have to fit into these different halls. So we tailor this production to three different possibilities: small, medium, and big, like in the Los Angeles Forum or in New York, in the Barclay Arena and in Chicago now. And so we have the right mix.

The interesting thing is that smaller, medium or the big places, the fans are the same, and that's the very important part. If you have this kind of combination to give them, you've hit the spot."

Again, time will tell whether Return To Forever (or, for that matter, the band's authorised documentary Forever And A Day, yet another piece of product with a milestone feel) will be the last we see from Scorpions. If it is, the band can bow out knowing that when it came to delivering on stage, they indeed went out on top—the Return To Forever show was bar none the most energetic and athletic performance of the year put on by any band with roots to the '70s, let alone the '60s.

However, there's one more piece of business that would and could excite the party faithful, and that's a reunion with Francis and Herman, something that it seems a heartily and hale Rarebell has put in proper perspective.

"After 20 years, they lost the court case against Francis," says a plain-speaking Herman, with no degree of malice to any of the parties. "After 20 years in court... after there was no more money to fight about, the lawyers then dropped the case, because the lawyers made the money on both sides. It just shows you. I was... me and Francis also has a big fight about this. One night, at dinner, Michael told me, 'Why don't you meet and talk?' So we met, we got drunk, and we solved it all in one night. We're best friends again. We thought, why didn't we do this before?! We're so stupid. Why did we pay hundreds and hundreds of thousands to lawyers, and in the end now we're playing together again? We talked it all out. I said to him, 'Tell me if you did something to me, I forgive you. Just tell me the truth.' So we talked it out and everything's fine. I wish the other three would do the same thing. They have Iranian stubborn... Bismarck said, an Iranian loves the detail, the small details, but he loses the overview. Bismarck. True. Very interesting. All they have to do is sit at a table and talk, okay? Couple bottles of wine and talk, talk, talk. 'You fucking fucked me up; why did you do this?!' 'No I didn't.' 'No, it was like this and this and this...' and then you could talk it all out. If you can't clean up this, well, you might as well go fight for the next 20 years—and make the lawyers richer."

Why this is even worth bringing up is the fact that Francis and Herman have been playing with Michael Schenker, working their way vigorously through material that is much more demanding than Scorpions songs, and doing it with energy and skill.

"I think they hear this," says Herman. "I'm sure Rudolf is aware of what his brother is doing. I'm sure he's listening to that. I'm sure, you know, when they really stop one day, then Rudolf will make an album with his brother, as the Schenker brothers. They wanted to do that for a long time. Obviously, they're going to ask me to play drums, Francis to play the bass. We are the rhythm section of the Scorpions. I wish we would've done an album, the five of us, a killer album, with Dieter Dierks producing, and show the whole world, 'Hey, we're still standing, we're still great.' This is not a good way to retire. But then again, they're not going to retire. They're still going to go on the next ten years, probably.

"Dieter is not well, so the time is running out," continues Rarebell. "What they all forget, we're all over 65 now. For sure, in 30 years, we're all gone. Then we would be 95. Who lives after that is lucky. I would like to make a final great statement to the world: 'Hey, we still can do it.' Look, all they have to do is get on the phone, and then you have the old songwriting team together. Klaus and Rudy. It's that simple. They don't have to pay me a hundred thousand dollars advance and all the shit."

"I took up the challenge to play with Michael, and it's no coincidence," notes Herman. "We both live in Brighton, and we didn't know we both lived in Brighton. One day I met him walking on the beach. I said, 'What are you doing here?' He says, 'Well, I live right here' (points). I said, 'I live here!' He just lives 300 yards from me. But the best news, Phil Mogg lives another 300 yards from him too. So one morning, I'm walking on the beach, like my fast walking, my sport, and Phil comes by with his dog, and he says to me, 'Herman, I've seen a guy that looks just like Michael!' I said, 'Yeah, he lives right here' (points). 'No!' And Michael comes to me, 'Herman, I saw a guy that looks just like Phil!'

'Yeah, he's living right down the road from you.' So it just goes to show, see, there's a coincidence there. We both ended up in Brighton. I still live there and he still lives there. Doogie, our singer, lives in London, so we do most of our rehearsals and creativity down there in Brighton. I love England. I came to England in '71. Michael, when he was a big star when he was with UFO, he was the one in '77 who said to me, 'Hey, my brother has a band in Germany called the Scorpions. What if you go there for an audition?' What he didn't tell me was that there were another 50 drummers there. But anyway, I got the gig, as you know. So this is a long friendship, and also you can hear that we are on the same wavelength musically. It is a great pleasure to play with him again."

So back to where all this might lead...

"Who knows?" laughs Herman. "Maybe when they get older, and maybe in the last minutes, their brain starts working again. Because the whole world is waiting for this, all the fans. I mean, the people like Pavel and they like James, but they have to copy what we created. If you listen to Francis and me, we are the original rhythm section. Now, different story. I was very lucky all my life. Very lucky, I feel very blessed from God that he gave me all this opportunity. I think also, you know, that I left the Scorpions, I don't regret, because I had a fantastic life. I've had the so-called golden years. I played on all the hits, so what more can you ask for?

I played in all the stadiums, all the big arenas. I picked James. I got him in the band, and it's always difficult for another drummer to copy what I created before. You know, it's easier though because you don't have to create it yourself. But I think he's a good drummer, and I think he's doing a good job there. So I think, you know, let's see what the time brings when they're really on their final tour. Maybe ten years from now. I think that the two brothers probably will play together again. I'm already there, Francis is already there, so you have already the original band there, you know?

"Everybody's in good health," reminds Herman in closing, a fact made abundantly clear at both Scorpions and MSG shows in 2015. "Everybody is. I feel very lucky that I'm still able to play at 65, and most of my friends are dead now. This is true. Cancer or through alcohol and drugs. When you look around you, other people like Jon Lord and Ronnie James Dio, who were regulars all those years—now they're gone. That just shows you that life is too short to waste it. It also shows you that you take nothing with you. You come naked, you go naked. This is the only fair thing in life."

Discography

I'm keeping this tight and disciplined for ya, folks, this discography being designed to be a handy, dandy guide you might flip back to and reference as you read along and ponder the albums, a quick checklist for you to see which songs hail from where. I've not put song titles in italics, the rule used elsewhere in this book, 'cos it would mean too many italics here.

Now, for live albums, given that with Scorpions, there aren't the usual spate of them, all tied up with DVDs and the like, I've left them within the flow. Compilations is another matter. Because there are in fact, a ton of them, and many just released in select territories, I've decided to open the window and chuck them out—no compilations.

For studio albums, I've included timings, but not with the live albums, 'cos it's not that important. As well, label is home country, in this case, Germany, and date of issue is earliest date, if dates are staggered. Also, as I usually do in my books, I've added a notes section to point out anything else I figured was important enough to make known, such as changes in band personnel.

Lonesome Crow (Brain, February 1972)
Side 1: I'm Goin' Mad / It All Depends / Leave Me / In Search Of The Peace Of Mind
Side 2: Inheritance / Action / Lonesome Crow
Notes: Production: Conny Plank. Band: Klaus Meine: vocals; Michael Schenker: lead guitar; Rudolf Schenker: guitar; Lothar Heimberg: bass guitar; Wolfgang Dziony: drums. Canadian copies on Bomb were red vinyl.

Fly To The Rainbow (RCA, November 1, 1974)
Side 1: Speedy's Coming / They Need A Million / Drifting Sun / Fly People Fly
Side 2: This Is My Song / Far Away / Fly To The Rainbow
Notes: Production: Scorpions. Bassist Heimberg is replaced by Francis Buchholz; drummer Dziony is replaced by Jürgen Rosenthal; guitarist Michael Schenker is replaced by Ulrich Roth.

In Trance (RCA, September 17, 1975)
Side 1: Dark Lady / In Trance / Life's Like A River / Top Of The Bill / Living And Dying
Side 2: Robot Man / Evening Wind / Sun In My Hand / Longing For Fire / Night Lights
Notes: Production: Dieter Dierks. Drummer Rosenthal is replaced by Rudy Lenners.

Virgin Killer (RCA, October 9, 1976)
Side 1: Pictured Life / Catch Your Train / In Your Park / Backstage Queen / Virgin Killer
Side 2: Hell-Cat / Crying Days / Polar Nights / Yellow Raven
Notes: Production: Dieter Dierks.

Taken By Force (RCA, December 4, 1977)
Side 1: Steamrock Fever / We'll Burn The Sky / I've Got To Be Free / The Riot Of Your Time
Side 2: 1. The Sails Of Charon / Your Light / He's A Woman – She's A Man / Born To Touch Your Feelings
Notes: Production: Dieter Dierks. Drummer Lenners replaced by Herman Rarebell.

Tokyo Tapes (RCA, August 1978)
Side 1. All Night Long / Pictured Life / Backstage Queen / Polar Nights / In Trance
Side 2. We'll Burn The Sky / Suspender Love / In Search Of The Peace Of Mind / Fly To The Rainbow
Side 3. He's A Woman – She's A Man / Speedy's Coming / Top Of The Bill / Hound Dog / Long Tall Sally
Side 4. Steamrock Fever / Dark Lady / Kojo No Tsuki / Robot Man
Notes: Production: Dieter Dierks. Live album.

Lovedrive (Harvest/EMI, February 25, 1979)
Side 1: 1. Loving You Sunday Morning /Another Piece Of Meat / Always Somewhere / Coast To Coast
Side 2: Can't Get Enough (2:35) / Is There Anybody There? / Lovedrive / Holiday
Notes: Production: Dieter Dierks. Guitarist Roth is replaced by Matthias Jabs. Michael Schenker returns for limited role specified as lead guitar on three tracks, but not in band picture.

Animal Magnetism (Harvest/EMI, March 31, 1980)
Side 1: 1. Make It Real / Don't Make No Promises (Your Body Can't Keep) / Hold Me Tight / Twentieth Century Man / Lady Starlight
Side 2: Falling In Love / Only A Man / The Zoo / Animal Magnetism
Notes: Production: Dieter Dierks. The band is back to two guitarists after the departure of Michael Schenker.

Blackout (Harvest/EMI , March 29, 1982)
Side 1: Blackout / Can't Live Without You / No One Like You / You Give Me All I Need /Now!
Side 2: Dynamite / Arizona / China White / When The Smoke Is Going Down
Notes: Production: Dieter Dierks.

Love At First Sting (Harvest/EMI, March 27, 1984)
Side 1: Bad Boys Running Wild / Rock You Like A Hurricane / I'm Leaving You / Coming Home / The Same Thrill
Side 2: Big City Nights / As Soon As The Good Times Roll /Crossfire / Still Loving You
Notes: Production: Dieter Dierks.

World Wide Live (Harvest/EMI, June 20, 1985)
Side 1: Countdown / Coming Home / Blackout / Bad Boys Running Wild / Loving You Sunday Morning / Make It Real
Side 2: Big City Nights / Coast To Coast / Holiday / Still Loving You
Side 3: Rock You Like A Hurricane / Can't Live Without You / Another Piece Of Meat / Dynamite
Side 4: The Zoo / No One Like You / Can't Get Enough (Part I) / Six String Sting / Can't Get Enough (Part II)
Notes: Production: Dieter Dierks.

Savage Amusement (Harvest/EMI, April 16, 1988)
Side 1: Don't Stop At The Top / Rhythm Of Love / Passion Rules The Game / Media Overkill / Walking On The Edge
Side 2: We Let It Rock... You Let It Roll / Every Minute Every Day / Love On The Run / Believe In Love
Notes: Production: Dieter Dierks (with the mutual understanding that it would be the last collaboration).

Crazy World (Vertigo, November 6, 1990)
Side 1: Tease Me Please Me / Don't Believe Her / To Be With You In Heaven / Wind Of Change / Restless Nights
Side 2: Lust Or Love / Kicks After Six / Hit Between The Eyes / Money And Fame / Crazy World / Send Me An Angel
Notes: Production: Keith Olsen and Scorpions.

Face The Heat (Mercury/PolyGram, September 21, 1993)
Alien Nation / No Pain No Gain / Someone To Touch / Under The Same Sun / Unholy Alliance / Woman / Hate To Be Nice / Taxman Woman / Ship Of Fools / Nightmare Avenue / Lonely Nights
Notes: Production: Bruce Fairbairn and Scorpions. Japanese bonus tracks are Kami O Shin Jiru and Daddy's Girl. Bassist Buchholz is replaced by Ralph Rieckermann.

Live Bites (Mercury/PolyGram, April 1995)

Tease Me Please Me / Is There Anybody There? / Rhythm Of Love / In Trance / No Pain No Gain / When The Smoke Is Going Down / Ave Maria No Morro / Living For Tomorrow / Concerto In V / Alien Nation / Hit Between The Eyes / Crazy World / Wind Of Change / Heroes Don't Cry / White Dove
Notes: Production: Scorpions for live material; Keith Olsen and Scorpions for studio tracks, Heroes Don't Cry and White Dove. US version deletes Ave Maria No Morro.

Pure Instinct (EastWest, May 21, 1996)

Wild Child / But The Best For You / Does Anyone Know / Stone In My Shoe / Soul Behind The Face / Oh Girl (I Wanna Be With You) / When You Came Into My Life / Where The River Flows / Time Will Call Your Name / You And I / Are You The One?
Notes: Production: Erwin Musper and Scorpions, except Wild Child and When You Came Into My Life by Keith Olsen and Scorpions. Japanese bonus track is She's Knocking At My Door. Drummer Rarebell replaced by session drummer Curt Cress.

Eye II Eye (EastWest, March 9, 1999)

Mysterious / To Be No. 1 / Obsession / Light Years Away / Mind Like A Tree / Eye To Eye / What U Give U Get Back / Skywriter / Yellow Butterfly / Freshly Squeezed / Priscilla / Du Bist So Schmutzig / Aleya / A Moment In A Million Years
Notes: Production: Peter Wolf. Drummer Cress replaced by James Kottak. Japanese bonus track is You And I (Butcher radio remix).

Moment Of Glory (EMI Classics, August 8, 2000)

Hurricane 2000 / Moment Of Glory / Send Me An Angel / Wind Of Change / Crossfire: Prologue (Midnight In Moscow/Crossfire) / Deadly Sting Suite: He's A Woman - She's A Man/Dynamite / Here In My Heart / Still Loving You / Big City Nights / Lady Starlight
Notes: Production: Scorpions and Chrstian Kolonovits. Expanded track list for video version. Bonus track in some territories is Hurricane 2000 (radio edit). Live album with additional personnel, The Berlin Philharmonic Orchestra. Band billed officially as Scorpions Berliner Philharmoniker.

Acoustica (EastWest, May 14, 2001)

The Zoo / Always Somewhere / Life Is Too Short / Holiday / You And I / When Love Kills Love / Dust In The Wind / Send Me An Angel / Catch Your Train / I Wanted To Cry (But The Tears Wouldn't Come) / Wind Of Change / Love Of My Life / Drive / Still Loving You / Hurricane 2001
Notes: Production: Scorpions and Christian Kolonovits. Expanded track list for video version.

Unbreakable (Sanctuary/BMG, June 22, 2004)

New Generation / Love 'Em Or Leave 'Em / Deep And Dark / Borderline / Blood Too Hot / Maybe I Maybe You / Someday Is Now / My City My Town / Through My Eyes / Can You Feel It / This Time / She Said / Remember The Good Times (Retro Garage Mix)
Notes: Production: Erwin Musper and Scorpions. Japanese bonus tracks are Dreamers and Too Far. Bassist Rieckermann is replaced by Pawel Maciwoda. Enhanced CD with Video Message, Picture Gallery and Biography.

Humanity Hour 1 (Sony BMG, May 14, 2007)

Hour 1 / The Game Of Life / We Were Born To Fly / The Future Never Dies / You're Lovin' Me To Death / 321 / Love Will Keep Us Alive / We Will Rise Again / Your Last Song / Love Is War / The Cross / Humanity
Notes: Production: James Michael and Desmond Child. Executive producer: Desmond Child. Japanese bonus tracks are Cold, Humanity (radio edit) and Love Will Keep Us Alive (radio edit).

Sting In The Tail (Sony, March 14, 2010)

Raised On Rock / Sting In The Tail / Slave Me / The Good Die Young / No Limit / Rock Zone / Lorelei /Turn You On / Let's Rock! / SLY / Spirit Of Rock / The Best Is Yet To Come
Notes: Production: Mikael Nord Andersson and Martin Hansen. US version omits Let's Rock. Japanese bonus track is Thunder And Lightning.

Comeblack (Sony, November 4, 2011)

Rhythm Of Love / No One Like You / The Zoo / Rock You Like A Hurricane / Blackout / Wind Of Change / Still Loving You / Tainted Love / Children Of The Revolution / Across The Universe / Tin Soldier / All Day And All Of The Night / Ruby Tuesday
Notes: Production: Mikael Nord Andersson and Martin Hansen. Japanese bonus tracks are Big City Nights, Still Loving You (Je t'aime encore) and Shapes Of Things.

MTV Unplugged (Sony, December 1, 2013)

Send Me An Angel / Where The River Flows / Passion Rules The Game / Rock You Like A Hurricane / Hit Between The Eyes / Rock 'n' Roll Band / Blackout / Still Loving You / Big City Nights / Wind of Change / No One Like You / When The Smoke Is Going Down

Notes: Production: Mikael Nord Andersson and Martin Hansen. Also a Studio Edits version and a Tour Edition. Album also known as MTV Unplugged In Athens or MTV Unplugged Live In Athens.

Return To Forever (Sony, February 20, 2015)

Going Out With A Bang / We Built This House / Rock My Car / House Of Cards / All For One / Rock 'n' Roll Band / Catch Your Luck And Play / Rollin' Home / Hard Rockin' The Place / Eye Of The Storm / The Scratch / Gypsy Life

Notes: Production: Mikael Nord Andersson and Martin Hansen. Also available in expanded form as Limited Deluxe Edition, iTunes Edition, Japanese Edition and US Deluxe Edition, variously adding anywhere from four to eight tracks.

Credits

Author Interviews

Bain, Jimmy—April 15, 2003; Branker, Don—2010; Buchholz, Francis—September 10, 2008 & April 22, 2015; Crosby, Bob—2010; Dokken, Don—May 15, 2000 & May 2, 2008; Frisch, Michael J—2010; Godwin, Rob—December 7, 2012; Jabs, Matthias—January 23, 2003; Krebs, David—2010; Meine, Klaus—August 29, 2007; Olsen, Keith—2010; Rarebell, Herman—February 4, 2006, September 26, 2006 & April 22, 2015; Rieckermann, Ralph—December 22, 2011; Rondinelli, Bobby—November 16, 2004; Roth, Uli Jon—November 7, 2000, January 20, 2004, August 28, 2008, December 12, 2011, January 29, 2012; Schenker, Michael—January 4, 2011; Schenker, Rudolf—June 10, 1999, June 25, 2001, June 14, 2004, August, 2007, December 21, 2011, September 24, 2015; Shulman, Derek—2009; Vallance, Jim—2010.

Additional Citations

Note: Some of these citations are incomplete as to date etc. If informed or corrected, I would be pleased to expand or amend any and all credits in future editions.

BraveWords.com. *Scorpions drummer James Kottak: We'll Really Be Done* By 2013 by Mitch Lafon. Jan 16, 2012.
Circus. *Scorpions—ten on the Richter scale* by Richard Hogan. Issue No.294. August 31, 1984.
Circus. *Home and away with the Scorpions' Mr. Schenker* by Rudolf Schenker. Issue No.311. January 31, 1986.
Classic Rock Revisited. Interviews with Jabs, Meine, Rarebell, and Michael and Rudolf Schenker by Jeb Wright.
Dmme.net. Interview with Phil Mogg.
Dmme.net. Interview with Klaus Meine.
Dunn, Sam. Interview with Uli Jon Roth.
Hit Parader. *Scorpions: over the top* by Hank Thompson. Issue No.228. September 1983.
Hit Parader. *Scorpions: Vocalist Klaus Meine Discusses New Album & Tour* by Andy Secher. Issue 232. Jan 1984.
Hit Parader. *Scorpions: loud and proud* by Andy Secher. Issue No.236. May 1984.
Hit Parader. *Roots: Matthias Jabs* by Bob Grossweiner. Issue No.238. July 1984.
Hit Parader. *Scorpions: the teutonic titans* by Rob Andrews. Issue No.242. November 1984.
Hit Parader. *Scorpions: the continental noblemen* by Winston Cummings. Issue No.245. February 1985.
Hit Parader. *Scorpions: on the road to rock* by Andy Secher. Issue No.250. July 1985.
Kerrang!. *Blackout record review* by Steve Gett. No. 12. March 25 – April 7, 1982.
Kerrang!. *Sultans Of Sting* by Malcolm Dome. No. 70. June 14 – 27, 1984.
Kerrang!. *World Wide Live record review* by Malcolm Dome. No. 95. May 30-June 12, 1985.
Kerrang! *Mama Ve're All Krazee Now!* by Don Kaye. No. 315. November 10, 1990.
M.E.A.T. *Scorpions: Crazy World* by Drew Masters. Issue No.18. November 1990.
M.E.A.T. *Scorpions* by Drew Masters. Issue No.46. October 1991.
Metalassault.com. *Interview with Rudolf Schenker and Klaus Meine* by Aniruddh "Andrew" Bansal. April 5, 2010.
Metal Edge. *Scorpions: Grande Teutons Return With Pure Instinct* by Adrianne Stone. Vol. 41, No. 5. Oct 1996.
Metal Hammer. *So You Wanna Be A Producer?* by Pete Makowski. Vol. 3, No. 11. June 6, 1988.
Metallion. *Love Stings* by Steve Gett. No. 1, Vol. 1. September 1984.
Metal-Rules.com. *Scorpions: Interview with Klaus Meine* by Marko Syrjälä. Translation by JP. 2003.
Music Express. *Scorpions On The Prowl* by Steffan Chirazi. Issue No.95. October 1985.
Record Collector. *Blackout record review* by Jon Sutherland. Vol. 6, No. 3. June 1982.
Record Collector. *Scorpions Conquer America* by Jon Sutherland. Vol. 6, No. 6. December 1982.
Rip. *The Scorpions: Rock-Tung!* by Robyn Doreian. November 1993.
Rip. *Scorpions Uber Alles* by Jon Sutherland. June 1994.
Rockmusicstar.com. *Interview with Matthias Jabs.* April 4, 2010.
Rolling Stone. *Blackout review* by J.D. Considine. Issue No.372.
Rolling Stone. *World Wide Live review* by Tim Holmes. Issue No.456.
Sounds. *Teu-Tone.* May 10, 1980.
Sounds. *The Unoriginal Sin* by Steve Double. August 23, 1986.

Photo Credits

Live photography comes courtesy of my own archive, as well as the rock 'n' roll vaults of Bill Baran, Kevin Estrada, Rich Galbraith, Greg Olma and Tom Wallace. Any photography besides the above are company promotional shots. If something other than that has slipped through uncredited, I would be pleased to rectify in future editions.
The following guys are old pros, and they do indeed have parts of their archives for sale:
Kevin Estrada can be reached at kevinestrada@sbcglobal.net and kevinestrada.com
Rich Galbraith can be reached at rtgenid@suddenlink.net.
Tom Wallace can be reached at tomwallace03@gmail.com.
As well, I'd like to thank Chris and his intelligently researched French fan site for some of the memorabilia shots.

About The Author

At approximately 7900 (with over 7000 appearing in his books), Martin has unofficially written more record reviews than anybody in the history of music writing across all genres. Additionally, Martin has penned 52 books on hard rock, heavy metal, classic rock and record collecting. He was Editor In Chief of the now retired *Brave Words & Bloody Knuckles*, Canada's foremost metal publication for 14 years, and has also contributed to *Revolver, Guitar World, Goldmine, Record Collector, bravewords.com, lollipop.com* and *hardradio.com*, with many record label band bios and liner notes to his credit as well. Additionally, Martin has been a regular contractor to Banger Films, having worked for two years as researcher on the award-wining documentary *Rush: Beyond The Lighted Stage*, on the writing and research team for the 11-episode *Metal Evolution* and on the 10-episode *Rock Icons*, both for VH1 Classic. Additionally, Martin is the writer of the original metal genre chart used in *Metal: A Headbanger's Journey* and throughout the *Metal Evolution* episodes. Martin currently resides in Toronto and can be reached through martinp@inforamp.net or www.martinpopoff.com.

Martin Popoff
A Complete Bibliography

Agent of Fortune - The Blue Öyster Cult Story (2016)
Wind of Change - The Scorpions Story (2016)
From Dublin To Jailbreak: Thin Lizzy 1969-76 (2016)
This Means War: The Sunset Years of the NWOBHM (2015)
Wheels of Steel: The Explosive Early Years of the NWOBHM (2015)
Swords And Tequila: Riot's Classic First Decade (2015)
Who Invented Heavy Metal? (2015)
Sail Away: Whitesnake's Fantastic Voyage (2015)
Live Magnetic Air: The Unlikely Saga Of The Superlative Max Webster (2014)
Steal Away The Night: An Ozzy Osbourne Day-By-Day (2014)
The Big Book Of Hair Metal (2014)
Sweating Bullets: The Deth And Rebirth Of Megadeth (2014)
Smokin' Valves: A Headbanger's Guiide to 900 NWOBHM Records (2014)
The Art Of Metal (co-edit with Malcolm Dome; 2013)
2 Minutes To Midnight: An Iron Maiden Day-By-Day (2013)
Metallica: The Complete Illustrated History (2013)
Rush: The Illustrated History (2013)
Ye Olde Metal: 1979 (2013)
Scorpions: Top Of The Bill (2013)
Epic Ted Nugent (2012)
Fade To Black: Hard Rock Cover Art Of The Vinyl Age (2012)
It's Getting Dangerous: Thin Lizzy 81-12 (2012)
We Will Be Strong: Thin Lizzy 76-81 (2012)
Fighting My Way Back: Thin Lizzy 69-76 (2011)
The Deep Purple Royal Family: Chain Of Events '80 – '11 (2011)
The Deep Purple Royal Family: Chain Of Events Through '79 (2011)
Black Sabbath FAQ (2011)
The Collector's Guide To Heavy Metal: Volume 4: The '00s (2011; co-authored with David Perri)
Goldmine Standard Catalog Of American Records 1948 – 1991, 7th Edition (2010)
Goldmine Record Album Price Guide, 6th Edition (2009)
Goldmine 45 RPM Price Guide, 7th Edition (2009)
A Castle Full Of Rascals: Deep Purple '83 – '09 (2009)
Worlds Away: Voivod And The Art Of Michel Langevin (2009)
Ye Olde Metal: 1978 (2009)
Gettin' Tighter: Deep Purple '68 – '76 (2008)
All Access: The Art Of The Backstage Pass (2008)
Ye Olde Metal: 1977 (2008)
Ye Olde Metal: 1976 (2008)
Judas Priest: Heavy Metal Painkillers (2007)
Ye Olde Metal: 1973 To 1975 (2007)
The Collector's Guide To Heavy Metal: Volume 3: The Nineties (2007)
Ye Olde Metal: 1968 To 1972 (2007)
Run For Cover: The Art Of Derek Riggs (2006)
Black Sabbath: Doom Let Loose (2006)
Dio: Light Beyond The Black (2006)
The Collector's Guide To Heavy Metal: Volume 2: The Eighties (2005)
Rainbow: English Castle Magic (2005)
UFO: Shoot Out The Lights (2005)
The New Wave Of British Heavy Metal Singles (2005)
Blue Öyster Cult: Secrets Revealed! (2004)
Contents Under Pressure: 30 Years Of Rush At Home & Away (2004)
The Top 500 Heavy Metal Albums Of All Time (2004)
The Collector's Guide To Heavy Metal: Volume 1: The Seventies (2003)
The Top 500 Heavy Metal Songs Of All Time (2003)
Southern Rock Review (2001)
Heavy Metal: 20th Century Rock And Roll (2000)
The Goldmine Price Guide To Heavy Metal Records (2000)
The Collector's Guide To Heavy Metal (1997)
Riff Kills Man! 25 Years Of Recorded Hard Rock & Heavy Metal (1993)
See martinpopoff.com for complete details and ordering information.